Alec Nove on Economic Theory

Alec Nove on Economic Theory

Previously Unpublished Writings, 1

Alec Nove

Edited by
Ian D. Thatcher
Lecturer, Institute of Russian and East European Studies,
University of Glasgow, UK

Edward Elgar
Cheltenham, UK · Northampton, MA, USA

Published by
Edward Elgar Publishing Limited
Glensanda House
Montpellier Parade
Cheltenham
Glos GL50 1UA
UK

Edward Elgar Publishing, Inc.
6 Market Street
Northampton
Massachusetts 01060
USA

A catalogue record for this book
is available from the British Library

Library of Congress Cataloging in Publication Data
Nove, Alec.
    Alec Nove on economic theory : previously unpublished writings /
Alec Nove ; edited by Ian D. Thatcher.
    Includes indexes.
    1. Nove. Alec. 2. Economic theory. 3. Marxian economics.
4. Socialism. 5. Soviet Union—Economic conditions. 6. Soviet
Union—Economic policy. 7. Soviet Union—Politics and government.
I. Thatcher, Ian D. II. Title. III. Title: Alec Nove on communist
and postcommunist countries
HB171.N72 1998
330'. 01—dc21   98–17086
                                                             CIP

ISBN 1 85898 829 2

Printed and bound in Great Britain by Bookcraft (Bath) Ltd.

Contents

Preface

Many tributes have been paid to Alec Nove (1915–1994). His bibliography has been researched and published,[1] several books and an issue of a leading journal have been dedicated to his memory,[2] and a Chair in Russian and East European Studies carries his name at the Institute he founded at the University of Glasgow.

Alec made substantial contributions to scholarship in several areas, most notably in our understanding of the Soviet economic system and its history, the intricacies of Soviet politics, and of a feasible socialist economics. In arguing for a practical, workable and humane combination of markets and socialism he was concerned not only to refute the case for a marketless economics advanced by Marxists, the main target of his *Economics of Feasible Socialism*, but also to counter the oversights of the highly influential neoclassical laissez-faire school so loved by Mrs Thatcher. In earlier books and articles he highlighted the weaknesses of the mainstream neoclassical school in the context of general equilibrium theory, notions of the firm, margins, and so on. Such a counter critique was so important to Alec because he witnessed the dire consequences of this ideology applied to the real world, for example the closure of a major (and previously successful) food shop after the hiring of 'myopic accountants'.[3] When the current volume was being edited the newspapers carried reports on the poor performance of the fragmented, privatised railways and the closure of branch lines;[4] the very things Alec had predicted and fought against! The blind application of the neoclassical mainstream to the postcommunist economies added an additional aspect and urgency to Alec's battle for a relevant economics. For long he had wailed against the deficiencies of the textbooks, the fact, for instance, that students were not taught the importance of 'quality . . . , function, duty, purpose or responsibility'. He set himself the task of producing a textbook that would, the manuscript of which, *The Economics of Relevance*, lay amongst the papers scattered around his study.

This had obviously been a project of several years standing. Alec sought to bring together a lifetime's thinking and experience of the economics of the real world, hoping, as ever, that his insights would be of practical value. In their appreciation of his life and work Sir Alec

Cairncross and Professor Archie Brown regret that the postcommunist Russian authorities have not paid more attention to Alec's thoughts on the role of government in the postcommunist transition.[5] One could make the same point to the British government in relation to Alec's critique of much of its economic policy since 1979. *The Economics of Relevance* should be required reading not only for students of economics in East and West, but also for the current Labour administration as it seeks to correct the economic mistakes of 1979 onwards.

As is clear from the letters published here, Alec did not confine his thoughts to this study, or to academic books and journals. He tried, not always successfully, to engage policymakers, or those giving advice to policymakers, in constructive debate. The issues that were central to Alec – of an efficient yet caring economics, one that accepts that humans respond to trust, that they care about providing a service and take pride in their work – are of course central to us all. It was surprising to him that economists paid so little regard to the obvious. He was frustrated and angered by the effects of 'myopic marginalism' wherever it was applied, whether to public transport or in the universities. Thanks are due to Edward Elgar for agreeing to publish Alec's unfinished (but almost complete) manuscript and papers on economic theory. He would have welcomed a wide readership and further counter-attacks. He cannot now answer them, but we can conduct the debate in his spirit of openness and honesty, remembering that economic theory should seek to provide a quality of life as well as quality of products.

Ian D. Thatcher

NOTES

1. Ian D. Thatcher, 'Alec Nove: A Bibliographical Tribute', *Europe–Asia Studies*, **47**(8), 1995, pp. 1383–410.
2. Jacques Hersh and Johannes Dragsbaek Schmidt (eds), *The Aftermath of 'Real Existing Socialism' in Eastern Europe*. Volume 1. *Between Western Europe and East Asia* (Macmillan, 1996); Mark Knell (ed.), *Economics of Transition. Structural Adjustments and Growth Prospects in Eastern Europe* (Edward Elgar, 1996); *Europe–Asia Studies*, **49**(3), 1997.
3. 'Alec NOVE' in Philip Arestis and Malcolm Sawyer (eds), *A Biographical Dictionary of Dissenting Economists* (Edward Elgar, 1992), p. 396.
4. See, for example, Zoe Brennan and Jonathan Leake, '"Unreliable" Virgin Rail heads passenger complaints list', *The Sunday Times*, 30 November 1997, p. 7; Keith Harper, 'Rail: fares up, quality down', *The Guardian*, 2 December, 1997, p. 2; Jonathan Leake, 'Private rail firms to close branch lines', *The Sunday Times*, 14 December 1997, p. 10.
5. Archie Brown and Alec Cairncross, 'Alec Nove, 1915–1994: An Appreciation', *Europe–Asia Studies*, **49**(3), 1997, p. 487.

PART I

The Economics of Relevance

Introduction: The economics of relevance

> When neither the hypotheses nor the implications of a theory can be con-
> fronted with the real world, that theory is devoid of any scientific interest.
> Mere logical, even mathematical deduction remains worthless in terms of the
> understanding of reality if it is not closely linked to that reality. (Maurice
> Allais, 1988 Nobel lecture)

INTRODUCTION

All theory must abstract from some aspects of a complex reality. Any
model must make some assumptions which do not fit some of the factors
which may influence outcomes in the real world. Thus, while real firms
may be affected by a heart attack suffered by a talented chief executive,
it is quite appropriate to abstract from coronaries in writing about
the theory of the firm. It is, however, less satisfactory to analyse the
firm while abstracting from much, if not all, of its raison d'être, or its
organisation and functions, indeed the role of management. Such considerations will receive much attention in subsequent pages. Nor can one
legitimately theorise about money in a universe of certainty, in which
most reasons for holding money are absent. No one, I trust, will write on
the economics of gambling while assuming that the gamblers know which
horse will win and at what price. Yet, I will submit, analyses of investment, which necessarily involve a degree of non-insurable risk, that is, a
sort of gamble, are gravely deficient, because of the conflict between the
commonly assumed equilibrium and the fact that profitable investments
require *dis*equilibrium, actual or anticipated. Marginal analysis, in textbook after textbook, is undertaken with little or no examination of the
rather complex meaning of the word 'margin' once one leaves the textbook for the real multi-level world. It seems incredible, but a search
through the index of most microeconomic textbooks reveals no entry at
all for *quality* or for *goodwill* (or else quality is considered only under the
heading of product differentiation), as if these were not vital elements in
the everyday business of life and, therefore, surely of microeconomics.

In short, this author is unhappy at what is taught in most of our economics courses, unhappy with mainstream neoclassical economics (and
even more with 'new classicals'). Of course he knows well that he is not
alone in this. Critiques have appeared bearing many names, from Janos
Kornai to Wassili Leontief, from Brian Loasby to Ludwig Lachmann.
Criticism has come from the 'Austrians', neo-Keynesians, neo-Ricardians.
To cite a few examples, here is Lawrence A. Boland, in his critique of
mathematical formalism in economics: 'Form is more important than
substance and logical validity by itself is considered more important than
difficult questions of empirical relevance.'[1] Henry Phelps Brown noted
that in 'economics at least those who devote themselves to the direct
observation of attitudes and behaviour have commonly been regarded as
playing in the 2nd XI',[2] that is, to be lower class scholars. S. Chakravarty
complains that 'explanation' now 'tends to be an explicit (preferably
mathematical) deduction from an axiomatically specified set of assumptions, where time is treated as fully reversible, expectations are fairly
stable (preferably "rational") and human beings are disembodied agents
. . .',[3] while Wynne Godley roundly asserts that 'I declare . . . the entire
notion of macroeconomic general equilibrium . . . to be a chimera.'[4]
Michio Morishima speaks of 'a dream world', out of touch with 'real
problems', in which 'entrepreneurs and bankers ceased to exist',[5] while
James Buchanan refers to 'intellectualised irrelevancies'.[6] Joan Robinson
wrote 'the concept of equilibrium is incompatible with history'[7] and
Keynes himself wrote:

> It is a great fault of symbolic pseudo-mathematical methods of formalising a
> system of economic analysis . . . that they expressly assume strict independence
> between the factors involved and lose all their cogency and authority if this
> hypothesis is disallowed . . . Too large a proportion of recent 'mathematical'
> economics are mere concoctions, as imprecise as the initial assumptions they
> rest on . . . .[8]

Intelligent defenders of the neoclassical schools, from Kenneth Arrow to
Frank Hahn, are well aware of the gap that separates general-equilibrium
theory from important aspects of reality. Some of the more skilled mathe-
maticians would be the first, indeed are the first, to express concern at the
excesses of mathematical formalism, the reluctance to recognise as genuine
economists those who tackle problem areas in which mathematics is of
little or no help. Unfortunately, mainstream economics remains largely
untouched by criticisms. As for the 'new classicals', more of them later.

So what can this author hope to contribute? Possibly (he hopes) a different angle, reflecting particular experience and concerns. Let me try to
define and explain them.

My own specialism was the study of Soviet-type economies, of economics of socialism, and to some extent also development economics. I am also very much concerned with the difficulties facing the British economy, and have been seeking to understand the blind-spots in the minds of those guiding Britain's economic policies in the Thatcher era, and this will also influence subsequent chapters. But let me return to Soviet-type economies, and to the Marxist thought-categories which, so it was claimed, explained and justified their system. It had been for upwards of 30 years my task to demonstrate the inherent *systemic* inefficiencies of centralised 'socialist' economies. I emphasize the word systemic because, as is sometimes forgotten, some errors and waste occur in all systems. I recall a conference in America in which it was demonstrated that, since in the Soviet economy the planners are bound to be imperfectly informed, which is true, therefore the outcome was bound to be well short of the production possibilities frontier, which is also true. But the conference was on comparative economic systems, and such a model implied that in a Western capitalist economy the decision-makers are perfectly informed, and also that, in the real world, the production possibilities frontier can be operationally defined. Surely this is no way to approach the subject! (Perhaps the author of that paper was a devotee of Panglossian economics: free market economies are already in the best of all possible worlds?) Be all this as it may, the bankruptcy of Soviet-type centralised planning is beyond dispute, and my own past analyses of that system do provide much of the needed explanation for that bankruptcy.

Marxist political economy was either irrelevant or useless as a guide to correct the deficiencies of the system, or even to analyse the causes of these deficiencies. Marx nowhere expounded his own model of socialism/communism, but various *obiter dicta* pointed to an imagined world of abundance, with no markets, money, prices, wages, state, police, bureaucrats . . . . He had no theory of value and price under socialism, since he imagined that under socialism production for exchange would be replaced by production for use, and he further imagined that this would be 'simple and transparent'. Finding that it was all neither simple nor transparent, that scarcity was a major problem, and that there was a need for prices, Soviet economists for long periods envisaged prices based on some sort of surrogate labour values, which oriented them towards a species of cost-plus pricing, which even in theory could measure only effort, not result. Yet it should have been evident that, in the absence of markets, two baskets which share only the characteristic that the goods they contain require the same effort to produce could not be of the same *value* to society, save by an unlikely coincidence. Then, far from being 'simple and transparent', marketless centralised planning proved to be

hugely complicated, necessarily bureaucratised, generating large diseconomies of scale. This is not the place to develop these and similar
arguments; I have done so at length elsewhere.[9] The bankruptcy of
Marxist–Leninist socialism is accepted today by most of my Russian
colleagues. What they are seeking is an alternative body of theory, as a
guide to practice. Suppose twenty bright Soviet economists were to be
sent to study in a typical American or British university, and were given
the standard neoclassical textbooks, what would they learn that would
help them to understand the functioning of a capitalist economy, and to
find the road towards fundamental change of their own? Where, in this
context, could one place general-equilibrium models? Or investment criteria? Or the needed institutional infrastructure? After all, to cite Frank
Hahn, a defender of neoclassical Walrasian tradition, 'a description of
the invisible hand in action is still beyond us', surely a very severe critique
of 'us'. I pondered similar questions when seeking to devise a course for
graduate students from the third world, and had irreverent thoughts on
the economics of irrelevance, and on textbooks and journal articles with
abstractions almost for their own sake.

This is not to say that mainstream economics has nothing to teach a
repentant central planner. It most certainly has. But, as my late colleague
Ely Devons used to say, and Alec Cairncross still says, 'in so far as economic theory is useful in enabling us to understand the real world and
helping us to take decisions on policy, it is the simple, most elementary
and in some ways the most obvious propositions that matter'. One can
make a list of such propositions: the interaction of supply, demand, and
price; the consequences of price control; or of printing too much money;
opportunity-cost; a theory of value which takes fully into account utility,
use-value, evaluation by the customer; the allocational functions of interest and rent. Cairncross referred to 'the marginal theory of value' in this
context, but here, for reasons to be examined at length later, I would distance myself because of the oversimplified and one-dimensional way in
which 'margins' are presented (Cairncross himself is aware of this deficiency, as his own writings show). It is indeed true that familiarity with
some basic and elementary economic principles was sadly lacking among
Gorbachev's advisors in the Soviet Union, and in Gorbachev's own mind
too (he had studied law). It is also true, however, that economists brought
up within the Walrasian world-view are sometimes unable to grasp points
which non-economists have no difficulty in understanding.

Thus it might seem self-evident to the layman that if Britain became a
net importer of cars, lorries, ships, electronics, computers, most consumer
durables, a high proportion of machinery and equipment, and recently
even cloth and clothing, with a large negative balance for manufactures as

a whole, this could lead to a balance of payments crisis of major propor-tions. Yet very few economists (Wynne Godley stands out as an honourable exception) felt it necessary to warn of what was coming, while the government and its myopic advisers thought that market forces were indicating that Britain's future lay with services and away from manufac-turing. There was even a theory that trade deficits did not matter, since they were just the obverse side of capital movements. The latter did indeed cover the trade and current account deficit as an accounting equivalence. This was true also of the large US deficit. But common sense – which some economists seem to lack – tells one that it is not possible to go on borrowing indefinitely, to go on and on living above one's means. (Of course, if the inward capital flow were investing in future production of goods and services, the picture changes; but to see if this was so one has to disaggregate.) The pound was in dire trouble as these lines were writ-ten. How many economists, how many macro models (including the British Treasury's) were able to foresee what should have been at least an obvious possibility? Milton Friedman, in a famous article, dismissed the importance of making realistic assumptions: what mattered was predic-tive capacity. By such criteria, there is much to criticise, and surely excessive abstraction from the real world is part of the disease. A (non-economist) Glasgow councillor, observing the collapse of all (and I mean all) industries for which the city was famous, sadly remarked: 'we no longer *make* anything'. (And indeed even the shirts worn by most Scottish sports teams are imported.) Yes, there are new jobs in services. Investment in large new shopping malls – selling mainly imported goods – has been impressive. But the effect on the import–export balance in tradeables has been strikingly negative.

How many economists have taken the trouble to study international trade statistics, or, for that matter, productive capacity? Thus Great Britain has an alarmingly high trade deficit even at a time (1992) of depressed demand. The government hopes that demand will recover. Will this not lead swiftly to an import surge and a balance of payments crisis? Related problems could arise in those East European countries that are liberalising foreign trade and moving towards convertibility, at a time of industrial (and agricultural) restructuring. Neither of the Heckscher–Ohlin general-equilibrium models would be of much help. Is there not a case so much for finding an adequate micro base for macroeconomics as for developing meso or mezzo economics to fill the yawning gap between them? To take one more example, some countries are much better able than others to channel savings into productive investment, and to make use of scientific research, to benefit from technical progress. These are matters of the highest importance, in west, east and south.

As these lines are written, economic (and political) crises are developing in West *and* East, and in some respects they are even similar. Thus Russia and Great Britain both face falling production and rising unemployment, and are set to make a bad situation worse by cutting state expenditures, especially on investment, because of fear that not doing so might unbalance an already unbalanced budget, fuel inflation and lead to further devaluation of the currency. Yet deflationary policies, designed to cut inflation, clearly can contribute to turning recession into slump in ways that should be familiar to students of the Great Depression. Similarly, in both Russia and Great Britain the ideologists that have the ear of ministers advise them that market forces and not any conscious industrial or energy strategy will provide the needed direction for investments, though it is becoming increasingly apparent that this is no answer to pressing problems. The stage is set, also in America, for a rethink on the role of government in the economy, and Japan has already adopted what look like Keynesian measures to try to deal with its recessionary wave.

In Great Britain, privatisation and the fragmentation of electricity generation has led not only to a political crisis over the rundown of the coal industry, as competing generators rush to install gas regardless of the long-term effects on the balance of payments, or the rundown of gas reserves, it has also eliminated the one central body that could try to estimate future demand for electricity (a homogenous product used by every household and firm in the land) and plan investments accordingly. I had imagined that the competing companies might fail to install sufficient reserve capacity to cope with periods of peak demand. But an equally likely outcome was that they would create an overcapacity, and it is this which appears to be occurring. Typically, an article in the *Economic Journal* which sought to compare investment decisions in the two situations (that is, one producer or several) ignored the decisive factor, that is, responsibility for estimating total future demand, which exists in the one case and not in the other, and assumed equilibrium which, for reasons to be discussed at length, is an inappropriate assumption if one is dealing with investment.

A devastating critique of British energy policy also mentioned that 'much . . . long-term thinking has . . . been thrown away. Two outstanding CEGB [Central Electricity Generating Board] laboratories have been shut down . . . , many lives ruined and much talent and vigour wasted', and this, 'not for some long-term energy strategy – this doesn't exist. For nothing other than a piece of mindless dogma.'[10] It is economic ideology that prevents the British government having an energy policy, or an industrial strategy. And, as we shall see, the same ideology stands in the way of an investment strategy in Poland, Russia, Czecho-Slovakia, and so on.

Anyhow, I use the above examples to show that my concern for economics of relevance relates not only to the 'east', but also to concerns much nearer home.

Finally, in this introduction, a word on history, or on its absence from the neoclassical (*and* 'new classical') theories. By this I mean not only the way in which *time* is treated, not only the tendency to neglect economic history and the history of economic thought. One is also struck by the prevalence in the journals of models which have no ante-natal existence, so to speak. The specifications are put there, but nothing is said as to their origin; to the causes of the situations which the models purport to analyse. Yet intuitively it seems clear that any recommendation for action is likely to be influenced by the circumstances that gave rise to the problem in the first place.

Thus if the money supply has been rapidly increasing, was this due to a credit boom and, if so, were credits used for investment or consumption? Or was a budget deficit and the means of its financing primarily responsible? Or take the Public Sector Borrowing Requirement (PSBR): was the money borrowed used to cover current-account deficits (for example, to finance unemployment benefit or to subsidise loss-making state enterprises), or for capital construction – for example, roads, ports, housing, electricity generation? These can also be seen as examples of the dangers of inappropriate aggregation.

Much attention will have to be paid also to the size of the public sector. While the need to 'marketise' is, and should be, accepted without question in the former USSR and Eastern Europe, they are at present receiving numerous visits from enthusiastic ideological missionaries from pure free-enterprise think-tanks, for whom markets are a magical wand and almost any action by public authorities an evil to be minimised, a stage on the road to serfdom. One wonders whether they would accept even the need for municipal street lighting! It is sad to see one extremism substituted for its opposite.

This is particularly dangerous given the evident need for major *structural* change, as well as large investments in infrastructure and in saving the environment, and all this under conditions in which *private* capital is plainly insufficient. In Russia especially there is also the need to impose priorities to deal with short-term emergencies, such as energy and food supply. Yet the policies prescribed by advisers approved of by the IMF concern themselves only with macro-stabilisation. Necessary though this is, can the micro and the 'mezzo' economy really be left to market forces? Chapter 7 in this book is called 'Economics of the Transition Period'. Very little can be learned, for this, from neoclassical models.

A long list of questions on which non-economists legitimately can expect answers from economists, include the following. Why (for instance) did the British motor industry and shipbuilding so rapidly decline? If labour productivity is much higher in Germany, why? Are trade unions to blame? Or management? Or under-investment? What explanations are there for the extraordinary success of Japan and South Korea? What are the reasons for higher savings and productive investment in Japan and Germany? Human attitudes? Institutional differences? Does labour participation (*Mitbestimmung*), German or Japanese style, or co-ownership, have significant effects on the quality and quantity of labour inputs? Has Britain been handicapped by its poor record on training, as compared (again) with Germany and Japan? What has been the role of the state and the public sector in the investment process of various countries, and with what (positive or negative) results? What social or political pressures, or perhaps false macroeconomic theories, explain the universal prevalence of inflation in recent decades (compared with relative price stability at certain periods in the last hundred years)? Why are some countries more inflation-prone than others? (And if someone answers: because their money-supply grows faster, then that is no explanation: *why* does it grow faster?). Are laissez-faire and the fragmentation of labour markets more or less likely to bring about wage stability than 'corporatist' central negotiations? What has been the experience in different countries and sectors with privatisation? Which public-sector activities in which countries have been efficient and which inefficient, and why? What are the appropriate efficiency criteria? How important are externalities, positive and negative, and in what sectors? What is the cost of seeking to correct for 'market failures' and external effects? What circumstances facilitate or obstruct innovation and technical progress? What are its effects on employment and on the environment? These are not matters to which general-equilibrium analysis is readily applicable. They are, however, part of relevant economics.

NOTES

1. Lawrence A. Boland, 'The Theory and Practice of Economic Methodology', *Methodus*, 3(2), 1991, p. 16.
2. E.H. Phelps Brown, 'The Underdevelopment of Economics', *Economic Journal*, **82**(1), 1972, p. 9.
3. 'Chakravarty, Sukhamoy (born 1934)' in Philip Arestis and Malcolm Sawyer (eds), *A Biographical Dictionary of Dissenting Economists* (Edward Elgar, 1992), pp. 75–6.
4. 'Godley, Wynne (born 1926)' in ibid., p. 199.
5. Michio Morishima, 'General Equilibrium Theory in the Twenty-First Century', *Economic Journal*, **101**(1), 1991, pp. 71–2.

6. James M. Buchanan, 'Economics in the Post-Socialist Century', *Economic Journal*, **101**(1), 1991, p. 20.
7. J. Robinson, *The Generalization of the General Theory* (Macmillan, 1979), p. xiv.
8. J.M. Keynes, *The General Theory of Employment, Interest and Money* (Macmillan, 1936), pp. 297–8.
9. A. Nove, *The Economics of Feasible Socialism* (Allen & Unwin, 1983), parts I and II, and in subsequent editions.
10. Norman H. Lipman, Letter in *The Independent*, 19 October 1992, p. 18.

1. Equilibrium and all that

Economists have virtually no theory of how individual decision-makers behave out of equilibrium. (Kevin Lancaster)

We have no good reasons to suppose that there are forces which lead the economy to equilibrium. By that I mean we have no good theory. If there is indeed order we do not understand how it is brought about. (Frank Hahn)

Readers are asked to look several times at the two quotations at the head of this chapter. Surely, given that we are out of equilibrium most of the time (and, in a dynamic economy, this should be seen as both necessary and desirable), these statements, if correct, represent a devastating criticism of the state of current theory. And this out of the mouths of two of its most intelligent and eminent practitioners. The title of Kornai's book, *Anti-equilibrium*, comes to mind. His critique has yet to be properly answered.

Yet the purpose of this chapter is not to dismiss the concept. No course on economics can dispense with it. But, so to speak, it should know its place, it must not dominate the discourse. What, then, is its place in a course on relevant economics?

First, Walras was an eminent theoretician, and refinements since his time of the theory or theories of general equilibrium must be studied and understood. I happen to agree with Shlomo Maital: 'A century ago, when economics faced a crossroads and had to choose between the pseudo-physics of Walras and the evolutionary biology of Marshall, it chose Walras . . . We chose wrongly.'[1] The attempt to set up a model covering all the interactions of a market economy was a worthwhile intellectual exercise, though to do so involved making many heroic abstractions, on which we have already had much to say and will say more. Michel de Vrouy, of the University of Louvain, headed an article, 'Walras et la sacrifice du réél'. The gain is the presentation of an elegant theoretical construction, which Hahn likes to call 'beautiful'. And it must be admitted that no alternative can match its rigour or its beauty. However, beauty is a quality this author appreciates more in the opposite sex than in economic theory, though agreeing that there is room for differing tastes on such matters.

To return to equilibrium. It remains an indisputable analytical tool. One finds it in Marshall too. His equilibria are often decried as 'partial', but there is good evidence that he failed to develop the notion of *general* equilibrium not through a lack of intellectual grasp, but because he was primarily concerned with the 'ordinary business of life', which cannot be conducted or analysed if one posits a general equilibrium. This because, as Hahn points out, it implies 'the termination of actual processes', while Marshall was interested in actual processes, as we should be. There has been recently some revival of interest in Marshall's many qualities as an economist.[2]

Equilibrium is a point of rest, around which there are fluctuations, departures from the equilibrium point, for example, overproduction of some commodity, or an attempt to overprice it, bring into action forces which tend to redress the balance. The most basic supply-and-demand analysis rests upon these elementary but essential propositions. Overproduction should cause prices to fall, and this would provide a stimulus to produce less, to switch to another product. At prices that are too high a portion of output cannot be sold, leading to pressure to reduce prices. The market does generate forces which, in the absence of artificial barriers, tend to bring supply and demand into balance. We will see that for various reasons markets do not always or even often 'clear'. But equilibrating tendencies do exist. Though there are countervailing forces at work, it is surely wrong to say, with Eatwell and Millgate, that prices have *no* effect on the size and composition of output.[3]

It is also true, as Hahn points out, that all economists of the past, Adam Smith and Marx included, have used equilibrium concepts at the heart of their analysis. Thus, in his exposition of the working of a capitalist economy, Marx's categories (for example, the labour theory of value itself, or 'prices of production') were within an equilibrium framework, even though another part of his analysis sought to show a process of evolutionary (and revolutionary) change, through contradictions. Fifty years later, Bukharin used the equilibrium concept repeatedly, whenever he wished to demonstrate the interrelationships of a system at rest, though of course he also spoke of contradictions within the system and knew that it was not at rest.

However, as Axel Leijonhufvud pointed out, economists differ fundamentally in their belief, or disbelief, in the self-regulating nature of markets, that is, in whether, left to themselves, market forces will tend to bring about equilibrium, to be self-balancing.[4] He concentrates on macroeconomics, and so, in due course, should we. But also in microeconomics, and particularly in the important and often neglected area between macro and micro, one can and should distinguish between self-balancing forces and their opposite, forces which make for cumulative *dis*equilibrium. It is important not to wear ideological blinkers, and to study the experience of the real world, in this and in all other respects.

Interestingly, this finds recognition in the rules of American professional football. The team that was least successful in the previous season has first pick of the most talented college players, thereby maintaining the intensity of competition and spectator interest. This is an example of deliberate (though non-governmental) interference with market forces, which otherwise would have deleterious cumulative effects.

A more serious example was cited over thirty years ago by Gunnar Myrdal. A town or region loses one of its principal factories, either by bankruptcy or by fire. The locality loses revenue and has to raise the level of local taxes. Some of the most energetic citizens move elsewhere. New investment is discouraged by the height of local taxes and also goes elsewhere. Again, a downward spiral. Conversely, reflecting the saying 'nothing succeeds like success', an area which is flourishing attracts capital, skilled labour. One has megalopolies such as Mexico City, Sao Paulo and Tokyo. In most countries this has led to some sort of regulation to check disproportions in regional or urban development, since these generate substantial social and external environmental diseconomies, and are *not* self-correcting.

All this becomes ideologically charged because at issue is the role of government, of public authorities, in the economy. Neo-conservative or neo-liberal (sometimes, one feels, neo-anarchist) think-tanks in America and Britain are devoted to the proposition that markets take care of almost all problems if left alone. In the USSR and Eastern Europe communist doctrines stressed the negative consequences of free markets (cyclical depressions, unemployment, and so on), while the positive elements were ignored or denied. With the intellectual and practical bankruptcy of this system and of its doctrines, many of their economists are prepared to listen to missionaries from the neo-liberal think-tanks, who preach the self-regulating nature of markets. There is a clear danger, pointed to by many critics, of illegitimately switching from the general equilibrium model and Pareto-optimality, that is, from a model of a fictional (and friction-less) economy, to advising real people what to do in the real world. It is therefore particularly important to approach such matters without ideological preconceptions. (Much more of this in a subsequent chapter.)

To take just one example, the price mechanism is indeed the key element in the functioning of a market economy, to be ignored or downgraded at one's peril. But, as Kornai pointed out, it remains true that few major decisions are ever taken on the basis of price information alone. This is one reason why Lange's model of socialism was inadequate, for it assumed (in line with the neoclassicals with whom he was arguing) that prices will provide the information on the basis of which socialist managers would proceed to equate marginal revenue with marginal cost – and this without explaining why they should in fact wish to do so. Today's price, and the response to it by other agents, will affect behaviour and thus also tomorrow's price. And, unless there is some form of price-fixing, tomorrow's price (future prices) *cannot* be known, without prior knowledge of how agents will respond to their anticipation of what that price would be. This, as we shall see, most especially affects investment decisions, which of their nature must take into account estimates of future prices of outputs and inputs. If these are *known* to yield a sizeable profit, then this knowledge could attract competitors, who by their actions will alter future prices and thereby perhaps eliminate the profit. More will be said about this when we discuss investment. Suffice it to say that rational behaviour of would-be investors cannot be fitted into the general-equilibrium paradigm, because profit can only be anticipated if there are grounds for anticipating *dis*equilibrium. Yes, there are futures markets, through which agents seek to reduce the degree of uncertainty. But no one pretends that these are sufficient. As for the general-equilibrium models that assume that transactions entered into today also cover the indefinite future, this is surely no more than a device to escape from time and from uncertainty, collapsing the future into the present. In this way all the real problems besetting any real economy, industry or firm, are removed by assumption. No wonder Hahn can say that 'of course it is absolutely correct to maintain that every basic feature of an actual economy which Keynes regarded as crucial is missing in Debreu',[5] in the formal exposition of general equilibrium, which won its author the Nobel prize.

What, then, is the justification of making this concept a species of centrepiece, as distinct from a theoretically interesting view of never-never land? Loasby described general equilibrium as 'social science fiction, and thus requires the willing suspension of disbelief'.[6] In her excellent *Evolution of Economic Ideas*, Phyllis Deane pointed out that, unlike the physical sciences, economics relates to a system

> in constant flux, its development is subject to a high degree of uncertainty and auto-correlation. Of all the innovations that Keynes tried to introduce into economic thought it was the notion of taking uncertainty into account that proved most difficult to absorb into the neo-classical paradigm. For a world of uncertainty is a world of perpetual disequilibrium and the neo-classical concept of a self-regulating system becomes irrelevant.[7]

(I am not sure that Deane is fair to all of Keynes's predecessors. One thinks of Knight's *Risk, Uncertainty and Profit*, which I read as a student, or, for that matter Marshall. But as a critique of the Walrasian tradition the point is well taken).

Hahn none the less sees general-equilibrium models as the culmination of 200 years of theorising, as what he calls the 'base camp' from which we should ascend the mountain of yet unsolved theoretical problems. While, as he himself wrote, all the basic features of an actual economy which Keynes regarded as crucial are missing, the construct still has value, in his view, 'in describing what would have to be the case if there were to be no Keynesian problem'.[8] But one does not have to be a Keynesian, or to adopt or support Keynes's views as to how these problems are to be resolved, in order to see that these problems rank high on the list of what exists in the real world! So is the base camp by the right mountain? What real-life problems are illuminated, rather than obscured or bypassed, by being considered within the general-equilibrium framework? Does it in fact help us to understand how the bits of an unplanned market economy all fit together? Hahn himself does not think so. To repeat: 'if there is order, we do not understand how it is brought about'.

Leijonhufvud wrote: 'some modern "pure" models are wonders of logical-mathematical precision, but the pursuit – necessary for that objective – of exact definition of the logical boundaries of the terms employed tends to drain them of assured association with the "messy" empirical data that is all the economist has to work with.'[9] The question is: where does the logical–mathematical precision take us in understanding any aspect of reality? To cite the same author again: 'Axiomatic models are capable of conclusive *proof* that *if* a world such as that postulated were to exist, it must have such-and-such properties . . .' Let us by all means accept that such intellectual exercises are legitimate, but surely the onus of proof as to their relevance to the real world lies with their authors. Kornai's *Anti-equilibrium* sets out the case against, but he would seem to be more tolerant of the general-equilibrium model-builders than most of them are of those economists who address other questions by other methods.

It is true that some economists in the neoclassical tradition have been building *dis*equilibrium models. One critic of such models, Henry Woo, argues that they tend to use 'disequilibrium as a merely reconciliatory expedient employed to reconstitute the disequilibrating concepts within the equilibrium framework'.[10] This would be a correct description of most of the papers presented at an Anglo–French conference on 'macroeconomics of disequilibrium', a report on which was published in the Bulletin of the Centre for Policy Research. The introductory note stated: 'For simplicity's sake, disequilibrium models often consist of three goods: product, labour and money. This gives rise to a series of equilibria with limited quantities.' Useful concepts emerge, like Edmond

Malinvaud's 'rationing' of a scarce factor, which acts as a bottleneck. There are examinations of equilibria with persistent unemployment, though this, as we shall see, presents methodological difficulties yet to be satisfactorily solved within the neoclassical paradigm. But missing from such models are two factors of vital importance in the real world. One could be called the pre-history: that is to say, *how* and *why* did the disequilibrium situation arise? Surely this would affect policy recommendations, and what actually happens in the disequilibrium situation. Second, the models tend to ignore the effect of disequilibria on human behaviour. Thus shortage (as Soviet experience showed) gives rise to hoarding, which exacerbates the shortages, to black markets and to corruption (as it does in London with, say, tickets for the centre court at Wimbledon). Or, to see the positive side, real or anticipated shortages provide stimuli for entrepreneurship, for human action designed to take advantage of the profit-enhancing nature of disequilibrium. This, to be sure, relates more to micro than to macro, but also to the grey area between them: industrial sectors, regions, exchange rates.

It is important, before leaving the theme of equilibrium and its neoclassical interpretation, to consider again the key role in real life of uncertainty and time. Leijonhufvud has defined the problem precisely: 'Pure decision theory, formalised as optimisation subject to constraints, is essentially timeless. The choice among the foreseen outcomes of alternative actions is a purely logical calculus that does not involve time in any essential way.' He added that

> probability distributions of outcomes (do) not alter the problem. In the Arrow–Debreu (general-equilibrium) construction, the rational choice of each agent is defined over all dimensions of the commodity-time contingency space: the result is that all decisions are made once and for all at the origin of time. To obtain a model in which decisions are made in temporal sequence, agents must be ignorant of some of the information that is necessary in order to calculate all optimal allocations at the beginning of time. Thus Shackle poses the problem with uncompromising force: . . . . 'the theoretician is confronted with a stark choice. He can reject rationality or time.'[11]

And indeed in many of his extremely stimulating works, G.L.S. Shackle challenges the validity of this entire approach. If rationality requires perfect foresight, then rationality there cannot be. (In my view, this is putting too great a precision into the term 'rationality'.) Sir John Hicks was well aware of the problem, and sought to find a solution by imagining a series of time-periods in which new price information enables agents to respond to new market-clearing prices, but Hicks himself found this unsatisfactory. What about the effects of current transactions and expectations?

Finally, in a spirit of self-criticism, he found that he was 'back in a static and so in a neoclassical direction'.[12] These last words should be repeated and underlined: '*a static and so in a neoclassical direction*'. Here lies the heart of the trouble, and the soul of the critique of neoclassical Walrasian economics.

The fact that some aspects of the future are unknown, including the responses of other agents, would seem to be too obvious to be worth discussing. Nor can one escape from this, as has already been mentioned, by assuming a probability distribution. The economy and economic decisions are not like a game of bridge, when the probability of a 4:1 or a 3:2 distribution of the missing trumps can be given precise mathematical expression. Shackle is particularly illuminating on these issues. Also, and this is surely vital, human capacity for assimilating information is limited, even if such information relates to today, let alone the day after tomorrow. A number of economists, notably Simon, and after him also Williamson and Loasby, espoused the (reasonable) idea of *bounded* rationality: one tries to act rationally within the bounds of the information one is capable of absorbing and assessing. It does appear to be a little extreme (other than for purposes of rigorous modelling) to assert that *either* one is perfectly informed, including about future events, *or* one cannot act rationally at all.

Oddly enough, Eatwell, while recognising that 'uncertainty is a fact of economic life', argues that

> such factors (that is, uncertainty and expectations) have no role to play in an economic analysis which is to have any definite content . . . Economic theory should be confined to those phenomena which may be analysed in terms of concrete behavioural relations of a market economy, and should eschew those phenomena about which nothing definite can be said . . . The market economy operates systematically in an uncertain world and it is these systematic operations which are the proper subject-matter for economists.[13]

And a contributor to that same volume, Magnani, speaks of Shackle's 'extreme hostility to every kind of "abstract" economic argument',[14] which surely is not the case. All this comes oddly from ideological *opponents* of the neoclassical paradigm.

However, many of the authors of the Eatwell volume are neo-Ricardians, followers of Piero Sraffa. To do full justice to the views of Sraffa would require much more space than is available here. Brevity is justified by the word 'relevant' in the title of the present book. Because Sraffa's ideas, expressed in *The Production of Commodities by Means of Commodities*, belong in a world as abstract as the most abstract general-equilibrium theorists. None of the problems of the real world – money, inflation, unemployment, unsold goods, actions by the state, growth, technical progress, organisation, power, and so on – are considered in his world. His ideas are helpful in understanding and modifying the theory of value inherited from Ricardo and Marx. But it is hard to see even one crumb of an idea which would help us understand better either the functioning of our own economies or to find anything from which repentant Soviet planners or ideologists could learn. Indeed, one aspect of the Sraffa model can, in my view, mislead. This is because GNP is divided between wages and profits, in a manner which seems to imply a purely zero-sum game: higher wages imply lower profits, and vice versa. In a simplified static model this is indeed the case. But in real life, growth (including growth in real wages) must involve investment, to create the needed extra flow of goods and services and in the model investment is financed out of profits. It is as if one had a simple 'corn' model, in which an increase in consumption of corn leads to a reduction in the amount available for seed next year. One encounters models (for example, by Garegnani) in which investment is accompanied by lower consumption, leaving one puzzled as to its purpose: if demand falls, where from the profit on the investment?[15] Surely one needs a more dynamic model, incorporating either technical progress or the bringing into use of unemployed human and material resources, or both, enabling growth to occur in both wages and profits, consumption and investment, such as has been the case in many countries after World War II.

The problem of rationality in the face of an uncertain future, which worried Hicks, has been tackled by the 'new classical' school, via 'rational expectations'. Time and uncertainty have both been taken care of, by assuming that rational agents tend to foresee the future – or if a few get it wrong, the bulk of them will correctly assess the available information. Lucas and his colleagues also assume that all things are at any given moment in equilibrium (hence the difficulty of accepting the very possibility of involuntary unemployment). They even, as we shall see, conceive of competitive equilibrium growth paths. And since rational agents can see the same picture as the government, they will discount anything a rational government is likely to do, and from this the (to me truly extraordinary) conclusion is drawn that the government cannot do anything effective. The theory also assumes instantaneous price adjustments which always ensure that all markets clear. This 'solves' the problem of how to reconcile rationality and uncertainty, but, it would seem, only mathematically. It seems quite impossible to bring this construction down to earth. Yet the 'new classical' school has influence, is taken very seriously. Perhaps these few remarks fail to do it justice. But it does seem not unlikely that, fifty years hence, people will puzzle over the popularity of this esoteric fashion.

So, to conclude, general equilibrium is indeed 'social science fiction'. What Joan Robinson called 'the neoclassical attempt to escape from time' guarantees its irrelevance to the real time in which we have to live and decide. Leijonhufhvd, in his already-cited piece on 'Ideology and Analysis in Micro-economics', divided scholars into two broad camps, *Interventionists* and *Automatists*, according to their world-view concerning the self-balancing or non-self-balancing nature of the system. On the whole question of state intervention, including intervention with counter-cyclical intent, one can have legitimate differences of view, especially bearing in mind that some forms of interventionist cures may be worse than the disease. The one thing that is surely illegitimate is to project onto the real world the never-never land of general equilibrium and Pareto optimality, that is, to derive from such models conclusions concerning how a real economy would or could behave under conditions of laissez-faire. Here the 'Austrians' are much nearer the real world of real people. To understand the need for markets, for money, for entrepreneurs, to understand the functioning (and appreciate the possible limitations) of the invisible hand, or indeed *any* real-life problem or perplexity, one must reject the Walrasian approach.

While recognising the vitally important role in analysis of the concept of equilibrium, one must also appreciate how any dynamism implies the existence of, or creation of, disequilibrium. Just so are human beings impelled to action by wants yet unsatisfied, while entrepreneurs and inventors seek to present people with new opportunities. Learning by doing, the emergence of yet unfelt wants, are inconsistent with the (static) assumptions about everyone having settled and fully informed and consistent 'preference maps'. And it is evident that future technical progress cannot be known today, or else it would not be in the future! Also that anyone today who decides to adopt or invest in some innovation (of production technique or product) is taking a risk. If capitalist market systems, despite various imperfections, are notably better at encouraging such risk-taking than are Soviet-type centrally planned economies, then (as Mises and other 'Austrians' would certainly argue) our paradigm must in no circumstances exclude or play down the imperfection of the knowledge of tomorrow. As for 'equilibrium growth paths', or such models as that of von Neumann, one is left wondering by what mechanism at the micro (or mezzo) level the various agents of which the economy is composed are supposed to be impelled to invest, since at any given moment there is equilibrium, that is, no abnormal profits to be made by satisfying wants yet unsatisfied (and if such existed, then there would not be equilibrium!). If, as Machlup has argued, equilibrium is 'a constellation of selected interrelated variables so adjusted to one another that no inherent tendency to change prevails in the model',[16] how can there be dynamic equilibrium?

It was after writing the above that I saw these very points had been well made decades ago by Ludwig Lachmann:

> Dynamic equilibria, maximum growth paths, and similar concepts are notions of economists with little interest in what matters in a market economy . . . Growth . . . has become a branch of applied mathematics, in which one is satisfied with the deduction of optimal solutions from given 'data', without having to be concerned with how many economic actors in the real world could possibly understand the meaning of these data . . . there can be no such thing as a dynamic macro-economic equilibrium.[17]

Well said! Investment, technical progress, growth, are inherently disequilibrium-creating. What answer can there be to such arguments? One fears that the 'mainstream' simply ignores them, as it has ignored Richardson. How can one introduce endogenous technical progress into an equilibrium model, other than formally-mathematically? Technical progress itself is most often a response to some unsettled problem: 'necessity is the mother of invention'. Yet equilibrium implies that there are no such problems. If one treats technical progress as exogenous, then surely the results of research get adopted either because an existing disequilibrium makes the risk (inevitable accompaniment of innovation) worth taking, or the innovation itself is expected to create the degree of disequilibrium which would yield the level of profits which would justify the needed investment and the associated risk.

Or take the individual, assumed to be in equilibrium. What, then, is his or her motive for innovative behaviour? Could Columbus have been in equilibrium when he took the risk of sailing westwards? Are authors of general-equilibrium textbooks in equilibrium when they decide to write them? Or not to write them? Are we not in the realm of misleading or unhelpful tautology? It is worth touching on the relationship between equilibrium and human action. Machlup has defined equilibrium as a situation in which there is no inherent tendency to change. Can one then explain or analyse *any* action on equilibrium assumptions, since action is usually either a response to change or aims to achieve change? It is doubtless possible to analyse routine action within the equilibrium paradigm. For example, it is true that we decide to eat because we feel hungry, which could also be seen as a sort of personal disequilibrium. But we all of us eat several times a day, so repeated eating in response to a repeated sense of hunger is constant with the individual being in an equilibrium state. So is a machine which is programmed to fill or drill a hole. Matters become more complicated when tastes change, perhaps under the impact of an advertising campaign (it is unclear to me how advertising can be fitted into a set of given and unchanging preferences), or if demand is frustrated (for example, by shortages, as in a Soviet-type economy, or by a decision by a food manufacturer or supermarket chain not to provide the desired item). But when one departs from routine and considers anything which is new or intended to change any existing situation, then the equilibrium paradigm is surely an obstacle to realistic analysis both of motive and outcome. A ship and its captain can be said to be in equilibrium when they sail twice a day between Dover and Calais. So is a peasant who takes vegetables to market every week. So, generalising, it would seem that the equilibrium paradigm is the basis of an analysis of the interconnections of a system at rest.

In the same spirit Jochen Röpke wrote, in defence of a much-needed 'evolutionary economics', that this 'offers the chance to replace or substitute the mechanistic view of the world, the clock-work modelling and equilibrium theorising, so prevalent even in those branches of economics that are specialising on the change and development of the system.' He went on: 'self-organising systems that display evolution are characterised by intrinsic non-linearities and irreversibility. Innovations as non-linear activities can become self-amplifying and change the very environment (the selective mechanism) hitherto dictating innovative behaviour.' And so 'it seems trivial enough to conclude that evolving systems can never be equilibrium systems (of the Walras–Arrow–Debreu type)'. Röpke imagines a kind of dynamic stability that includes Schumpeterian creative destruction, but this sort of stable system 'can never be in equilibrium'. Indeed, 'if we employ the rationality criteria of equilibrium economics, we would have to characterise an evolving economy as a system misallocating scarce resources or by the non-optimising behaviour of its elements . . . Firms working as neoclassical optimising machines lack the potential for absorbing uncertainty and producing uncertainty for others.'[18]

Investment and growth, however, require a separate chapter.

To conclude, let us note the tendency to assume that inefficiencies of virtually any kind will already have been eliminated through competition in the market. Indeed, equilibrium represents the ending of actual processes. But relevant economics is about actual processes.

It is important to restate the position here defended, and attacked. There *is* an important role in economics for the concept of equilibrium. I agree with Amartya Sen that the attack is more justified on

the *use* of equilibrium-based reasoning. Sometimes this type of economics is invoked in a starkly simple form, drawing instant political conclusions – for example, about the efficiency of the market mechanism . . . The methodological difficulties of equilibrium economics do not lie in the idea itself. They lie in the rather narrow and simple way the idea is often interpreted and the over-extensive use that is frequently made of this one concept.[19]

Agreed! Just as there is nothing inherent in neoclassical economics that should prevent attention being paid to variations in quality, and the role of goodwill as a 'quality-maintainer'. It is just that a legitimate simplifying assumption – that one is dealing with a homogenous good of a *given* quality – has been carried so far that most textbooks on microeconomics barely mention either quality or goodwill. But more of this in other chapters.

NOTES

1. Shlomo Maital, 'Observing by Watching: Putting People Back into Methodology', *Methodus*, **2**(1), 1990, p. 48.
2. See, for example, the articles in the 'commemorative' issue of the *Scottish Journal of Political Economy*, **37**(1), 1990.
3. J. Eatwell and M. Millgate (eds), *Keynes's Economics and the Theory of Value and Distribution* (Duckworth, 1983), p. 16.
4. A. Leijonhufvud, 'Ideology and Analysis in Macro-economics', in P. Hoskowski (ed.), *Economics and Philosophy* (Tübingen, 1985).
5. F. Hahn, *Equilibrium and Macroeconomics* (Basil Blackwell, 1984), p. 65.
6. Brian J. Loasby, *Choice, Complexity and Ignorance* (Cambridge University Press, 1976), p. 26.
7. P. Deane, *The Evolution of Economic Ideas* (Cambridge University Press, 1978), p. 223.
8. Hahn, *Equilibrium and Macroeconomics*, p. 65.
9. Leijonhufvud, 'Ideology and Analysis in Macro-economics', p. 188.
10. H. Woo, *What's Wrong with Formalization in Economics?* (Victoria Press, 1986), p. 91.
11. A. Leijonhufvud, 'Hicks on Time and Money', Conference Paper, pp. 27–8.
12. J. Hicks, *Economic Perspectives* (Oxford University Press, 1977), p. vii.
13. Eatwell and Millgate (eds), *Keynes's Economics*, pp. 13–14.
14. Marco Magnani, '"Keynesian Fundamentalism": a critique' in ibid., p. 249.
15. See, for instance, Pierangelo Garegnani, 'Notes on consumption, investment and effective demand' in ibid., p. 23.
16. F. Machlup, 'Equilibrium and Disequilibrium: Misplaced Concreteness and Disguised Politics', *Economic Journal*, **68**(1), 1958, p. 9.
17. L.M. Lachmann, *Capital, Expectations and the Market Process* (Sheed Andrews and McMeel, 1977), pp. 117, 246.
18. J. Röpke, 'Evolution and Innovation' in K. Dopfer and K.F. Raible (eds), *The Evolution of Economic Systems* (Macmillan, 1990), pp. 111, 114, 115, 116.
19. A. Sen, 'Economic Methodology: Heterogeneity and Relevance', *Methodus*, **3**(1), 1991, pp. 70, 71.

2. Maximisation and rationality

Profit maximisation has no unequivocal meaning outside economists' models. (B. Loasby)

No one is assumed to maximise anything. (P. Earl)

It is not clear in a sequence economy what it is that a firm should maximise. (F. Hahn)

Firms maximise profits. Individuals maximise individual utility. For textbook after textbook, for model after model, these are axiomatic truths. I accept that as rough approximations to real behaviour, such assumptions have their uses, but as scientific propositions they have some difficulty in standing up. For they can neither be proved nor disproved, they are inherently unfalsifiable. Let me illustrate by using the name of Johnnie Walker, which is a well-known whisky firm and also the name of quite a few individuals in Scotland.

Suppose the firm of Johnnie Walker makes a grant to Scottish opera, or to Conservative party funds, or doubles its directors' fees, or sponsors a football team, or does none of these things, while earning a 10, 15 or 20 per cent return on its capital, this would all qualify as 'maximising'. For how could one prove it was not? This would be so if its directors devoted twelve hours a day seven days a week to their business, or if they took off to Honolulu for a month (after all they might come back refreshed and energetic). Some textbooks assert that firms that do not maximise profits would be forced out of business by the competition of those who do, and use this as an argument against accepting Herbert Simon's 'satisficing' alternative. But this seems to be yet another example of the intellectual penalties paid for the static-equilibrium approach. To cite Hahn, 'it is a fair question whether it can ever be useful to have an equilibrium notion which does not describe the termination of the actual processes.'[1] In equilibrium the less efficient firms have already been eliminated. So whatever is, must conform to the maximising axiom, which is then devoid of meaning.

Galbraith as well as Simon have long been stressing the relevance, in this context, of the division between ownership and management. As Galbraith several times observed, it is extraordinary how little this has influenced 'mainstream' presentation of managerial motives. Simon's 'sat-isficing', in the sense of adopting a profit and dividend strategy that keeps the shareholders from protesting too much, seems an acceptable way of presenting the situation in corporations, where the 'owner' is barely even definable. (Institutional investors – pension funds, insurance companies, investment trusts – buy and sell corporations' stocks and shares with other peoples' money.) It is surely valuable and important to observe and note the contrast between behaviour and motives of the *owner*–entrepreneur and the corporate executive. Yet, as Shlomo Maital has pointed out: 'Economists do very little research built on direct obser-vations conducted personally by the researcher.'[2]

But, as will be pointed out when discussing theories of the firm, within the equilibrium paradigm management has virtually no function, no role. In which case this species of economist might consider research into actual managerial behaviour a waste of time. It is odd to find Marxists arguing that such theories are a form of apologetics for capitalism, for what role is there, in general equilibrium, for capitalists or entrepreneurs (as the Austrians have been rightly pointing out).

In the most recent years attention has been focused on the very large increase in company executives' remuneration. It has risen very much faster than average earnings in general, and in an extreme case cited from *Business Week* in *The Times*,[3] the chief executive of United Airlines 'earned' \$18 million in 1990, a year in which the profits of the company *fell* by 73 per cent! The above example is typical of a trend, which has been the subject of a well-researched book by Graef Crystal.[4] The gap between the pay of the 'boss' and the average employee appears to have multiplied tenfold in recent years. And no correlation can be found between remuneration and managerial performance. On a very much lower level, anyone who moves from the civil service or a university into the business world cannot but be struck by the lavish expenses from which executives benefit (from stretch limousines with built-in whisky bottles all the way to 'gold-topped desks'). Is this maximising profits?

In this connection, it may be useful to adapt Tullock's and Buchanan's 'public choice' theories to the present instance, that is, to 'private choice'. It will be recalled that such theories assert that public servants, politicians, bureaucrats, are seeking to maximise their own individual utility (incomes, promotion, and so on). It will be argued that this can be an example of methodological individualism taken too far. But let us look at the corpo-ration executive from this point of view. If he is the owner, or a major shareholder, then clearly he (or she) is directly interested in profit. The tra-ditional image of the protestant ethic has the entrepreneur denying himself luxuries, ploughing back earnings into the firm, to the benefit of his own long-term fortune and glory. But the non-owner executive need have no long-term commitment; indeed, according to a recent survey, in the United States he moves to another corporation on an average within five years. His (rarely her) motive may be seen as maximising personal income, subject to the 'satisficing' constraint: the scale of his takings must not be such as to goad shareholders into forming a coalition against him.

The situation may not be totally unlike that of a president of a central American republic. He can take as much as he thinks he can get away with. And no one considers that this has any connection with his marginal productivity. Whether what he actually takes represents a 'maximum' in any meaningful sense is a question with no answer, as is also the case for the corporation executive. And both can fail to assess correctly the tolerance of colleagues.

In theory the shareholders can set limits, can bring to heel and dismiss incompetent and excessively greedy executives. There is a growing literature on the relationship between principal and agent, though most of this is concerned with situations in which there is one clearly-defined principal, which is far from being the case in most corporations. In the real world too there are instances where shareholders can take action, and there can be takeover bids, which discontented shareholders could support. It is a matter of empirical research to evaluate their countervailing *power*. The answer cannot be derived from abstract theoretical formulations. Kurt Rothschild, many years ago, deplored the lack of attention paid to 'power in economics'.[5] It surely affects both decision-making and income distribution. It equally surely is absent altogether from neoclassical models, except in the context of applying games theory.

An interesting question arises: if executives had the power all along to award themselves very high personal incomes, why is it that their remuneration has soared far above average earnings in the past 10–15 years? Statistics clearly show this to be the case. Is it a byproduct of the spirit of Reaganism–Thatcherism? Or is it that chief executives have become relatively scarce in relation to demand? By what mechanism is their remuneration determined? Has this mechanism changed? All these questions seem to imply some modification of the 'profit maximisation' axiom.

In any event, why assume maximisation? Is there *any* reason, other than that of mathematical convenience of exposition? Why is it not sufficient to note that, other things being equal, a higher profit is preferred to a lower profit? One must then also discuss the long-term versus the short-term issue: the two may conflict. Then there are questions linked with goodwill, discussed at length elsewhere – the desire to maintain stable relations with customers and suppliers, the effect on one's competitors, actual or potential, and of one's price policies. Even to raise such

questions requires one to depart from the assumptions of perfect competition, for reasons already gone into. It affects monopoly theory too.
There is William Baumol's valuable concept of 'contingent competition':
a monopolist's monopoly power may be conditional upon it not being
abused, for that might make it worth a potential competitor to enter the
field. Here again the neoclassical paradigm can be not just irrelevant but
harmful to understanding. To cite Frank Hahn yet again: 'if price
changes are themselves the outcome of the rational assessment of their
consequences for the agent making the change, then we can no longer
take the neoclassical axiom for granted'.[6] Hahn goes on to defend the
axiom, yet he would surely be the first to agree that administered prices,
decided upon after at least an attempt at the rational assessment of the
consequences, are the rule and not the exception.

The reader should now refer back to the three citations with which this
chapter began.

Let us now turn to *individual* utility-maximisation, that is, to my (imaginary) *Mr* Johnnie Walker. Some of the same objections to the axiom at
once spring to mind. It is, again, unfalsifiable. If Mr Walker gives money
to charity, if he beats his wife, if he takes drugs, if he works a twelve-hour
day, if he prefers leisure, if he derives pleasure from doing his job well, or
he shirks whenever he can get away with it, if he takes bribes, or refuses
to take bribes, he thereby reveals his preferences. He must be (by definition) acting to maximise his utility, *whatever he does*. In the hands of
Becker this sort of analysis extends beyond economics, even to the choice
of a wife, or whether to have a child, thus proving that tautology has no
disciplinary limits.

No wonder that Hahn can write that 'no meaning can be given in classical general equilibrium theory to the notion of equilibrium with
involuntary unemployment',[7] and Lucas is logical when he regards unemployment as 'leisure preference' (or job search), since he considers
whatever exists to be equilibrium, while neoclassical theory does tend to
assume that every individual is always in equilibrium.

How can one escape from tautology? Possibly by limiting oneself to
maximising income or wealth, subject to constraints. But in doing so one
is compelled to abstract from the complexities of human motivation, even
within that which should properly belong to *homo economicus*. Adam
Smith noted two centuries ago that curates have a long and expensive
education, yet they earn less than journeymen stonemasons.[8] This brings
one to the case made by Tibor Scitovsky in his aptly titled *Joyless
Economy*.[9] While orthodox theory does recognise that some jobs carry
with them more disutility (pain, unpleasantness) than others, the idea of
job satisfaction, of pride in work well done, seems not to be taken seri-

ously. Indeed Scitovsky had problems in getting his book published. Among the points he makes is – as statistics prove – that anyone who feels he is working for him- or herself, with control over work time, tends on average to work much longer hours than individuals who work for others. I used this in a critique of the then minister for higher education, Jackson, who had been proposing a fixed working week for university staffs. These are, of course, in a formal sense employees, but have considerable control over what they do and when they do it, and so feel to some degree self-employed. According to the textbook this should lead to widespread shirking, yet, although our profession does contain some shirkers, evidence suggests that longer hours are worked by most than the 9 to 5 routine which might be imposed on them. (It used to be said: 'If they compel me to come in at 9, I will leave promptly at 5').

It is intuitively evident that efficiency depends *inter alia* on work commitment, the desire to do the job well, a reluctance to shirk even when opportunities to shirk do exist. This applies to a wide range of occupations, from university professors to office cleaners, from managers to mechanics. Indifference and lack of commitment can and does result in inefficiency. It is important to note that below the top officials employees can seldom see the connection between what they do (or fail to do) and the firm's profitability. To some extent, therefore, doing the job well becomes a 'good' in itself. Indifference and apathy can be encountered in all systems. Thus poor work performance in Soviet industry, agriculture and trade was widely attributed to 'alienation', to being ordered about, to being at the receiving end of arbitrary decisions. There are other reasons too: the effect of over-full employment on labour discipline, the frequent non-arrival of needed inputs, and so on. The point is that human motivation is far too complex to be seen in terms of maximising either income or utility, except in the tautological sense which deprives the term of meaning.

This has a direct bearing on the applicability to the real world of what has come to be known as the theory of *public choice*. It is surely right and proper to question the commitment of public officials at any level to the ill-defined (and probably undefinable) 'general interest'. Officials, politicians and bureaucrats are human, are subject to pressure from interest groups, and have interests of their own. Thus far there is nothing to quarrel with. Where Buchanan and his colleagues appear (to me) to go too far is that their interpretation is purely one of *individual* maximisation. This surely is too narrow a conception, whether applied to the public *or* the private sector. The head of a research laboratory in the private or the public sector has a commitment to the research laboratory. Buchanan himself has a commitment to his institution and to the spread of the ideas in which he believes. Whoever is in charge of kindergardens, public parks, a city's police force, water supply, sanitation, a university library, or whatever, is concerned for the sectors for which he or she is responsible. True enough, the 'public interest' is indeed indefinable operationally, but what tends to happen is that each of the individuals mentioned will press for more resources to be devoted to the research laboratory, kindergarten, parks, police, library, and so on, identifying this with the public interest as he or she conceives it. Yes, in varying degrees, the individuals will indeed be concerned also for personal income and advancement. But by focusing exclusively on *individual* advantage the 'public choice' school show their ideology. True, they allow for occasional outbursts of 'altruism'. But the parks superintendents, librarians, and so on, are not 'altruist' by identifying with their jobs. They are behaving like normal human beings, as do individuals within private corporations, too. The ideology shows because 'public choice' theory is used to justify privatisation and a reduction in the regulatory or other active role for public authorities.

An interesting contrast was recently demonstrated in Great Britain. Managing directors of newly-privatised utilities (water, electricity, gas) awarded themselves huge pay increases, causing even the Conservative prime minister to express disapproval. The degree of the individual financial ambitions (greed?) of the individuals concerned was surely unaltered. It was just that in the *public* service the income controls were tighter. Since these were the same individuals 'before' and 'after', it could not be that higher salaries were needed to attract them to the job they were in already. If 'public choice' theory implies that in the public service there are greater opportunities for feathering one's own nest, or 'rent-seeking', this particular experience suggests the contrary.

Indeed, one wonders, as did Schumpeter long ago, whether a society can exist in which all seek nothing but their own short-term advantage. If *all* citizens are supposed to be pursuing their individual profit maximisation, does this extend to judges and police officers? Should university teachers sell degrees or degree grades to the highest bidder? Prostitution becomes a comparatively honest profession in a society so organised. But can any society be so organised and survive? (This does not matter, if one supposes, as did Mrs Thatcher, that 'there is no such thing as society'. There will be more to say about the excesses of pure individualism.) Do we wish doctors to act as profit maximisers? How many good doctors wish to be so regarded, or so regard themselves?

The excesses of naive and axiomatic individualism have not been immune from criticism. Amartya Sen, for example, noting that 'self-interest maximization has become the standard – almost universal – assumption used in modern economics', considers this 'rather remarkable given the fact that many other types of objectives and values clearly do have a role in human thinking and action'. It is assumed that 'rationality requires maximization of self-interest'. He rightly remarks that, 'Even if it were the case that a relentlessly profit-maximizing individual would do better in a society where others in that society were inclined in other directions, it does not follow at all that a society in which everyone is self-interest maximizing would do better than another in which self-interested behavior is standardly constrained by systematic adherence to "rules of conduct".' He added: 'Human behavior is influenced by a variety of considerations that go beyond the narrowly economic.'[10] Quite so! Many of us have no one maximand: we may be interested in archaeology, mountain-climbing, charity, horses, the violin, the Talmud, ice-hockey, interior decoration even womanising. In pursuing these or many other activities, while *also* trying to increase our income, are we being 'irrational'? Or are these 'constraints', or are they to be in the individual's utility function? Which of us single-mindedly pursues just one objective? Schumpeter declared his aims in life to be the greatest economist, the greatest horseman and the greatest lover (but that unfortunately there were no horses at Harvard!). Was Schumpeter then not an 'economic man'? The distinguished Russian economist V. Novozhilov was an excellent violinist. So was Einstein. The composer Borodin was an eminent professor of chemistry. And so on.

What *is* 'rationality'? Some ask: can we meaningfully assert that no one can behave rationally unless the future is at least stochastically 'certain'? What is theoretically new about the concept 'rational expectations'? After all, everyone, from Adam Smith to Keynes inclusive, was well aware that action is deeply influenced by what agents expect to occur, and that, despite a human tendency to extrapolate, most people know most of the time that the future is not likely to be precisely similar to the past. Also it seems evident that people are not omniscient, that human attention span and ability to assimilate information are limited, that the amount of information potentially available (and particularly with the boom in information technology) vastly exceeds anyone's ability to cope with it. We have seen the development of the concept of *bounded* rationality.

There is a considerable 'methodological' literature on the subject both of rationality and on the meaning to be attached to 'economic man'. J.G. Merquoir denied that *homo economicus* is a 'heartless and tasteless philistine', or 'a vile materialist'. He or she 'calculates', 'weighs things', 'chooses', 'evaluates', but 'nothing prevents the objects of his desire from being amongst the most human, the most "noble" that we have.'[11] Rationality then is simply acting in a consistent manner in pursuit of *any* objective. Though David Hume long ago asserted that 'reason is, and must be, the servant of the passions', reasonable men act rationally. Thus if A's motive to travel to Edinburgh is to see his beloved, it would not be rational for A to go to Waterloo station in London. Or to cite A. Wildavsky: 'only means may be said to be rational, not ends'.[12]

Almost any action can be described, *post factum*, as rational, given the constraints and the uncertainties. Tautology is an ever-present danger. Since we pursue several objectives in life simultaneously, and have imperfect knowledge, we often seem to act inconsistently – but then one man's inconsistency can be subsumed under the heading of constraints: thus Novozhilov's time in playing the violin was limited by his work as an economist, and vice versa. Stalin's desire to have efficient generals who could beat the Germans was constrained by fear of efficient generals who might conspire against him, so he had most of them shot on the eve of the last war; he could be judged to be 'rational' whether he shot them or no, after the event, whatever it was.

More will be said in a subsequent chapter about individualism. But it is relevant in the present context to cite Jerry Evensky's critique of Gary Becker's concept of Man as a 'substantially rational' being, whose beliefs and desires are a sort of unchanging data, and whose origins remained unexamined.[13] For me Becker is tautology *à l'outrance*: generosity, meanness, altruism, workaholism, sobriety, *any* action or inaction, in any field, can be fitted into the utility maximisation principle. As I see it, it explains everything, as thus nothing.

In discussing Adam Smith's and David Hume's ideas on the subject of self-interest, Stephen Holmes notes that 'Smith repeatedly states that self-interest, however robust, is merely one motive among others', while for Hume 'the very idea of interest-driven behaviour is meaningless . . . , unless we can identify behaviour which is *not* interest-driven'. Like this author, Hume argued against 'binary schemes' like egoism–altruism, there are also 'passions', including 'non-selfish murderous behaviour', as well as 'benevolence'.[14]

Those who advocate the acceptance of 'rational expectations' ask their critics: do you then assert that people act on *irrational* expectations? This appears to me to be a play on words. One can ask them: do they then believe in *unbounded* rationality? It would seem that what the rational-expectation theorists have done is to smuggle in uncertainty (or at least stochastic, probability-certainty) where it is needed to make models determinate on paper. Models based on maximisation under constraints, on general equilibrium, do face logical difficulties in introducing the uncertainty that goes with real time. This is indeed a logical-mathematical obstacle. This the models seek to overcome. There is a Russian saying: *bumaga vsyo terpit*, 'paper can bear anything'. But what of the real world? Here we must indeed stress the vital importance of expectations.

But the future can be seen differently by people who try rationally to weigh up the contradictory factors that might determine, for instance, the dollar–yen or dollar–mark exchange rates, which, as everyone would agree, have a sizeable effect both on micro and the macro economy. It is precisely *because* of such differences of view that, at any given moment, some are buying and others are selling dollars and yen and marks. Some agents interpret the same factors differently, others have taken cognisance of different bits of information which their particular interests or interest have caused them to focus on. What on earth can be the meaning of 'perfect information' when, as already stressed, there is so much more of it than anyone can encompass. There is another Russian saying: *Nel'zya obyat' neobyatnoe*, 'one cannot encompass the unencompassable'.

The 'new-classical' version, or extension, of the neoclassical paradigm has an inner logic to it, insofar as some puzzles left unanswered in neoclassical models are made mathematically determinate. It is, one presumes, their answer to Lachmann, who argued that 'We must therefore conclude that expectations, and other subjective elements, constitute an alien body within the organism of formal model analysis. The conflict remains unresolved.'[15] Have they resolved it? They may have found an answer, but surely at the cost of assuming an unacceptable degree of knowledge of the future. The Archbishop of York has written: 'Omniscience does not entail knowing what cannot be known, and since the future does not yet exist there is a proper sense in which God can be said not to know it.'[16] Can Lucas, Muth *et al.* envisage agents who know more than God? An earlier generation of economists, or a resurrected Marshall, would be puzzled: what purpose, other than mathematical determination, do such theories serve? One accepts, of course, that people act in accordance with their expectations, and that, in forming their expectations, agents do try to be 'rational' – though just what they are supposed to maximise is another question (see above).

The existence of Walrasian general equilibrium, in which all agents maximise subject to constraints, is said to have been 'proved' by theoretical developments since his time, especially by the Arrow and Debreu models. The word 'proved' has puzzled me, along with the word 'existence'. After all, we are not in a state of general equilibrium, and never have been. What has been proved is that it is possible to define conditions in which it *would* exist, the mathematical problem of exposition has been solved. But *could* such conditions exist in real life? The solution, as has already been stressed, neglects, or assumes away, the problems connected with time and uncertainty, and also (as Loasby pointed out) choice. Fully predetermined choice is a contradiction in terms: where real choice exists there *must* be uncertainty, if only about what others will choose. So general equilibrium models have to assume that the choices have already been made, covering in predetermined contracts the present and the future.

The temptation then exists, and some have not resisted it, to move from this theoretical construct to real mother earth, and to neglect process, the passage of real time, the inevitable degree of partial ignorance of agents (if only about what other agents will choose to do) and the existence of errors, inefficiencies and, as will be shown, adopt the philosophy of Dr Pangloss.

Rational expectations, market clearing prices, agents who exercise perfect or all-but-perfect foresight, add up to an optimal world. Imperfections of organisation, which result in unnecessary transaction costs, will have been eliminated, for if they existed there would be neither general equilibrium nor Pareto optimality.

It becomes difficult even to contemplate error. If individual actions are 'rational' (purposeful), and he or she has the needed information, then mistakes cannot be rational, even though McKee and West have allowed for what they call 'rational ignorance', that is, doing one's best subject to informational constraints. They then reach the conclusion (I quote P. Nicolaides) 'that government intervention to correct market distortions is both impossible and unnecessary, because *economies function optimally*.'[17] This position is clearly related to Lucas's 'new-classical' view that the economy as well as all individuals, is at any given moment in equilibrium. '[T]he status quo cannot be improved upon because individuals always exploit any potential benefits. Any apparent unexploited benefits imply that individuals are somehow constrained either because of hidden costs or because of imperfect information which would be too costly to improve upon.'[18]

Dr Pangloss, thou shouldst be living at this hour! Surely Alfred Marshall would not have accepted this as economics. Thousands of bankruptcies occur every year, and common sense suggests that businessmen, though doing their best to be 'rational', make mistakes, and it should not require philosophical circumlocutions to recognise the obvious. Errors apart, this (in my view illegitimate) distortion of the static equilibrium concept would lead us to suppose that competition will already have rendered impossible the existence of poor quality of any good or service, that abnormal profits and losses will already have been eliminated (for otherwise there is not equilibrium), that British managers do not come into work late or have long 'business' lunches, that secretaries are not hired with an eye to their beauty rather than their productivity, that nepotism cannot exist in profit-maximising business, or race-prejudice either . . . (that they ought not to exist in a '_____al' timeless equilibrium is another story). Such work as Hirschman's *Exit, Voice and Loyalty* on the correction of defects is then clearly superfluous, since the defects will already have been corrected.

Let us take a contemporary British and Japanese example. In the late 1980s there was a boom in office building. Let us suppose that this was due to the (rational?) expectation of high rents, due to shortage of modern office space. Unfortunately, many property developers observed this possibility, shared this expectation, and there was an over-reaction, not dissimilar to the 'cobweb' in agriculture. Result: fall in rents below expected levels, losses and bankruptcies in the property sector, a sharp fall in activity in the building industry. It is unnecessary in accounting for these events to assume that anyone was acting 'irrationally', but plainly there were mistakes. The problem, in theory *and* practice, is that the mistakes could only have been avoided if every agent knew every other agent's intentions, but in the competitive model such knowledge is difficult to conceptualise. Now it so happens that the British government, for good or bad reasons, curtailed public-sector housing construction. It also found it necessary to resort to historically very high real rates of interest, which depressed the private housing market. Suppose the government then decided to encourage municipal housing and also double the authorised investment in railways, roads, ports, school-building. This would make no difference to the real economy? Or to unemployment? Or to profits? Of course, one must take into account the opportunity-cost of whatever is done, but unless one makes the preposterous assumption that employers in the building industry prefer near bankruptcy and their workers prefer leisure, *and* that any capital used in these investment programmes will 'crowd out' other investments that would have been undertaken, there can be cases where government intervention makes a difference, because economies do not necessarily 'function optimally'.

I agree at once that neoclassical economics need not lead to such inherently implausible conclusions. But it does help to train a cast of mind for which these conclusions do not seem inherently implausible.

So, finally, what could and should one say, to the earnest student from Moscow, Warsaw or Calcutta, about 'maximisation', of profit and of utility? I suggest: stress the ambiguity of the concept of maximisation, the evident danger of tautology in using the terms. At the same time, it is also proper to stress the drive for profit, and for income and status, as powerful motivating factors which must be harnessed in the pursuit of efficient production of goods and services. Failure to do so, the attempt to substitute administrative orders, and attaching rewards to the fulfilment of plan-orders were among prime causes of the failure of Soviet-type economies.

At the same time the students need to be warned of the complexities involved in distinguishing long-term and short-term profits, and of the possible consequences of the separation of ownership from control (management). The student may find 'public choice' theory congenial, since in the USSR that state (and the one Party) can be shown to have pursued policies designed to enhance the power and privileges of the ruling stratum. They may need reminding that corporation executives can behave in a similar fashion, and that the countervailing forces which should prevent abuses in both the private *and* the public sector do not always countervail.

NOTES

1. F. Hahn, *Equilibrium and Macroeconomics* (Basil Blackwell, 1984), p. 48.
2. Shlomo Maital, 'Observing by Watching: Putting People Back into Methodology', *Methodus*, **2**(1), 1990, p. 48.
3. Philip Robinson, 'US bosses' pay soars above staff', *The Times*, 29 April 1991, p. 21.
4. G. Crystal, *In Search of Excess: The Overcompensation of America's Executives* (Norton, 1991).
5. K.W. Rothschild, 'Introduction' in K.W. Rothschild, *Power in Economics. Selected Readings* (Penguin, 1971), pp. 7–17.
6. F. Hahn, *Equilibrium and Macroeconomics*, p. 85.
7. Ibid., p. 84.
8. A. Smith, *The Wealth of Nations*, Volume 1 (Oxford University Press, 1909), pp. 147–8.
9. T. Scitovsky, *Joyless Economy* (Oxford University Press, 1976).
10. Amartya Sen, 'Economic Methodology: Heterogeneity and Relevance', *Methodus*, **3**(1), 1991, pp. 74, 75, 76.
11. J.G. Merquoir, 'Death to *Homo Economicus*?', *Critical Review*, **5**(3), 1991, p. 356.
12. A. Wildavsky, 'Accounting for Political Preferences: Cultural Theory vs. Cultural History', *Critical Review*, **5**(3), 1991, p. 311.
13. Jerry Evensky, 'The Role of Community Values in Modern Classic Liberal Economic Thought', *Scottish Journal of Political Economy*, **39**(1), 1992, esp. pp. 23–7.
14. S. Holmes, 'The Secret History of Self-Interest' in J.J. Mansbridge (ed.), *Beyond Self-Interest* (University of Chicago Press, 1990), pp. 268–70.
15. L.M. Lachmann, *Capital, Expectations and the Market Process* (Sheed Andrews and McMeel, 1977), p. 249.
16. John Ebor, Letter in *The Times*, 9 October 1991, p. 19.
17. Phedon Nicolaides, 'Positive and Normative Conflicts in the Expanding Domain of Economics: Induced Distortions and Rules', *Methodus*, **2**(1), 1990, p. 12. Emphasis added.
18. Ibid., p. 14 (n.b.: this is not Nicolaides's view!).

3. Margins, marginalism and the firm

One speaks of the 'marginalist' revolution as having taken place over a hundred years ago. Along with equilibrium, the textbooks are full of phrases implying that marginal this must equal marginal everything else, to borrow a phrase from Shubik. The marginal product, the marginal labourer, marginal costs, marginal cost pricing, and so on. As presented, it seems simple: one is speaking of the product attributable to the addition or subtraction of one labourer, of one unit of capital, or of land of a given quality, or of one additional item of product, such as a batch of footwear or a bushel of wheat. The same goes for marginal rates of substitution. The concept of 'margin' is indeed of great importance, the anti-marginalism one found in Marx's followers required to be criticised. Yet, as Cairncross put it, 'marginal theory is usually taught in terms of a single margin when in fact there are a great many'.[1] I could add: and they are multi-level. A similar caveat may be found in the work of Axel Leijonhufvud:

> It [the neoclassical production function] does not describe production as a process, that is, as an ordered sequence of operations. It is more like a recipe for bouillabaisse where all ingredients are dumped in a pot (K, L), heated up, $f(\cdot)$ and the output, X, is ready . . . [The] neoclassical production theory gives no clue to how production is actually organised.[2]

And Kenneth Boulding refers to 'what I have sometimes called the "cookbook theory of production" – that we mix together land, labour and capital, and out come potatoes'.[3]

Let us leave aside for the present the issue of substitutability, and concentrate instead on the fact that most firms are multi-product, and that production takes place in interrelated sequences, involving several processes, through time. The omission of any one of these processes, or the withdrawal of whosoever carries it out, would bring production to a halt. What, then, is that person's marginal product? To take a quite different example: an oil pipeline from Siberia crosses to Ukraine on its way to central Europe. If the Ukraine blocks it, losses to producers and consumers alike would be severe. Negotiations are in progress about transit fees. These cannot be based on any incremental or marginal analysis, though light can be shed by application of games theory to the bargaining process, which would take into account the many factors 'external' to that segment of pipeline. How can one evaluate any of these sequential and interconnected tasks or processes other than by reference to totality? Here, by the way, is a more important reason for the existence of firms (as coordinators) than the 'transaction costs' approach, as will be argued later. As Leijonhufvud also points out, each process may differ in respect of economies of scale. Perhaps this is what Hahn had in mind when he wrote: 'there are logical difficulties in accounting for the existence of agents called firms at all unless we allow there to be increasing returns of some sort.'[4]

Suppose, as is frequently the case, a marginal decision relating to one part of the interconnected whole can have an effect, positive or negative, on other parts of that whole. Then this effect needs to be taken into consideration by the decision-maker. Indeed, unless the whole does contain interconnections, 'internalities', indivisibilities, complementarities, it is difficult to see why it should exist at all. Imagine any firm, divided into *n* sub-units, concerned with such activities as acquisition of material inputs, several distinct processes of manufacture, testing, storage, transport, marketing, after-sales service. Each of these activities may be presumed to have some individual in charge of them, each of whom must be presumed to have some decision-making powers. However, the firm will have rules, under which certain types or magnitude of decision require to be referred upwards. Such rules are needed to ensure that *internal* effects (that is, effects on other parts of the firm, or on the firm as a totality) are taken into account. Marginal decisions can, and should, be seen as multi-level, with, corresponding to this, a hierarchy. It is this that explains the hierarchy's existence. Within any organisation or firm, what appears to be the rational thing to do depends in some degree on the area of responsibility of the decision-maker. This is because a particular decision-maker may simply be unaware of the effect of his or her decision on other parts of the organisation, or, even if aware, would give priority to his or her department's interests. Therefore changes in organisation, in defining areas of responsibility, can and often do affect decisions. A moment's thought will surely provide any number of examples from the experience of any reader of these words. Yet this elementary point is, to my knowledge, *never* made in textbooks on microeconomics, as if the rationality of marginal decisions is unaffected by the organisational structure. Margins are presented one-dimensionally, and decisions are related to the market, and not to other decisions or other parts of the organisation. No wonder there have been difficulties in defining the reasons why firms exist.

Part of the problem lies in the silent assumption that the interests of the whole are but the sum of the interests of the parts. This aspect of 'methodological individualism' led to what I have called 'fragmentation-ism'.[5] For if the whole is only the sum of its parts, these can be costlessly hived off, and money can be saved by selling head office and disposing of the corporation's bureaucracy. More will be said about all this in a moment in connection with O. Williamson's concepts. At present it must simply be stressed that hierarchies exist, and some categories of decisions are referred upwards, because marginal or incremental decisions taken at lower levels, in terms of local interest as seen at these levels, can have deleterious (or disproportionately positive) effects elsewhere, and one reason for having firms and hierarchies is to *internalise* what would other-wise be externalities.

It also appears to be silently assumed (the contrary is not stated) that every decision and transaction is or should be profitable, that loss-making should not be covered by profits from other activities, for that would be cross-subsidisation, and cross-subsidisation is seen as irrational. While some kinds of cross-subsidisation may indeed by economically inefficient, one can produce a long catalogue of examples where this is emphatically not the case. Failure to acquaint students with such examples can lead to regrettably short-sighted decisions, which I like to call *myopic marginal-ism.* Let us look at some.

Suppose a firm aspires to be your city's equivalent of Fortnum and Mason of London, or Fauchon in Paris, or Yesileyev in old Moscow, that is, to be known for its vast choice of foodstuffs. In an actual instance, a new owner employed myopic-marginalist accountants. They made a long list of items which moved slowly, were seldom demanded; to stock them appeared unprofitable. The resultant sharp reduction in the assortment of products had the effect of destroying the shop's raison d'être. People no longer had any reason to take the trouble to visit it from afar. Soon it closed. Moral: in deciding whether or not to stock caviar, or smoked salmon, or truffles, marginal decisions all, you should not only calculate the (marginal) saving which would follow from cancelling the order, but also the possible effect on the shop as a whole. If profit is said to be obtained from the reputation of having a wide choice, this involved stock-ing some items which, if evaluated separately, would appear to be loss-making. This is but one example of the importance of *goodwill,* which links *all* transactions of any firm with each other: reputation for quality, choice and reliability pays, the reverse does not. It is to me incredible that so vital an element in real-life microeconomics gets barely a mention in textbooks.

Any supermarket which has a free (or loss-making) car park 'cross-subsidises', and would be foolish not to. Or take another decision which can be characterised as marginal: should trains to the suburbs run after

7 p.m., since after that hour they make a loss. Before deciding, it is surely necessary to consider the effect on those passengers who normally travel before that hour, any of whom may be called upon to work (or play) later. They might then travel in by car, to be sure of being able to get home. So, once again, decisions must be seen in contexts. A loss from activity A might be a precondition for profit from activity B undertaken by the same firm.

Mention of railways reminds one of an almost classical example of the disease I have in mind. The late Denis Munby, referring to a rail network, recommended that each segment of line, station, marshalling yard, be as far as practicable regarded and evaluated separately. In other words, disassemble the system, externalise internalities. It is this sort of logic which underlies the present British government's transport policy: the idea is to divide up the railway system and urban transportation. The *network*, the interrelationships, disappear from view. A less ideological view is taken in other countries from America to Switzerland inclusive. (More on transport in a subsequent chapter.)

In an earlier work, I cited an example of the perversity of the outlawing of cross-subsidisation. Suppose a feeder service of any sort operates at a loss, but its closure would inflict a bigger loss onto the service into which it feeds. This is a simple case of the marketing of externalities: it would pay the 'fed' to subsidise the 'feeder'. But suppose both are under the same ownership: then this becomes 'cross-subsidisation', and so apparently irrational!

Other examples spring easily to mind. Suppose there is an island, and on it there is a hotel complex. Transport to the island could be by boat, or by air. Any marginal decision relating only to the boat or airfield must surely take into account the impact, positive or negative, on the hotels. It may be that the hotels (or the island's local authority) may wish to own and operate the boats or the airfield. More will have to be said about the externality/internality issue later, and about infrastructure too. The essential point is that the separate consideration of the profitability of boat or airfield could be inconsistent with the needs of the tourist industry as a whole.

The 'no cross-subsidisation' rule can produce perverse or even comic results. Should public lavatories in stations be closed if they do not pay? Should the Edinburgh Festival or the Barcelona Olympics be regarded as *economically* unjustified even if the subsidy they receive is a fraction of the extra revenue which it brings to the hotels and shops of Edinburgh and Barcelona? Or, to take a university example, does one close down the department of Italian (which has few students) without considering the effect on the teaching of comparative romance philology for which that university has a high reputation? Or disregard the contribution of the existence of a department of statistics in the teaching of economics? In any system or network of activities, the parts *interrelate*. Decisions are taken in contexts, and exactly the same 'micro' information could lead quite rationally to a different decision if the context (or the firm's strategy) is different. Obvious? Yes, to a non-economist. It is not a matter that comes naturally into the purview of a mathematically-minded neoclassical economist. His models lead his thoughts elsewhere.

More examples come to mind as these words are written. Thus the *New Yorker*, in an article on New York's Chinatown tells us that buses that take gamblers to Atlantic City (where gambling is legal) are subsidised by the gambling houses. Were they 'irrational' in so doing? An article whose author deplores cross-subsidisation in transport was published in the London *Times*, which, since it is priced the same in northern Scotland as in London, cross-subsidises *its* transport costs, as does any firm which charges (and advertises) a price nationally. Within any transport network, which charges any standard fare by zone or by distance, there must be an element of cross-subsidisation, since costs and revenue per passenger-mile differ widely. In a sense individuals, like firms, having chosen a role, find themselves 'cross-subsidising' when they take the rough with the smooth. Example: correcting examination scripts is an activity which, evaluated in isolation on a pleasure–pain scale, will most certainly rate 'pain', and this university teacher would not undertake it, were it not part of a chosen role (teaching and research) which, by giving job satisfaction (and income), more than compensates for the pain of reading these tiresome scripts. This is indeed obvious, and should not need saying. Yet texts relating to firms imply all things that they do, if separately evaluated, are or should be profitable.

This relates also to the issue of reserve capacity, mentioned in the introduction. When demand is uneven, or there are other uncertainties, reserve capacity is necessary to avoid loss of goodwill and market share under 'imperfect' (that is, real) competitive conditions. Under monopoly it could be commercially more profitable to have customers queue or to ration them, unless one has a sense of duty, or has such a sense imposed by regulators. To take another footballing example, Arsenal F.C. Ltd. keep a loss-making reserve team because, in the event of injury, replacements are needed, and the management would be held responsible if they were not available. A shuttle air service attracts passengers by guaranteeing them an unreserved seat, even though the standby plane and crew are loss-makers (to repeat an earlier example). But there is unclarity in the case of electricity after privatisation in Great Britain. While there are competing generating companies, none are responsible for estimating the *total* demand, for a homogenous product used by everyone. This had been the responsibility of the Central Electricity Generating Board. In France it was and is that of Electricité de France. While in Britain there will be a multiplicity of supply contracts, for supply via the national grid, the possibility exists that reserve capacity will be run down, and indeed a number of power stations have already been closed. This is not the place to go into detail, merely to note that, if one silently assumes that all one does will be profitable as such, the very possibility that such a problem could arise would not come to mind.

The problem is not privatisation as such. The issue is *responsibility*, as noted in the football example above. A private firm anxious for success will bear the loss involved in providing reserve capacity, but only if it would bear also the consequences of not doing so. Another recent negative example in Great Britain was the privatisation of Royal Ordnance. This state-owned and operated undertaking existed (for centuries!) to provide weapons and ammunition for the armed forces, and, clearly, in the absence of wars, demand for current output was modest. The (Thatcher) government, inspired by ideology, sold it to a private firm. Within months it had closed several factories, since there was greater profit to be made by selling the sites. The provision of reserve capacity for weapons and ammunition was not that firm's responsibility, so it acted rationally; what was irrational was unconditional privatisation, because it was clearly the *government*'s responsibility to decide whether this reserve capacity was or was not needed. Which was why it was *Royal* Ordnance in the first place! In the case of electricity, to repeat the point made earlier, once the electricity enters the grid, it is no longer clear who originally generated it, since all kilowatt-hours are alike and therefore it will not be clear which of many privately-owned power stations is to 'blame' if total capacity proves insufficient. Whereas, to take a different example, if the capacity of (say) Bass breweries proves insufficient to meet demand in a hot summer, it would be clear that the 'fault' would be that of this firm (and thirsty customers could drink Carlsberg or Watney's beer instead). Experience (including my own) suggests that the neoclassical marginal (incremental) approach is unable to focus on such issues as reserve capacity, because of the silent assumption that each act, or segment, or decision, is or should be profitable if separately evaluated.

One must not labour the point, but its omission from nearly every textbook justified restating what should be obvious: without in the least denying the importance of the 'marginal' concept, one must bear in mind that margins are, so to speak, both numerous and multi-dimensional, that one can say that to a hierarchy of margins there corresponds a hierarchy of decision-makers, the existence of one relating to the existence of the other. Much naturally depends on the context within which any decision is considered, the strategy pursued by the firm, what it considers itself (and is considered by others) to be responsible *for*. Exactly the same micro-circumstances can result in different decisions in different contexts without ceasing to be rational. Thus consider the 'marginal' power station and the standby plane in the two above examples. The context would determine whether they are worth investing in, or maintaining.

Marginal cost pricing is impeded both by the difficulty of identifying marginal cost in a multi-product multi-process enterprise, with sizeable overheads, but also by the identification of the margin itself. I recall Alan Day recommending marginal cost pricing for London's transport. I wrote to ask: *which* margin? The No. 13 bus? The No. 13 bus after 7 pm? The Northern line from Kensington to Morden? Buses north of the Thames at weekends? The 8.10 train from Orpington? I had no reply.

Nor is this obscurity exceptional. Lorie Tarshis is credited with the view that 'in the real world, the estimate of marginal cost for a multi-product firm is based on so many assumptions, each of them of doubtful validity, that the effort of estimating hardly seems worth it'.[6] Which has not prevented textbook after textbook referring to marginal cost (and marginal revenue) as clear and unambiguous concepts. Dennis C. Mueller, in a challenging article, draws attention to the words of Hall and Hitch, who cast doubt on the general applicability of conventional analysis of price and output policy in terms of marginal cost and marginal revenue, and, after citing other evidence, concludes that 'evidence gathered over two decades . . . directly contradicted the assumptions upon which most economic modelling of pricing was at that time, and is today, based'.[7] Like Galbraith before him, Mueller was pointing to the reluctance of the neoclassical mainstream to draw conclusions from the real behaviour and structure of the modern corporation. Of course, one could assert that management follows the marginal rule without knowing it, like Molière's Jourdain speaking prose, since it is the rational thing to do. But such a conclusion would be far-fetched. Outside of simple textbook examples, marginal cost is an ill-defined category. There is also the further complication that if an enterprise is working below its full capacity, which many if not most do much of the time, and if fixed overheads are significant, as they mostly are, then the cost of an additional unit of output would be *below* its average cost. Neoclassical economics dislikes increasing returns, since these are seen as inconsistent with equilibrium, though in a dynamic as against a static economy they are frequently encountered. (Adam Smith regarded their existence as a prerequisite and consequence of technical progress through the division of labour.) Maurice Allais also has little use for 'contemporary theories of general

economic equilibrium which are based on the hypothesis of general con-
vexity of the fields of production, a hypothesis that is disproved by all the
empirical data and leads to absurd consequences'. Marginal productivity
of any individual labourer or group of labourers is often rendered meaningless if, as Leijonhufvud has written, 'the labour of individual workers
become *complementary* inputs'.[8]

There is a contrast worth noting between a manufacturing (or service)
firm with high fixed costs and the situation likely to be encountered in
agriculture. It *is* realistic to envisage (say) a farmer cultivating land of
diminishing marginal fertility, and so facing increasing marginal costs. So
if a fall in demand leads him to reduce production of a given crop, he
would presumably withdraw from the less fertile field, which would
reduce his average and his marginal cost. If and when market conditions
change for the better, this field can again be sown. A factory, or a railway,
which suffer from a reduction in demand would be much more likely to
face higher unit costs. It can be different if one analyses an industry; a
fall in demand could lead to the elimination through bankruptcy of the
weaker firms, which, it may be surmised, were producing at higher costs
than their competitors, so *industry*'s average costs could fall as a result of
their elimination (a point unlikely to occur to the many 'neoclassicals'
who deny the analytical significance of the very concept 'an industry',
which occupies the vacant space *between* micro and macro). However,
unlike the agricultural example, a firm once eliminated cannot be speedily
resuscitated; when demand increases it no longer exists to meet it. This is
one reason why in Great Britain, after the closures which accompanied
the policies of early Thatcherism, the upsurge in demand led to a sharp
rise in imports. 'Eastern' economists who listen to those Western advisers
who advocate stern measures to close down loss-making enterprises
should not lose sight of the permanency of closures, or of the balance of
payments constraint. The once-proud British shipyards, now nearly all of
them eliminated, could not even bid for construction of large passenger
ships, as and when demand for them recovers. They are dead, too dead
for artificial respiration to revive them.

For economic laws to have an effect through the behaviour of economic
agents, these agents must be influenced by the manifestation of these laws,
whether or not they are aware of their existence as laws. An example from
the Marxist canon of an invisible, non-functioning and therefore invalid
'law' is the supposed tendency towards equality of rates of exploitation.
One can see forces which might tend to equalise rates of profit, since capital must be expected to move to the more profitable sectors, and profits
can be seen and measured. The same applies to wages. But no one, not the
employer, not the wage-earner, has any concern for what the 'rate of

exploitation' (*v/s*) might be, and it is surely evident that any sector with above-average 'organic composition of capital' (*c/v*) will tend durably to have above-average rates of exploitation, in Marx's sense of these words. Marginal productivity is a non-operational concept, if one cannot identify the marginal labourer. And in any event, as employers well know, it frequently 'pays' to pay more, so as to retain the goodwill and loyalty of reliable members of the labour force, which is one reason, among others, for the much-discussed 'downward-stickiness' of wages.

Here again, as in the case of the luxury food store example, 'marginal' action in respect of labour must keep in mind the wider effects, a point never forgotten by Japanese firms, who understand that goodwill and confidence among their employees, as well as their customers, is good for business. And goodwill, as argued earlier, is not only a saleable asset, it also costs something to acquire.

Long ago, Andrews found not only that there was no attempt to relate marginal costs and revenues at any particular time; 'it is not rational to do so if it is recognised that today's sales are dependent on yesterday's price, and today's price affects tomorrow's sales'.[9] And the last word on multi-level margins can be left to Brian Loasby:

> Even in economics, where the proliferation of multi-level interdependencies is the essential basis on which the subject has been built, very drastic simplifications are the rule. Highly complex subsystems, *such as firms* or even whole sectors of the economy, containing within themselves many layers of complexity, are regularly treated as simple elements, while components of a complex system are analysed as isolated units.[10]

Or finally Kornai: 'It is surprising that economics should have neglected for so long the problem of multi-level phenomena'.[11]

So, via hierarchies of margins and a multi-dimensional view of decision-making, one can pass on to the discussion of *theories of the firm*.

Non-economists would see no problem at all in accounting for the existence of firms. A series of closely interrelated processes requires to be run by a management responsible for all of them. So it may surprise those unfamiliar with Walrasian neoclassicalism to learn that here was a puzzle to be solved. And solved it has been, first by Coase, then by Penrose and finally by Williamson. The difficulty arises from two elements in the neoclassical, perfectly competitive, general-equilibrium paradigm. The first has been well defined by Harold Demsetz: perfect competition is really *perfect decentralisation*, within which none of the problems of coordination of the parts can possibly arise, since all the sub-units are coordinated solely through the market, in which the product (single and homogenous) can by definition be sold without effort at *the* price at which markets will clear. Firms are then just 'production functions', with no function.[12] And, second, Loasby: 'Despite the overwhelming theoretical emphasis on the working of a disaggregated market, it is not at all clear why in economic equilibrium one person should not decide everything, since in equilibrium there is nothing to decide.'[13] The same point is made by the German economist Helmut Arndt: in such a model 'the manager or entrepreneur . . . are totally deprived of function . . . What they "do" could just as well be left to a robot!'[14]

Williamson, and Coase before him, found the key to explanation in *transaction costs*. One cannot cover all the joint activities required for production by negotiating prior contracts, and then ensure that they be observed, which is costly, and one runs the risk of 'opportunism', or 'self-seeking with guile', on the part of partners in the market place, so it is often cheaper and more secure to rely not on market but on hierarchy.

This is not seen as satisfactory by Demsetz: he asserts, rightly, that 'the function of coordination is itself productive'. This suggests, also rightly, that the key to explanation does not lie in the cost of transactions, however the word 'cost' is defined. Perhaps greater clarity would dawn if one considered the role of the subcontractor. It is true that many firms face the choice of whether to undertake an activity or to hire someone else to do it. Thus a firm could use its own employees to operate a fleet of lorries, or it could hire a transport contractor; a building firm could employ painters, or hire a firm of painters, and so on. This can be seen as a choice between 'hierarchy' and 'market', but must not obscure the fact that the firm, as the principal, retains control and *responsibility* (a word which recurs frequently in this book, but is strangely absent from textbooks on microeconomics). This is not the same as just purchasing an input made by an independent producer, for example, buying a lorry or paints. For example, airport management must ensure that runways are kept in repair, luggage handlers are hired, food is available, there is a shuttle bus between terminals, there is toilet paper in the loos, an information board in the departure lounge, and so on. Any one of these activities can be bought in, but they would not happen by magic or by invisible hand. Someone must be *responsible* for them all, for otherwise the airport would fail to function. True, a subcontractor might fail to observe the letter or the spirit of the contract, and so Williamson's approach does help us to understand when it is that the firm chooses to do it itself ('hierarchy') or hire a subcontractor ('market'), but surely its existence is prior to the taking of such decisions. It is not only a matter of coordinating sequential and interrelated tasks, though this is indeed a vital role for any firm's management. It must also decide whether the given transaction (the key unit of Williamson's explanation) is worth undertaking at all, whether it fits into the firm's strategy, its chosen role in the market. Management internalises what otherwise could be externalities, subordinates the interests of the part to that of the whole when they conflict, as they must at times do.

And, of course, real firms in the real world do not face a perfect market in which they can sell any quantity of their (homogenous and single) product at the price announced by the mythical Walrasian auctioneer. If, as argued by Arndt, in the equilibrium model 'enterprise management cannot affect price, quality, assortment, personnel, finance, sales or investment policy', and other such matters, including design, new techniques, testing, negotiating with suppliers, market research, not to mention risk-taking and entrepreneurship, then indeed what room is there for a theory of the firm. It is functions like these which require the organisation of a firm under the leadership of a management. This should be as obvious as that a ship must have a captain, who cannot predetermine the actions of the crew in all and any circumstances in a previously-drafted contract. Actually, if they have not read neoclassical general-equilibrium texts, our 'eastern' colleagues would find these points too obvious to bother with. What *would* puzzle them would be the fact that, on the assumptions made in such texts, a firm seems to have no reason to exist. I go along with Earl: 'The [neoclassical] theory simply assumes that firms know the nature of "given" preferences and supply perfectly appropriate products. I wanted a theory that could be practically applied and which did not assume all of the interesting informational issues out of the way in order to reach determinate solutions in a highly formalised manner.'[15] Yes, indeed.

Here one must applaud the 'Austrians'' critique. In view of their stress on the need for and value of entrepreneurship, they naturally have little use for the equilibrium paradigm within which entrepreneurship cannot flourish. Indeed, the theory itself shows that profits would tend to zero, with no reward or opportunity for entrepreneurship, which usually takes the form of utilising actual or anticipated *dis*equilibrium. One can take issue with the 'Austrian' tendency to identify management with ownership, but surely their critique needs to be made known to the students, from East and West alike.

One should draw upon the ideas of Simon and Cyert and March, and from organisation theory. A firm should not be seen as a 'black box'. It is wrong to fail to differentiate between General Electric and the local ice-cream store, to borrow the thought from Shubik, treating them both impartially as 'firms'. There are also the multinationals, about which legends abound in third-world countries. What firms actually do, and how they decide to do it, must surely be a part of economics, and not the least part.

So difficult is it to fit a real-world firm into a paradigm that a recent article by Nyman spoke of the need for reintroducing the entrepreneurial function into the theory of the firm. Its author duly noted the realistic approach of Marshall, who stressed the role of entrepreneurial initiative, and, since he was not unduly influenced by the equilibrium concept, he also noted that some firms are led by energetic managers, others can gradually decay. While this is visibly the real state of the real world, instead one finds substituted a production function, with 'equilibrium firms with identical cost structures facing identical market situations'. The author quotes Baumol: 'The management group becomes a passive calculator that reacts mechanically to changes imposed on it by fortuitous external circumstances over which it does not exert, and does not even attempt to exert, any influence', and entrepreneurs are absent 'because there is no way in which they can fit into the model.'[16] Oddly (from my point of view) Nyman limits the entrepreneurial function to 'institutional innovation', that is, reorganising, rather than extending the argument to the more promising role of product and production innovation and marketing initiatives. But he does point to a gap, whose existence yet again provides evidence for the view that after Marshall economics may have taken a wrong turning.

For reasons already advanced when discussing 'margins', internal organisation matters and affects decisions by affecting what subordinate management takes into account. Also important are the success criteria of management at various levels, the kinds of incentive schemes which are introduced. Students of Soviet-type economies are, or should be, familiar with the problem: how does one evaluate the performance of subordinates? Anecdotes abound to illustrate how distortions can arise. Thus if subordinates are rewarded for reaching or exceeding some target, it is in their interest that this target be a modest one, and they may withhold or doctor information to that end. (When I spoke at a management conference organised by a large oil company, and cited this deficiency of Soviet-type economies, I found that they were quite familiar with this same problem in the oil industry!). Also relevant are the possible consequences of pressure to increase short-term profit (the 'bottom line' for the quarter), at the expense of longer-term profits, the much discussed 'short-termism'.

In any large organisation there is also the issue of centralisation versus decentralisation. This was particularly vividly portrayed by Ely Devons in his *Planning in Practice*, based upon his experience in the wartime Ministry of Aircraft Production, but the same problems exist in *any* large organisation, public or private. Those on the spot know the local details, but, as the centre is bound to point out, cannot see the effects of their actions on the organisation as a whole, while those on the spot can cite instances when rules made by a remote headquarters do not fit the local circumstances. There is bound to be argument and conflict over who is entitled to take what decisions, and organisational structure can affect *what* is decided, as well as by whom.

Such considerations tend to be ignored in neoclassical textbooks, partly because of a (usually unspoken) assumption that the competitive process has already produced the optimal form of organisation. This is another instance of the appearance of Dr Pangloss as a neoclassical economist: Dennis Mueller is one of many who made a similar point. The efficiency of organisational forms raises questions 'the economist does not even ask, since in his models an inefficient organisational unit could never even be created.'[17] Or, if created, be already eliminated by the competitive process. Which is one reason why neoclassical mainstream and institutionalism have had little to say to one another. To cite Hahn again: 'it is a fair question whether it can ever be useful to have an equilibrium notion which does not describe the *termination* of actual processes',[18] so that any necessary changes will already have occurred. In any case, the Walrasian concepts leave management with so little to do, that organisation simply does not matter.

Interestingly, Williamson approaches the basics of the problem but then (in my view) shies away from facing the implications of his own argument. He noted that economists tend to assume that, 'subject only to the condition that transactions are technologically separable, each transaction can be priced and metered independently. I submit, however, that technological separability is merely a necessary and not sufficient condition for transactions to be regarded independently.' Good, said this reader, he will at last say that transactions by a firm react upon other transactions by that same firm. But no. He went on: 'Attitudinal separability must also be established', and speaks of '*attitudinal* spillover . . . at the margin' (emphasis added). Yes, transactions affect and are affected by the attitudes and behaviour of members of the firm and by what it does in the market. Yet the words 'customer goodwill' are absent, and he does not further investigate the relevance of his insight to the internal organisation of firms.

It is also worth applying Buchanan's 'public choice' theory to corporate behaviour, that is, to 'private choice'. Opportunities for what Williamson has called 'opportunism', and which he confines to the behaviour of firms or individuals hired in the market, exist also *within* any large organisation. (Nowhere more than in the largest organisation, the traditional centralised Soviet economy!) A divisional chief, or head of research, in a corporation, in pursuit of career and income, or just because he is committed to his or her task and naturally regards it as important, can and does apply for resources, tending to understate cost and to be overoptimistic about the likely result. Again, a phenomenon familiar to students of the Soviet economy, but by no means confined to it. (Indeed every one of us, as university teachers, when applying for a research grant, make the best case we can, and this without conscious dishonesty.) It is a blinkered 'theory of the firm' that fails to refer to such matters as these. Can we really believe that the forces of (perfect?) competition will have eliminated such behaviour, as they should also have eliminated such phenomena as gold-topped desks and multimillion payments to chief executives?

Some people have faith in their ideology, others in religion. The question of what is or is not maximised has been discussed already in Chapter 2.

NOTES

1. A. Cairncross, *Economics and Economic Policy* (Gregg Revivals, 1986), p. 5.
2. A. Leijonhufvud, 'Capitalism and the Factory System' in R.N. Langlois (ed.), *Economics as a Process* (Cambridge University Press, 1986), pp. 203–4.
3. 'Boulding, Kenneth E. (born 1910)' in P. Arestis and M. Sawyer (eds), *A Biographical Dictionary of Dissenting Economists* (Edward Elgar, 1992), p. 52.
4. F. Hahn, *Equilibrium and Macroeconomics* (Basil Blackwell, 1984), p. 50.
5. A. Nove, 'The Fragmentationist Disease', in *Studies in Economics and Russia* (Macmillan, 1990), pp. 164–70.
6. 'Tarshis, Lorie (born 1911)' in Arestis and Sawyer (eds), *A Biographical Dictionary*, pp. 575–6.
7. Dennis C. Mueller, 'The corporation and the economist', *Economics Alert*, No. 3, May 1993, p. 2.
8. A. Leijonhufvud, 'Capitalism and the Factory System', p. 209.
9. See P. Earl, *The Economic Imagination. Towards a Behavioural Analysis of Choice* (M.E. Sharpe, 1983), p. 37.
10. B. Loasby, *Choice, Complexity and Ignorance* (Cambridge University Press, 1976), p. 30. Emphasis added.
11. J. Kornai, *Anti-equilibrium* (North-Holland Publishing Company, 1971), p. 84.
12. H. Demsetz, 'The Theory of the Firm Revisited', *Journal of Law, Economics, and Organization*, **4**, Spring 1988.
13. B. Loasby, *Choice, Complexity and Ignorance*, p. 131.
14. H. Arndt, *Irrwege der Politischen Okonomie* (Beck, 1979), p. 218.
15. P. Earl, *The Economic Imagination*, p. 8.
16. Neil B. Nyman, 'The Entrepreneurial Function in the Theory of the Firm'. See further, F. Machlup, 'Theories of the Firm: Marginalist, Behavioral, Managerial', *American Economic Review*, **57**(1), 1967, pp. 1–33.
17. Dennis C. Mueller, 'The corporation and the economist', p. 3.
18. F. Hahn, *Equilibrium and Macroeconomics*, p. 48. Emphasis added.

4. Prices, values, money

Prices in general equilibrium models, determined either by Walras's Auctioneer or through haggling in the market, are such that supply and demand balances, and everything that is produced can be sold at that price. 'Markets clear' is a phrase very frequently encountered. It is, of course, also known that under oligopoly or monopoly firms are not price takers but (within limits, to be sure) price makers. Book after book relates prices to marginal costs. It has already been argued in the previous chapter that this equality is seldom encountered in real life, because of the ambiguity of the 'margin', especially in multi-product, multi-process firms, with all the interdependencies and indivisibilities that exist more often than not. Marginal cost is seldom known, at least in manufacturing and in many if not most services, and so many if not most managers adopt an average-plus-cost the conventional-profit-rate approach to pricing.

So it may make little sense to instruct repentant Soviet planners to 'adopt' marginal cost pricing, or to teach their management to do so. They would not follow them. But it may be useful to teach them in what respects Western pricing practice differs from the one they were familiar with in the old Soviet Union, which was also notionally based on average-cost-plus.

The key difference relates to customer choice. In the Soviet system, production decisions were taken by the monopolist state. In so far as the customers were other state enterprises, they were tied to their suppliers by the plan, that is, were not free to seek supplies from other state enterprises. Furthermore, they had no economic incentive to seek cheaper variants of material inputs, since *their* prices were also cost-based, and their success indicators emphasised not profit but (in many instances) value of turnover. Customers' influence was minimal, the (cost-plus-based) price supposedly represented the planners' *ex ante* evaluation of the 'worth' of that good or service. With plan targets unavoidably aggregated, the specific needs of the user, and quality considerations generally, carried little weight. As for consumers' goods, the customer did have the right and possibility to refuse to buy if he or she regarded the price as too high, but choice was limited, 'goods hunger' a widespread phenomenon, with a 'take-it-or-leave-it' attitude on the part of the retail trade. In all these circumstances, a cost-plus price could have little connection with use-value, save by an improbable coincidence.

In a normal Western economy the user does have choice and must be expected to reject a product which seems to him or her overpriced. Or there could be a bargaining process. And, as already argued, the monopolist's power to raise prices is limited both by the existence of close substitutes and by fear of attracting a competitor. (Unfortunately, as a Czech economist once remarked in conversation, 'there is nothing so monopolistic as a socialist monopoly'.) The market, even an imperfect market, even with widespread oligopoly, brings use-value and cost-plus prices closer together, reacts via backward linkage on the willingness of the producer to incur costs if these are at a level at which he or she would anticipate difficulty in selling.

These last words are of vital importance. Janos Kornai long ago stressed that producers and traders should face a buyers' market, since this and only this would provide them with a powerful incentive to seek user satisfaction, to maintain or improve quality and service. But then it would be wrong to see prices as just clearing the market, that is, to define an optimum as one in which supply just equals demand. Markets do not clear. Markets *should* not clear, once one makes the elementary and realistic assumption that choice implies unpredictability, that perfect micro knowledge even of today's demand, let alone tomorrow's, is beyond the bounds of possibility.

Furthermore, full utilisation of resources is inconsistent with competition if this is viewed as a process. For if all resources are fully committed, what is there to compete *with*? If all customers are satisfied with what they already have, what is there to compete *for*? Choice and competition are intimately linked; one cannot have one without the other (as Marxist economists obstinately failed to note). And both choice and competition require excess supply.

We see around us innumerable examples of supply regularly exceeding demand. It is not just a matter of random error, due to imperfect foresight, for that would be consistent with there being as many cases of demand exceeding supply as vice versa. Yet this is clearly not so. And it is a precondition of real choice that it should be not so. If this is an 'imperfection', it is a necessary imperfection. *Supply normally exceeds demand.*

A few illustrative examples will suffice. Imagine that the number of restaurant seats just equals demand for restaurant meals. And that in every restaurant the amount of food in the kitchen just equals total requirements. Or the total supply of books equals demand for (all) books. Since the exact nature of 'micro' demand for specific books, or the customers' preference for roast duck or sirloin steak are not known in advance, this would not be a tenable form of competitive behaviour: the bookstore and the restaurant will knowingly keep excess supplies. There will normally be 'too many' restaurant seats and dishes (and bookshops and books) because micro demand is not predictable. If one deliberately plans for equality between demand and supply, the result will be shortage of some desired item. This in turn would create a climate in which it would seem advantageous to hoard, which would make shortages worse. Such shortages could only partially be remedied by price manipulation: goods and services are only to a limited extent substitutable. If one seeks piston-rings, or roofing material, or a textbook on vertebrate sociology or chicken, it is little consolation to be offered carburettors, window-glass, a textbook on biochemistry, or sardines, and these at *any* price.

Or else the customer does acquire a substitute. For example, suppose the restaurant has only one meat dish available, or a shopper in Moscow who went to buy beef found himself purchasing sardines instead. The transactions might take place, but they no longer reflect the buyer's revealed preferences. This becomes an important, though unquantifiable, factor in comparing welfare and living standards. Choice should be seen as a good in itself, its absence (usually) a 'bad'. Worse still, there were many instances of 'conditional sales': 'We will sell you A only if you also buy B'. Then there is absolutely no preference, even relatively to shortage, for B. Yet the transaction is duly recorded, and statistics will not record its involuntary character.

Excess production, items that cannot be sold, or excess productive capacity, not capable of being profitably utilised, are not the same as 'inventories', that is, what could be called normal reserves. Perhaps the best way of envisaging the distinction is to note the difference in intention. An unsuccessful attempt to sell, offers to customers which the customer declines to accept, are not quite what is customarily envisaged when one speaks of 'inventories', even if the latter also represent materials or products not in current use.

Since, in the real competitive world, firms seek to maintain or increase their market share, it is important for them to have reserve capacity, inventories and labour, available to deal with the unexpected, knowing that future demand (or even the requirements of a customer in ten minutes' time) cannot be known in operational micro detail. To keep such reserves incurs a cost. It has already been argued (Chapter 2) that this represents one of many exceptions to the rule that every decision or transaction should yield a profit for a profit-seeking firm, and is yet another reason for seeing marginal cost pricing as belonging more to the textbook than to the real world.

One of the reasons for chronic shortages at micro level in Soviet-type economies was precisely the conscious aim of fully utilising all material and human resources, so that, when micro-imbalances were identified there were insufficient reserves to cope with them. Fear of such an outcome then leads to predictable forms of behaviour: if any durable (be it soap, sugar, or bricks, or spare parts for tractors) becomes available, there is a rush to buy it in case it is unavailable in the future, thereby providing a reason for future unavailability. A Soviet-type enterprise, as a monopolist, has no need either to struggle for market share or to seek customer goodwill. In this situation, if it is instructed to behave 'commercially', in the sense of paying more attention to its profit-and-loss account, it will find no good reason to maintain reserve productive capacity for output (as distinct from hoarding inputs). To take another simple example, a retail store will improve its 'efficiency' indicators, including turnover per employee, if customers stand in line all day. To add another employee would doubtless reduce queuing, but 'worsen' measured performance. Unless the dissatisfied customer can go elsewhere.

It is also essential to give due emphasis to the prevalence of non-price competition. Aware that price wars – though they do occur – can damage the interests of the oligopolists, informal agreements not to cut prices are very frequently encountered, providing yet another reason for seeing marginal cost pricing as the exception rather than the rule. The phenomenon of non-price competition should remind us of the importance of non-price aspects of product differentiation, and the importance of such dimensions of quality as after-sales service, punctuality, reliability. One is then reminded of the naiveté of assuming that price signals can convey all the needed information. Also it points to a cause of a major weakness in Soviet-type economies: they were notoriously poor at after-sales service, punctuality, reliability, which requires to be provided at a cost, which, in the absence of competition, becomes an avoidable cost. Goodwill does not matter under monopoly.

Adam Smith saw clearly the connection between the size of the market and the opportunities for lowering costs through division of labour and mechanisation, so he at least had no doubt that in a dynamic 'growth' economy one encounters increasing returns. This helps explain the tendency for firms to grow, and in the real world some are in fact in a process of growth. Growth is limited not only by the fact that at some stage costs (including the costs of administering large and complex units) will indeed start to rise. But at least equally important, as a limit on the growth of the firm, is the size of the market, and of its share in it. At any given moment of time, some firms are at a stage of increasing returns, others not, just as some firms make higher than average profits, while others will shortly go bankrupt. The danger posed by analysis based on timeless equilibrium is that such evident aspects of everyday reality are obscured: in equilibrium the inefficient will already have been weeded out, firms on an increasing returns curve will already have expanded, and indeed all firms will be alike.

As already argued earlier, a distinction should be made between firms and industries in respect of increasing/decreasing returns. Suppose, for any reason, demand for commodity A falls. Firms find themselves producing at a level below capacity. Given the importance of overheads, unit costs may, often do, rise. However, if in the given industry there are some high-cost producers, they may go out of business, and in that case industry-wide average cost may decline. Conventional micro-theory is unhappy with increasing returns, and it is theoretically more tidy to present a U-curve with the firm at the stage of decreasing returns. However, Maurice Allais has already been cited as expressing a critical view of such an assumption, and Kaldor has repeatedly drawn attention to the importance of increasing returns in manufacturing.

The importance of the price mechanism, acting at the same time as a measure of cost, a stimulus to and a signal to producers, an invaluable source of information, an irreplaceable means of exercising consumer choice, could scarcely be overestimated, especially when for decades the Soviet planners and economic ideologists either ignored or profoundly misunderstood it. Marx is to some degree to blame. The labour theory of value had as its evident purpose the de-legitimation of income from property, demonstrating that the owner of capital and of land exploits the employees and tenants, appropriating the fruits of their labour. As such it is as defensible a value-judgement as the opposite view – that the owner of land and capital makes a contribution to production by allowing his property to be used. It is (in my view) arguable that a very rich man who inherits from great-grandparents a high-value estate in the centre of a big city is not entitled to enjoy vast riches while doing no work at all. Economics written from the standpoint of working people is very likely to devise a theory of value which lays especial stress on the role of human labour. As Tugan-Baranovsky observed almost a hundred years ago, if horses could write economics there would be a horse theory of value!

However, Marx was misleading in several respects. First, in his anxiety to establish the existence of exploitation, he downgraded the role of capital and land (as well as of the capitalist and the landlord). This led to endless complications over the 'transformation problem', differences in organic composition of capital, an allegedly equal rate of exploitation. Of this I have written in my *Economics of Feasible Socialism*. But of greater importance in the present context is a failure to understand or even try to measure the specific contribution of physical capital, a refusal to use interest rates, and, worse still, the belief that land is a free good. I will not enter into an argument over whether these gaps in Soviet official thinking were or were not due to misunderstanding Marx. The fact remains that when decisions were taken involving the 'drowning' of thousands of acres of land in a hydroelectric scheme, or ruining land through industrial waste or oil spillage, land was not seen as having any value.

Second, Marx downgraded use-value. Of course he was not so foolish as to deny that goods must have use in order to have value; labour devoted to the production of useless goods is itself valueless. But in a well-known passage he stressed that use-values are incommensurate, that (say) ink, sausage and a lathe have completely different uses, and that the one thing they have in common is that labour is devoted to their production. (Which did not prevent him and Engels from imagining that under socialism the planners would choose what to produce by comparing the 'social use-value' of alternative products, though how this was to be done, in what units and by whom, was never discussed.[1]) This led Soviet official economists into what their (Soviet) critics described as 'a cost-based theory of price', a theory of value which purported to be based on human effort (of past as well as present labour). However, it is surely obvious that two goods, both of some use, sharing only the characteristic that the same amount of labour (of whatever quality) was devoted to their production are not for that reason of equal *value* (in the sense of use-value) save by unlikely coincidence. If machine A is more productive than machine B, or dress A is more attractive than dress B, the user plainly would prefer A to B in both instances, yet A and B may require the same number of hours of human labour to produce. B would not be valueless, of course. In a market economy, its output would presumably not yield a profit, so it can be plausibly argued that market forces would cause A rather than B to be produced, with a tendency to link together the cost of production and the value-in-use of the product. But Marx, and the traditional Soviet planning system, did not rely on the market, they wished to eliminate the market. Those who decided what to produce were supposed to know its use-value. Indeed Marx argued that in this sense labour under socialism would be 'directly social', that is, its product would have its value-in-use known *ex ante*, instead of having it imperfectly valued *ex post* by the market. Accepting that perfect markets exist only in textbooks, this is none the less quite unsatisfactory: how can any planner know in advance that the right decision was taken, other than by some validation *ex post*? Marx did not have a theory of socialist price, as he did not expect that under socialism there would be any prices (or money, or profit, or wages). However, his followers did in fact continue to use prices, and in the absence of any alternative, planners fixed the prices of what they chose to produce by reference to planned average costs (these excluded rent and, until recently, interest), plus a profit margin. These, they held, were a sort of surrogate labour values. When Leonid Kantorovich sought to introduce the concept of 'objectively determined valuations' (that is, values derived from a programme, reflecting scarcities by reference to the programme), he was met at first with ideological hostility: these were not labour values. The same fate befell V. Novozhilov, when he sought to explain the concept of opportunity-cost, which also involves taking relative scarcities into account. They had an uphill struggle, but gradually they found support among a younger generation of economists, who stressed the need to measure not only effort (cost) but also the usefulness of the outcome. (That was the title of Novozhilov's last major work: *Izmerenie zatrat i rezultatov*, 'The Measurement of Cost and Results'.) It is odd in retrospect to read the dogmatists' negative response, their deep distrust of anything that smacked of a subjective value theory.

All this said, at least this author is not altogether happy with the other extreme, that is, a *purely* subjective theory of value, which downgrades the importance of the circumstances (and techniques) of production. As in a number of instances one finds a more satisfactory approach in Marshall. He saw both the conditions of supply and of demand (utility) as playing their part, as if two blades of scissors, though with demand fluctuation the decisive short-term influence on price. The following old *New Yorker* cartoon can serve as an illustration of what I have in mind. A senator addresses a meeting and says: 'When I was elected senator, ballpoint pens cost a dollar-fifty. Now you can get them for 29 cents.' Clearly, what had changed drastically – and led also to a vast upsurge in both demand and production – was the technique of making the pens. It was argued 170 years ago by the first economist–academician at the Imperial Academy at St. Petersburg, A. Shtorkh [Storch], that, contrary not only to Marx (whom he could not have read) but also to Adam Smith (with whom on this point he disagreed), goods do not acquire value because labour is expended on them, labour is expended on them because they have value – *are valued*.[2]

Theory must also take on board the concept of diminishing marginal utility; it was also surprising to find the older dogmatic Soviet generation of economists resisting recognising the self-evident influence on value and price of relative scarcity. They also had severe problems with joint products, but these create problems also for the neoclassicals, as another example of interrelationships (a species of indivisibility: one cannot separate the sheep's meat from its fleece while the sheep lives) which make conventional marginal analysis untidy. As well as joint products, there are instances of joint *production*: in order to produce A there may be needed items Y and Z in technologically given proportions; or, to take another example, ships require docks to tie up at. (But much more about infrastructure later.)

While the former Soviet planners will most certainly need to be instructed in the vital importance of the price mechanism, as well as the role within it of interest and rent, they most surely also need to be warned about its limitations. One of the most important of these relates to the future. Though futures markets and long-term agreements exist, the fact remains that future prices are not known, and this most plainly affects investment decisions, when the would-be investor has to estimate the likely prices of both inputs and output (not to mention interest and exchange rates) at some future date or dates. Errors in estimating costs, prices, the level of demand, are a major cause of thousands of bankruptcies, and uncertainty inhibits long-term investment.

As Kornai observed, few major decisions are (or can be) taken on the basis of price information alone. It is this, *inter alia*, which renders impracticable the model developed by Oscar Lange: he imagined a central planning board able to set parametric prices (he also envisaged prices being determined in a 'socialist' market), and managers of state-owned enterprises would then apply the marginal rule; these would be socialist 'Walrasian' prices, at which the output would be sold. But, first, the marginal rule can be applied unambiguously only in books, for reasons already advanced, and Lange, like the neoclassicals with whom he was debating, abstracted from increasing returns. Second, all decisions relate to an uncertain future, and prices could not provide sufficient information even about next week, let alone what a socialist (or any other) manager wants to know regarding investment. Third, it was never explained why the imagined socialist managers should act in the way Lange desired; what material advantages would they obtain by so doing? Or what penalties would follow from not so doing? Fourth, and finally, far too many theories and models refer to two dimensions only: quantity and price. Of considerable importance are such things as durability, reliability, punctuality, and a whole list of quality characteristics, not to mention delivery dates, credit terms, and so on. In his excellent book, Oscar Morgenstern reminded us that many firms offer discounts which remain unreported, so that even our knowledge about actual prices is far from perfect, especially as the scale of the discounts can vary with the business cycle.[3]

But of course it was not only Lange but also his critics who tended to assume that the price mechanism carries all the information needed by entrepreneurs.

These warnings apply also to the issue of control over monopolies. As already argued, the price behaviour of monopolies in the real world is constrained by their desire not to attract potential competitors, or, in some cases, regulators. An example of the latter is occurring in America as I write these lines. Cable TV companies, with monopoly franchises in many areas, and no longer subject to regulation, caused a storm of protest by repeated and substantial rises in their charges. The result: Congress is proposing to reimpose regulation. However, it is also important to recall the importance of quality, which cannot be covered by control or regulation confined to price. Thus, if anything goes wrong (with TV, car, telephone, gas appliances, whatever) how soon will they be repaired? Will the necessary spare parts and mechanic be available when needed? What remedy does the dissatisfied customer have? (In this context, as in others, Albert O. Hirschman's *Exit, Voice and Loyalty* is very much to the point). There is also the experience of various forms of regulation of public-utility monopolies in the United States, by such bodies as the Interstate Commerce Commission. There are those who preach demonopolisation as the solution, but this has only limited application in cases of 'natural monopolies', such as water-supply; and only in Thatcherite Britain does one encounter the notion (regarded as odd throughout the rest of Europe *and* the United States and Canada) that public transport in conurbations should be fragmented and run on a competitive basis. But we will return to public services (and public service) in a subsequent chapter.

Price theory should, of course, also refer to the standard neoclassical 'Walrasian' analysis, under timeless conditions of perfect competition, as a species of extreme, ideal case. It may be approximated in agriculture, in the sense that, there being many producers, all are price takers. However, precisely for this reason (and not only because of the pressure of interest groups), prices are not allowed to fluctuate freely. Mention has already been made of the 'cobweb'. Over-reaction to price signals, when crops require many months to grow, could lead to excessive price fluctuations, excessive in the view both of the producers and the users. A degree of stability is a precondition for rational decision-making. Price and wage 'stickiness' are therefore not necessarily 'imperfections'.

Inflation, however, is a matter that worries us all, regardless of ideology. In open or hidden form it has affected centralised as well as market economies, and has been particularly violent in the period of transition, as can be seen by the experience of Poland and the (former) Soviet Union.

Inflation is, everywhere, a monetary phenomenon. Yes, Friedman is right, but such a formulation does not even begin to tackle causes. *Why* does the supply of money (in the various senses of that word) rise more rapidly at one period than another, in one country than another? Is it appropriate to 'blame' Keynes, as some (for example James Buchanan) are apt to do, for legitimising budget deficits? This is odd, for several reasons. One: the record deficit in the United States under Reagan occurred when anti-Keynesians were in the ascendant, and in circumstances which would surely have been deplored by Keynes (it was a time of boom!). Two: Keynes's doctrine was developed because of the impact of the mass unemployment of the Great Depression. Was the appropriate remedy at that time one of cutting budget expenditures (as was indeed done, on 'orthodox' advice, in Germany, which helped to bring Hitler to power)? Three: some inflations are generated not by budget deficits but by excessive credits by private institutions, such as the so-called 'Lawson' boom in Britain in 1988–90, when there was a budget *surplus*. Finally, one really must take issue with the (surely ideologically-driven) assertion by Friedman that even the Great Depression was due to errors of monetary policy committed by his chief villain, which has to be the state. A crash such as that in 1929–32 naturally cuts borrowing heavily, many banks collapse, so money supply goes down. While not denying that government policy in these years (and not only in Germany!) made matters worse, it is surely a travesty to reverse cause and effect, and make the public authorities' incorrect reaction to collapse the cause of that collapse. And it was precisely Keynes who was among the advocates of a government policy designed to stimulate sagging demand, a policy the consequences of which would have been an increase in demand for and supply of money. In other words, Friedman's policy of maintaining money supply growth at a steady level at a time of slump would have required Keynesian measures.

There is, of course, much more to be said about monetarism and the demand for and supply of money of different kinds. In his dispute with Friedman, Kaldor pointed out that 'nobody would suggest (not even Professor Friedman, I believe) that the increase in note circulation in December is the cause of the Christmas buying spree.'[4] If in this or other circumstances the authorities sought to limit note circulation, all kinds of substitute-money would appear, and has in fact done so; and one way (mentioned by Kaldor) is 'to delay paying bills', that is, involuntary inter-enterprise and interpersonal credit. This has in fact occurred in all ex-communist countries in 1990–92 in response to attempts to apply a tight monetary policy.

It would certainly be important to stress the importance of monetary aggregates, to emphasise that money does indeed matter. However, it would also be necessary to note the sheer practical difficulty of controlling money supply, achieving specific monetary targets, given the large number of actual and potential money creators (banks, other financial institutions, even, as when Irish banks went on prolonged strike, IOUs written by men of good standing). Charles Goodhart has noted the distorting effects of attempting to control the quantity of money on the measurement of that quantity, given definitional ambiguities.

The temporary triumph of what could be called crude monetarism, and the reaction against it, were well described by Benjamin M. Friedman (*not* to be confused with Milton!) in the *NBER Reporter* (Summer 1992):

> As of the late 1970s, much of the newest research in monetary economics embraced the view that the growth of the money stock (however defined) satisfactorily summarised the macroeconomically relevant doings of the central bank; that money growth affected real economic activity only to the extent it was unexpected; and as a direct consequence of the first two notions, that a central bank could achieve disinflation with little if any cost in terms of foregone production, employment or incomes, simply by reducing money growth according to a schedule publicly announced in advance . . . The events of the 1980s, especially in the United States [in Britain too!] were not kind to disinflation, and the progressive globalisation of financial markets, standard relationships connecting money growth to either income growth or price inflation more or less collapsed. The conventional 'Ms' not only no longer seemed sufficient to guide monetary policy; they no longer provided much empirically identifiable information about anything of interest in a monetary policy context.

It is not that money ceased to matter. But (Milton) Friedman's notions about controlling the money supply, when financial institutions were deregulated and money in all forms could flow freely across national borders (which conformed to his laissez-faire philosophy) proved inapplicable in practice. And deregulation led to less, not more, stability in financial markets.

The old formula MV = PT still retains validity, despite claims that V (velocity of circulation) changes little in the long run; in the short run it can and does alter, and one influence upon it could be an attempt to control M (whether M0, M3 or some other measure). If, as in Britain after the 'Lawson' boom of 1988–90, the attempt takes the form of high real interest rates, it has a number of side-effects: higher mortgage rates, higher cost of capital and so a fall in investment, a redistribution of income from borrowers to lenders (and so to savers and away from investors), with a fall in output and business activity which has among its other results a fall in the money supply and of budget revenues.

It is right and proper to criticise the doctrine, held by some who thought themselves to be Keynesians, that 'money does not matter'. Of course it matters. But it is also necessary to stress the importance of forces which *cause* money supply to vary, the difficulties in the way of acting directly on the money supply. Take two examples: the first relates to wages: upward pressure on wage rates was much greater in Britain than in Germany, and was a significant cause (*inter alia*) of the higher inflation rate in Britain, since it is hard to conceive of purely financial measures which would prevent the higher wages from being paid. Would it be not superficial in the extreme simply to explain why inflation was higher in Britain (or Italy) than in West Germany by the fact (the undoubted fact) that money supply in all its forms grew more rapidly in Britain and Italy? Is it more enlightening than to say that a firm that loses money does so because its expenditures exceed revenues? The struggle to achieve stability in Poland involved direct government intervention to prevent wages from rising as fast as prices. A second relates to Russia at the time these words are being written. The chairman of the state bank is under attack for printing so many roubles at a time when the government is trying to halt hyperinflation. However, as he points out, if personal incomes and an unregulated volume of credits from the new commercial banks create much higher demand for currency, how can he *not* print it? In 1992 arrears in wage and pensions payments built up in Russia because they were unable to print and transport bank notes fast enough, and inter-enterprise debt has multiplied. The point at issue in the above examples is that one must examine the *causes* of changes in money supply. Friedman's view that the level of wage demands does not matter, provided one firmly controls money supply, is oddly myopic: it plainly *does* matter. What one can or should do about it, by way of incomes policies, or via high unemployment, is another question.

To make the point in another way, suppose one seeks an explanation of the fact that in all warring countries there were strong tendencies to inflation. If one confined one's attention to the monetary aspects, then it might seem sufficient to show that money supply rose faster than the (reduced) supply of goods and services to the population. This would be a true statement. However, the underlying reason was surely war and all that went with it. I favour at all times the motto of my alma mater: *Rerum cognescere causas.*

Which in no way diminishes the importance of the aim of macroeconomic stabilisation, or the harm done to the reform process, especially in the former Soviet Union and Poland, by reckless disregard of the consequences of budget deficits and money creation. However, one must also be aware of the *cost* of giving priority to combating inflation. Even in Great Britain today, high interest rates and high unemployment contribute to recession and to bankruptcies, while discouraging investment. In Russia, as we shall see, drastic cuts in state expenditure, and credit controls, are leading to a collapse of investment, production, social services, rising unemployment, and this threatens not only social convulsions but also the process of macroeconomic stabilisation. A comparative study of how inflation has been combated, and with what consequences, is of evident value, and this would include Russia's own experience in 1923.

Monetary theory and equilibrium analyses do not live well together. Uncertainty, the difficulty of forming rational expectations, is at the very heart of the desire to hold money, just as, as already argued, investments are made in the anticipation of *dis*equilibrium. Similarly, if the equilibrium price is known, and all deals are made at that 'Walrasian' price, it is impossible even to begin to analyse the role of many kinds of market traders, arbitrageurs, stockbrokers. To seek to establish what might be the optimal level of money supply under conditions of general equilibrium is to ask a question devoid of meaning. It is almost like estimating the number and behaviour of gamblers if one assumes perfect knowledge of outcomes.

A quotation from Shackle: 'For the conduct we are free to choose is future conduct, but the circumstances we are able to know are past circumstances. That is why the Theory of Value in its strict form, the theory of rational conduct, must place itself in a timeless world of a single moment which has neither past nor future.'[5] But is this where *we* must place ourselves?

Many questions arise over public finance. A Russian economist will have been brought up on the Soviet all-inclusive budget. All-inclusive in two senses: it incorporated the total revenues and expenditures of *all* public authorities, from the Union to the rural district. It is as if the British state budget also included those of Yorkshire and the city of Hull. It was like the traditional Russian doll, with budgets contained one within the other. It also included both current and capital expenditure, and all kinds of revenue, including that from the sale of state bonds. For a number of years, as we know, the budget was secretly in deficit, this being covered by advances from the State Bank, included in an undifferentiated item called 'Other revenues', along with revenues reflecting the accounting profit of foreign trade (that is, the difference between the domestic and world price, both converted into roubles at the official rate of exchange; if the difference was negative, this appeared under budget expenditure, though 'appeared' was the wrong word; the figure was not separately published).

All this has changed. While the Union was collapsing the budget deficit soared, and was a principal cause of the collapse of the rouble, eventually resulting in treble-digit inflation. There will be much to say about this in a subsequent chapter. Here I will be concerned with what my imaginary repentant planners might learn about Western practices. The first lesson, presumably, is that the biggest budget deficits in history, in absolute terms, are to be found in the United States, whence comes the stern advice about the need to eliminate deficits, advice which successive American presidents ignore. True, American deficits are not inflationary, insofar as they are financed by bond sales. Russian economists must sadly note that this option is not available to them, since amid political and inflationary uncertainties few are likely to purchase Russian rouble bonds. The second would be that provincial, city and rural district budgets should be separate, with locally generated revenues to sustain them, supplemented by grants from the centre (for example, in Great Britain, towards education and public expenditures).

There would be much to learn about various forms of taxation, direct and indirect, the levels of progression, if any, the balance between direct and indirect taxation, about costs of collection, and means of evasion, and about various kinds of local taxes (local income tax, property tax, sales tax, the ill-fated British poll tax, and so on); also about some doubtful practices.

One of these is a confusion between current and capital expenditures, and revenues too. No commercial corporation would use revenues from the sale of capital assets to finance current dividends. Yet the British government did exactly this: it included the proceeds from the sale of state-owned enterprises (that is, capital assets) in current revenue, and then cut income-tax rates. Then there is failure to make distinction between three different kinds of expenditures: what might be called 'redistributive' (for example, on old age pensions), the provision of government services, and, finally, capital investments in the public sector. Borrowing to cover the first two would be analogous to a firm borrowing to finance its losses on current operations. But firms do not, as a rule, finance their capital expenditures out of current revenue. They either borrow or use their own accumulated reserves.

The British government abandoned the separation of the capital from the current account, which was practised in the first post-war years. It also denied nationalised industries access to the capital market, forcing them to borrow from the Treasury, and then only with permission, with the Treasury seeking to hold down the Public Sector Borrowing Requirement (PSBR). Furthermore, with this aim in view, especially after 1979, nationalised industries were pressed to finance the bulk of their investments out of current revenues, thus causing them to raise prices by more than the rate of inflation, thereby contributing to the rate of inflation. (This was described by some critics as 'fattening them for privatisation'.) Criteria for public-sector investment became distorted by the priority given to keeping down the PSBR. Only an ideological hostility to the public sector could explain a policy which seemed to judge a given investment project less on its merits than whether it was in the public or private sectors. Yet the effect on the real economy of an investment in a new airfield runway, or power station, or in rail electrification, was surely identical regardless of who owned them. And giving priority to holding down the PSBR at a time of recession, when this recession adversely affects ordinary current revenues, has the effect of preventing capital expenditures on public works of many kinds, which could have useful countercyclical effects.

As we shall see in a later chapter, all ex-communist states are compelled by past financial mismanagement to cut budgetary expenditures. However, in the absence of a normal capital market and of accumulations of (legitimate) private capital, drastic cuts in publicly financed capital spending can result in drastic cuts in capital spending in general, which cannot but have a negative effect on reconstructing productive capacity.

Another problem, handled differently in different Western countries, is the financing of, and control over, local government expenditures. In such federal countries as the United States and Germany, the constitution defends the right of the states and the Länder. In Britain, which has no constitution, the centre can, and in recent years emphatically does, tightly control not only local authorities' expenditure but also what they are permitted to do with their money (for example, it can prevent them from building houses or running a bus service). Local authorities used to be free to borrow in the capital market, and in some countries they still are, but not in Britain (this part of government control over the PSBR). California, New York, Rhineland-Westfalia, Hamburg, cannot be ordered about in such ways, and local democracy should be more highly valued in ex-communist countries than it has been in Britain in recent years. In the former Soviet Union in its last years, with the breakdown of the tight centralised controls over finance (as well as over most other things), the various republics and localities failed to limit expenditures, and by 1991 the combined budget deficits soared to over 20 per cent of GNP, with a corresponding decline in the value of the rouble. Plainly, this is intolerable. It is worth studying how similar problems are handled in Western countries other than Britain (where the degree of central control over local authorities is surely excessive, and unprecedented in British experience). American states and cities are much freer to decide what to do and how to do it, but by law must cover current expenditures out of current revenue, though they are permitted to borrow, at least for capital projects. A similar degree of financial soundness is imposed on German Länder and municipalities. This is a subject worthy of careful study.[6]

Of course there is much more to be said on theories of value, price, monetarism, inflation, public finance, incidence of taxation and financial controls under federalism. It remains for me to stress, not for the first time, the limited light that can be shed on these problems within the neo-classical and general-equilibrium paradigm.

NOTES

1. See my critique of Bettelheim in 'Market Socialism and Its Critics' in A. Nove and I.D. Thatcher (eds), *Markets and Socialism* (Edward Elgar, 1994), pp. 383–401.
2. For detailed references see A. Nove, 'Three Early Russian Economists', in *Studies in Economics and Russia* (Macmillan, 1990), pp. 3–23.
3. O. Morgenstern, *On the Accuracy of Economic Observations* (Princeton University Press, 1963).
4. N. Kaldor, *Further Essays on Applied Economics* (Duckworth, 1978), p. 9.
5. G.L.S. Shackle, *An Economic Querist* (Cambridge, 1973), p. 38.
6. In 1936 I won an essay prize at the LSE on local government finance in France and the United States, but have not returned to the subject since!

5. Investment, growth, ecology and 'macro' economics

In centrally planned economies, investment decisions, the share of GNP devoted to accumulation and the priorities of different sectors, were the responsibility of the supreme political authority. Though there was a size-able literature about investment criteria (rates of return, pay-off period, and the like), this made little impact on decision-making, save to the limited extent to which it influenced the choice of means, that is, alternative ways of achieving a given objective, for example, to expand electricity generating capacity by X kW. But even this was influenced by other factors too: since prices of inputs bore no relationship to their relative scarcity, they served poorly for an evaluation of alternative means, and this meant that there was plenty of opportunity for administrative intrigue, 'pull', influence, as different groups competed for investment resources, which for them appeared to be a free gift. Priorities decided by the political leadership were in any event decisive in the allocation of investments between sectors.

The result was a great deal of misallocation, unnecessary waste. A book could easily be filled with citations from Soviet authors pointing this out. There was a persistently high rate of accumulation. Priority was given to 'heavy industry', with long-term neglect of consumers' goods and services, and also, in recent decades, of transport and other infrastructure. In the competition for investments, victory in the 'administrative market' tended to go to the big battalions, that is, to those sectors and regions which were already large and therefore headed by influential people. Thus steel or oil, or the province of Chelyabinsk, had more 'pull' than textiles or retail distribution, or the province of Tambov, because the officials in charge of the former had higher rank than those in charge of the latter. Only when some sector fell scandalously behind, and the topmost leadership noticed this, was there a revision of priorities. The *locus classicus* of such a tendency was the chemical industry. In the 1950s it was very poorly developed, with fertiliser, plastics, detergents and artificial fibres very far behind the West. When this came to Khrushchev's attention, he ordered an increase in investments in chemicals so vast as to cause considerable disruption, and the plans had afterwards to be modified downwards.

Investment planners were also influenced by their own 'material balances', that is, a primitive form of input–output tables. They too, based inevitably on coefficients derived from the past, tended to exercise a conservative influence.

It proved hard to incorporate technical progress, innovation, into investment planning. The centre desired innovation, but seldom had the information to enable it to issue detailed plan-instructions of operational significance. Managers, rewarded primarily for the fulfilment of current plans, were risk-averse, but even if they were willing to take risks they were frequently unable to obtain the necessary inputs, or the approval of the planning bureaucracy. Furthermore, as a massive literature bears witness, the investment process was characterised by extremely long delays (the so-called *dolgostroi*, 'long-build'), due to a chronic tendency to start more investment projects than could be completed with the available material and human resources, so that, even if the original project incorporated some technology which was new at the time the project was drafted, eleven or more years later, when the plant was finally in operation, that technology was already obsolete.

Since the so-called 'scattering' of investment over too many projects had been the subject of criticism from the highest authorities for upwards of 30 years, it is worth considering the reasons for its persistence, and persist it did, all the way to the collapse of the Soviet system. This despite the fact that investment, undertaken in the context of an all-inclusive development plan, should have been a strong-point of centralised 'socialism'. The reasons include: the power of sectional interests, interested in expanding their sectors and attracting budgetary funds for the purpose, which overcame the countervailing power of the plan-coordination agency, Gosplan. Investment funds seemed to be free to the recipient, since even if financed from enterprises' profits, the latter would otherwise be transferred to the state budget. There was a systematic and conscious underestimate of costs, both of the actual project and of the need for complementary investments. Local officials were colluding with economic interest groups in pressing for more investments for their locality, which would enhance their importance in the party hierarchy. No amount of party and government orders to desist could counteract the tendency to commit more resources than could actually be made available.

Other notorious causes of misallocation included a preference for large and ambitious projects, a neglect of small-scale, of mechanising auxiliary tasks. One sees this particularly vividly in agriculture: many were the complaints from farm management that the planners imposed on them the construction of large-scale livestock complexes ('palaces for cows'), which, as one source put it, had the effect of doubling the cost of milk and halving the life-expectancy of the cows. A whole ministry (*Minvodkhoz*, literally of 'water resources') engaged in large-scale drainage and irrigation work, which provided little return but which enabled the ministry to fulfil its plans, which, like much of the new construction, were in terms of roubles *spent*, that is, extravagance was actually rewarded, economy penalised.

Since investment planning had perforce to be divided between different parts of the central bureaucracy, one also had frequent instances of failures of coordination. Thus a decision to increase substantially the production of fertiliser was unaccompanied by the required expansion of storage space, means of transportation and spreading machines, and many (including Khrushchev) drew attention to the large amounts of fertiliser left out in the open at railheads. Failure to provide essential infrastructure has been a major cause of heavy losses of farm produce.

This brief summary of what was wrong with the investment process in the USSR is included here so as to give one some notion of the kind of problems with which planners of the old Soviet Union would be familiar. So now imagine them turning to Western textbooks, Western advisers, Western experience. What will they see? What *should* they see?

As already argued earlier, it is hard to 'fit' investment into a general-equilibrium paradigm. Profits from investment can be foreseen under conditions of relative and temporary *dis*equilibrium. Equilibrium growth paths, within any model in which at the given moment the system and the parts composing it are in equilibrium, represent contradiction in terms. For growth to occur there must be some net investment (or the introduction of new cost-saving techniques). The investors or innovators must face some inducement to act, a profitable opportunity which they hope has not been observed by others. In other words, they must anticipate disequilibrium.

They must also hope that they have information not (nor not yet) available to their competitors, and/or they have made or will make a long-term tie-up with their customers (and probably also with suppliers of complementary inputs). The role of the state in this area, as a source of information, coordination, support with low-interest loans and protection from foreign competition, has been substantial in such (successful) countries as Japan, South Korea and Taiwan.

Thus in a paper devoted to this subject, Waltrant Urban notes the role in South Korea and Taiwan of 'a strong state committed to economic growth', with

perennial economic plans or rather economic programmes of the government. Extensive use is made of subsidies and other financial and non-financial incentives to implement economic programmes, but without putting the market mechanism itself into question . . . The rather close relationship between government and the private business sector is another important characteristic of their economic system. Public enterprises, too, play an important role. The working of the system in general is highly dependent on a well trained and well functioning bureaucracy.[1]

(This last point is important too; lack of such a bureaucracy is a serious handicap in ex-communist countries and much of the third world.)

Yet Western advisers, such as Jeffrey Sachs, in Poland and in Russia, apparently convey the notion that an optimal investment pattern would emerge under conditions approximating to free competition. And this when private capital is exceedingly scarce, a capital market barely exists, and when a distorted capital structure had been inherited from the communist regimes. The very words 'investment strategy' are seen as reminiscent of centralised planning and so excluded from consideration. This is a theme to which we will return in a later chapter.

It is G.B. Richardson, in his *Information and Investment*, who highlighted the theoretical gap. On the assumption of perfect markets and information, all will see the profitable opportunity and, to cite his words, 'a profit opportunity equally available to everyone is in fact available to none at all'. So it is not only that investments are made in anticipation of a (profitable) disequilibrium, they are made when the would-be investor has reason to believe that he or she sees what others do not see, knows what others do not know, or there are other so-called 'imperfections' (of competition or of information) already referred to. Brian Loasby correctly derives from all this the conclusion:

> Richardson demonstrates that, in the absence of the auctioneer, formal perfect competition provides no plausible basis for expectations, whereas oligopoly does at least define the apparently relevant set of competitors, and may well promote the exchange of information which gives firms the confidence to make commitments. It is perfect competition which is indeterminate. The imperfections are what makes the system work.[2]

Joan Robinson noted the 'uncertainty as to future profits' as limiting entrepreneurial borrowing.[3] T. Koopmans stated: 'To my knowledge no formal model of resource allocation through competitive markets has been developed, which recognises ignorance about all decision makers' future actions, preferences, or states of technical information as the main source of uncertainty confronting each individual decision maker.'[4] Nowhere is this more obvious than in the area of investment decisions. Koopman's essays were published 35 years ago, but the gap remains. As Frank Hahn rightly put it, investment 'is deeply mysterious under perfect competition'.[5]

Most 'neoclassicals' seem simply to have ignored Richardson's unanswerable comments. In my own experience there is here an area of mutual incomprehension. At a conference a few years ago I asked an eminent orthodox economist on what institutional basis (for example, about the possible conduct of competitors, future prices, and so on) the decision to invest would be taken in his model. My colleague looked at me in genuine puzzlement and replied: 'But I am assuming profit maximisation!' It was and is a source of puzzlement to me that he thought this was an answer to my question.

Nor, as already pointed out, is it remotely clear how one can speak meaningfully of 'dynamic equilibrium', or 'equilibrium growth paths', when, as Lachmann correctly pointed out, such 'concepts are notions of economists with little interest in what happens in the market economy . . . Growth theory has . . . become a branch of applied mathematics.'[6] One cannot sufficiently repeat a point which has been so persistently ignored: given that a 'macro' magnitude such as 'investment' is made up of a multitude of micro decisions to invest, taken by thousands of hopeful investors, any model with any pretensions to realism *must* assume anticipated (*rationally* anticipated) micro *dis*equilibria or some other so-called 'imperfections'.

In Britain too there are blind spots, which can be traced to the gaps in the theory. While very orthodox economists would readily admit that in the real world perfect competition and perfect markets do not exist, it is silently assumed that the nearer one can get to perfection, the better. We have seen that it is emphatically not the case in the area of investment, if the word is taken to mean long-term expansion of productive capacity. In passing it has to be said that Keynes had remarkably little to say about productive capacity, though he and his school were well aware of the importance of expectations in informing what Keynes himself called the 'animal spirits' of entrepreneurs. Worse are the so-called 'supply-siders'. They had in fact no concern for supply: they believed that lower taxes would stimulate demand, and so were 'demand-siders', though no doubt they thought that supply would respond. They also said they believed that lower taxes on the rich would stimulate them to be more active and to save, though precisely at the time their doctrine had the greatest influence (Reagan's presidency) US savings fell to an all-time low.

In Britain the Thatcher government has been committed not only to privatisation, but also to maximising competition by putting as much as possible out to competitive tender, as well as fragmentating: thus electricity generation and public transport were to be the responsibility of numerous competing firms.

In Europe it is all quite different. Swedish transport has a long-term tie-up with Volvo, German municipal undertakings with Renault-Berliet,

French railways with Alsthom, Italian railways with Breda, Italian buses with Fiat, Dutch buses with DAF. All investment involves risk, but a long-term relationship with major customers reduces that risk and gives the would-be investor grounds for confidence. I am sure that British economic advisers would see in the above links a form of half-disguised protectionism, and this may not be wide of the mark. But my point is a different one: it would apparently not occur to such advisers that the greater the degree of uncertainty created by competitive tendering plus fragmentation, the less likely it is that investments will be made by suppliers. The decline in the output of British manufacturers of means of transportation, the huge increase in imports, have many causes, but surely this is one of them.

Long ago Schumpeter noted the link between large-scale commitment to research and innovation and the actual or potential domination of the market by large firms. True, there are counter-examples, especially in electronics and computer software, but it is surely important to remind those who know all about the distortions of centrally planned investments in the old Soviet system that, in this area at least, the maximisation of competition can paralyse action. As already argued earlier, a profit opportunity available to everyone is in fact available to none.

In a challenging article, W. Baumol pointed out that collusion, joint expenditure on R&D by two or more firms, could be an effective and rational strategy if viewed dynamically, though it would be regarded as inefficient in orthodox static analysis.[7] Nor can one disagree with Galbraith's view that 'economic success requires technological advance. This in turn requires capital to finance research. It also requires organisation to undertake the development of technological breakthroughs and to use their fruits. Since only large firms have such capabilities, only they can invest in technology'.[8]

If market domination is an 'imperfection', it is, again, a necessary one, though maybe one needs at least a fear of oligopolistic competition to overcome a tendency to rest on one's laurels, or inertia. A degree of monopoly may be a precondition for large-scale investment, but too much of it can have the opposite result.

It also matters greatly what is invested in. Cairncross complained of

capital as an undifferentiated aggregate that yielded a flow of income and profit . . . But for some purposes it made a great deal of difference what concrete form the capital took: housing, public utilities, machine-tools, inventories and so forth . . . Whenever generalisations could be made in relation to the aggregate – and many of them seemed to me very doubtful – it was necessary to supplement them with a clear understanding of the behaviour of the constituent parts.[9]

This is of clear importance in any country, but particularly in Great Britain at the present time; did the so-called 'Lawson boom' of 1986–89 contribute significantly to British productive capacity? Only a disaggregated study can begin to answer the question. To cite Kenneth Boulding, 'land, labour and capital were hopelessly heterogeneous aggregates'.[10]

Also of great importance are the circumstances in which savings can be effectively channelled into productive investment. The role here of 'close links between financial institutions and operating firms – links like those found in contemporary Japan and Germany or in the turn-of-the-century United States (for example, J.P. Morgan) – are an important part of a well-functioning financial system to channel savings to investing firms in growing high-technology industries', to cite an NBER 'research summary' by J. Bradford De Long. The author also agrees with the view that there are 'large gaps between private profitability and the social utility of investment'. He sees 'clear and convincing evidence of stock market irrationality', and concludes that 'we have few grounds for confidence that America's present institutions are the financial institutions that best help the stock market fulfil its role as a social calculating mechanism for guiding the pace and direction of investment.'[11] There is much that 'eastern' economists (and our own theoretically-minded colleagues) could learn about the functioning or malfunctioning of real (not textbook) capital markets.

Also relevant here is the relationship between ownership and control. Who decides whether to invest? It is not satisfactory to contrast the entrepreneur-owner with, for instance, the employee-managed enterprise or a cooperative, noting that the latter may be more interested in short-term income-maximisation rather than in long-term investment. The point to make in the present context is that separation of ownership from control in large corporations can also result in what has been repeatedly labelled 'short-termism': management's success criteria becomes the quarterly profit statement, the 'bottom line', or its own income. If, as is frequently the case in the United States, executives expect to move every few years to other corporations, their personal commitment to the long-term prospects of their firm may be no greater than that of a member of the board of an employee-managed enterprise.

How are investments to be financed? What kinds of capital markets exist, or should exist? 'Eastern' economists would learn little about such matters in Western textbooks. The stock exchange in Britain and America provides surprisingly little investment capital. It has a role in *valuing* enterprises, since their stocks and shares are repeatedly bought and sold – though the behaviour of stock exchange prices are a source of puzzle and of a sizeable literature, seeking to find rational explanations for what sometimes look like random fluctuations. But most investment is financed out of retained profits and firms' reserves. It is otherwise in Germany and Japan, where financial institutions, notably the banks, have long had a commitment to long-term investment, providing venture capital. The lack of such commitment, the difficulty in obtaining venture capital and securing a long-term financial base for investment, has been the subject of much comment in the media, but has received little academic attention. Yet the functioning and efficiency of the capital market is a matter of great importance for countries seeking to move towards a market economy. Here, as elsewhere, a detailed study of institutions is required, and plainly one must avoid making any assumption implying that whatever exists is the best of all possible worlds.

Stock exchange valuations do serve a positive purpose, since they reflect, though imperfectly, the capital market's judgement of the firm's prospects, and this can serve as a guideline for the behaviour of management as well as would-be investors. However, it is important here to distinguish between two acts, both of which can be called 'investment', but which have quite different economic effects. Suppose that firm A is expected to do well, firm B not so well. Institutional investors and individuals buy more shares in firm A, which, as a result, rise by (say) 15 per cent. The opposite happens for firm B. As was pointed out as long ago as 1815 (and not just by Joan Robinson in the 'Cambridge versus Cambridge' capital controversy), the valuation of capital assets depends on anticipated future earnings, and not on the initial cost of this capital, whatever this might be. After the adjustment, upwards or downwards, by 15 per cent, and other things being equal, the rate of return for new investors in firm A and firm B would tend to be similar: the higher profit expected would be reflected in the higher capital valuation and the higher share price. In any case, the buying and selling of shares in the two firms would not have generated any investment activity in the other sense of that word: that is, expansion of capacity to produce goods or services. Those who already had shares register a capital gain. The firm's higher profits, if not paid out in dividends, would make possible higher real investment out of retained profits, of course. But there is a distinction to be made between 'investment' which takes the form of dealing, in purchases and sale of existing stocks and shares, and new capital which is used for real expansion of capacity.

There is a sizeable literature on project evaluation, an essential part of the investment decision process. However, some of it is 'sidetracked' onto the comparatively trivial question of whether 'internal rates of return' are inferior to calculation in terms of 'discounted cash flow'. The point is trivial because it is very doubtful if a single investment error can be quoted which could be ascribed to the difference between the two. If there were an error, it would be due to some mistaken expectation about a necessarily uncertain future.

Another point which is worth stressing, because it is so widely ignored, is the difference between *whether* and *how*. Let me explain. A large proportion of investment decisions are related (via complementarities, indivisibilities, and so on) to other decisions. Thus the question of investing in oil extraction in Alaska (or West Siberia) is a 'whether' decision. Once it is made, there are then a multitude of 'how' decisions, relating to transport facilities (for the oil and for inputs), pipelines, pumping stations, housing, drilling equipment, the location of processing plant, and so forth. Criteria for the 'how' decision concern the best way to achieve a *given* result. In each of the above instances, failure to invest would put into jeopardy the project as a whole. This is another instance of the multi-level nature of decisions in the real world, which so many textbooks present in a fragmented way, as related directly to the market.

Savings and investment can be equal only in a formal accounting sense, except by coincidence. The acts of saving and of investment are separate, even if sometimes undertaken by the same persons or institutions. Already Malthus drew attention to the possibility that savings may not be invested, that this was a cause, among others, for departures from Say's Law, according to which supply creates its own demand in the aggregate. Current income may or may not be saved, income saved may or may not be invested. It also greatly matters: invested in what? Savings in both America and Britain during the Reagan–Thatcher decade were heavily 'invested' in real estate, office building, in loans to finance-leveraged takeovers, and, in Britain's case, also abroad. The contrast with Germany and Japan has been widely noted. Yet the former communist-ruled countries, who have inherited a distorted capital structure and have relatively little non-governmental capital, are being advised to let investment be taken care of by market forces. They are to learn not from the experience of such countries as Japan and South Korea, or from that of Western Europe in the first years after the war, but from the textbook world in which investment goes automatically where it can be most effectively utilised. There will be much more to say about this in Chapter 7.

A critical view is also needed of the rate of interest, which fulfils in modern interconnected economies a number of potentially contradictory functions.

Interest rates should, in theory, reflect the 'time-preference of the community', and serve to bring demand for capital into line with supply, with savings. In practice, in an interdependent world with free or largely free capital movements, other factors frequently intervene to cause major distortions, as also do political uncertainty and inflationary expectations, or balance of payments problems. Numerous factors have influenced the level (very high by historical standards) of British interest rates in and after 1990, for instance: the felt need to slow down credit-financed consumption, pressure on the pound in foreign exchanges, a rise in interest rates in Germany for purely German reasons, to name but three. Severe pressure on borrowers, whether these be householders with mortgages or firms seeking credits, has contributed to a decline in business activity and in investment, engendering a record level of bankruptcies and house-repossessions, as well as to rising unemployment. In a country such as Poland, seeking to introduce a market economy, inflationary pressures push interest rates to very high levels, 50 per cent and more. While in 'real terms' such rates may seem modest, if inflation is also close to 50 per cent, the effect of such interest rates is to inhibit borrowing for any long-term investment, since there are acute cash-flow problems, and the peasants too are complaining about the effect of such rates on their costs. The relation between all this and either real time-preferences or the marginal productivity of capital seems remarkably remote.

It may be useful, for those who have been persuaded that Adam Smith is an apostle of laissez-faire, to quote from the *Wealth of Nations*: there he quite specifically advocated discrimination in lending in favour of those who really do borrow to invest, as distinct from those he called 'prodigals and projectors'.[12] So, in modern terms, Smith would have no qualms in charging higher rates to those who borrow to finance leveraged takeovers, or, in today's Russia, for purely speculative purposes. Conversely, he would have had no objection to policies such as those pursued by South Korea with conspicuous success; there, according to a report by the National Bureau of Economic Research there was:

an active, interventionist government policy that was credible, consistent, and coherent. Investment to promote exports received top priority, and the economy was led through a fundamental industrial restructuring. Korea instituted a series of five-year plans (beginning in 1962) that determined the level of investment necessary for a desired level of growth, and singled out sectors to be stimulated, focusing especially on exports. The close link between government and business in Korea made this strategy work.

Neither the IMF, nor the economic advisers of whom Jeffrey Sachs is a typical example, seem to believe in the desirability of an investment strategy, although the capital structure inherited from the communist regimes is known (also to them) to be highly distorted, and although investment capital is in very short supply, they see no need to direct or persuade it towards 'bottleneck' sectors. They are concerned with macroeconomic balance. The need for such balance is beyond dispute, and the chapter on the transition period, below, will give due emphasis to the task of establishing such balance. However, two theoretical weaknesses then combine to contribute to (what to my mind is) blinkered judgement. One is the well-known gap between macro and micro (and the lack of intermediate, or 'mezzo', categories). The other, already enlarged upon, is the poverty of the treatment of investment within neoclassical economics. There will be much more to say about the relevance of this for economics of transition in Chapter 7.

A somewhat different question, also of great relevance to my imagined 'eastern' ex-planners, is the extent to which, once established, macro-equilibrium or balance is self-sustaining. As already argued earlier, the profession is divided on this point. Some persist in emphasising the forces which speedily restore equilibrium. Others – surely with over a century of various theories of trade-cycles behind them – give greater emphasis to booms and slumps and the ways in which they can have cumulative effects: a fall in demand, however caused, leads to lower employment, lower profits, a further fall in demand. Eventually a recovery occurs, but, just as a ship in rough sea does tend to right itself, passengers feel less sick in a ship equipped with stabilisers. Or, to change the image slightly, Leijonhufhvd imagines that, in rough weather, the ship's cargo could have shifted, requiring action by the crew. And of course the storm could be so severe as to threaten shipwreck, as in 1933.

Macroeconomics has Keynesian roots, yet it became fashionable among right-wing neo-liberal economists to criticise Keynes, or even to blame him for inflationary excesses. Some 'eastern' economists had expressed the view that Keynes had found the solution to the trade-cycle problem which had plagued capitalist economies before World War II, but now are being influenced by the neo-liberals and the monetarists, and even by the new-classical 'rational expectations' school. These critics share a deeply-ingrained ideological revulsion against any systematic action by the state, other than in the area of money supply – though there are also extremists who believe in private money, reversing one of the oldest economic laws known: that good money would drive out bad. They also seem oddly to combine the belief that the state cannot achieve anything (positive), because its potential actions will have already been discounted by economic agents, with the not-altogether-consistent belief that the state can do serious harm. Such a mind-set can be reinforced by the 'public choice' school, which can convince its adepts that state officials are only concerned with their personal utility anyhow.

It is odd that under Reagan and Bush there were all-time records in budget deficits, which for a time did stimulate the economy, and this in circumstances in which Keynes would most certainly have advised against such a policy. It should be recalled that his *General Theory* was developed against a background of deep depression and mass unemployment, and was critical of those whose 'cure' would have made (did make) the depression worse, by cuts in public expenditure in pursuit of balanced budgets. The *locus classicus* of such policies was Germany in 1931–33, and it made a major contribution to Hitler's coming to power.

If one discusses growth, it is not irrelevant to cite a saying attributed to Kenneth Boulding: 'Anyone who can think that exponential growth can go on for ever is either a madman or an economist.' There will be much more to say about ecology under the heading of 'externalities'. In the present chapter it is only necessary to warn about the facile assumption that high growth rates are a 'good' in themselves, regardless of the effects on the environment. One need not adopt the more extreme interpretations about imminent ecological catastrophe to realise, first, that planet earth is limited in space and in resources; second, that population growth continues to be rapid; and finally that measures to protect the environment are almost always costly in terms of growth-opportunities foregone.

Socialist theory implied that environmental questions would be given due weight by planners, supposedly committed to the long term and able to internalise externalities (indeed having this as a principal task and duty). By contrast, capitalists, concerned with sectional interest and profit, would tend to ignore the effect of their behaviour on the environment. It was therefore something of a surprise to find that virtually every 'socialist' country was in the front of the polluters. The reasons will be discussed later, in the context of externalities in general, which, it turns out, can be just as much of a problem when boundary-lines are administrative as they are when they are based on separation of ownership. Clearly, environmental damage must be taken into account in investment decisions, but to do so requires a basic departure from the principles of laissez-faire. This is perhaps why, after having rightly criticised communist regimes for their neglect of these issues – some of the most shocking examples of air and water pollution were the work of these regimes – their successors, having adopted 'Chicago' ideology, now soft-pedal the issue. For even if one seeks a 'market' type of solution, such as that embodied in the slogan 'let the polluter pay', conscious action by government is needed, if only to compel payment.

In this area, there is little indeed to be learnt from the neoclassical mainstream.

A word of warning would be appropriate about econometric macro-models. Naive enthusiasts could be referred to the article by E. Leamer, with the excellent title, 'Let's Take the Con out of Econometrics'.[13] The author is himself a distinguished practitioner of the art, and clearly there is a legitimate area for econometric models. However, there are dangers in being what in my army days was called being 'blinded by science'. The sophistication of the methodology may distract attention from the fact that the conclusion is built into the specifications, in the initial assumptions. Thus Wynne Godley wrote: 'I know that the Treasury model says devaluation is always fully offset by inflation. But the model says this is because Treasury economists have programmed it this way'.[14] A second example, a few years old, relates to Wynne Godley himself. He devised a model which purported to show how import restrictions could have positive effects on the British economy, but here again there were built-in assumptions (about supply response, inflationary effects, retaliatory measures, and so on) which were programmed to produce the desired result. One can also cite Worswick's remark about econometricians, who have a 'marvellous array of pretend-tools which would perform wonders if ever a set of facts would turn up in the right form'.[15]

NOTES

1. W. Urban, 'Economic Lessons for the East European Countries from Too Newly Industrializing Countries in the Far East?', *Forschungsberichte*, **182**, April 1982, of the Vienna Institute for Comparative Economic Studies.
2. B. Loasby, *Choice, Complexity and Ignorance* (Cambridge University Press, 1976), p. 187.
3. J. Robinson, *The Generalization of Economic Theory* (Macmillan, 1979), p. 14.
4. T. Koopmans, *Three Essays on the State of Economic Science* (McGraw-Hill, 1957), pp. 146–7.
5. F.H. Hahn, 'Of Marx and Keynes and Many Things', *Oxford Economic Papers*, **38**, 1986, p. 360.
6. L.M. Lachmann, *Capital, Expectations and the Market Process* (Sheed Andrews and McMeel, 1977), p. 117.
7. W.J. Baumol, 'Horizontal Collusion and Innovation', *Economic Journal*, **102**(1), 1992, pp. 129–37.
8. Galbraith's views are here summarised by Steven Pressman in P. Arestis and M. Sawyer (eds), *A Biographical Dictionary of Dissenting Economists* (Edward Elgar, 1992), p. 166.
9. A. Cairncross, 'From theory to policy-making', *Banca Nazionale del Lavoro Quarterly Review*, March 1982, p. 9.
10. 'Boulding, Kenneth E. (born 1910)' in Arestis and Sawyer (eds), *A Biographical Dictionary*, p. 52.
11. *NBER Reporter*, Summer 1992, pp. 9, 11.
12. A. Smith, *Wealth of Nations*, Volume 1 (Oxford University Press, 1909), p. 400.
13. E.E. Leamer, 'Let's Take the Con out of Econometrics', *American Economic Review*, **73**(1), 1983, pp. 31–43.
14. Wynne Godley, 'Lamont is leading us towards catastrophe', *Observer*, 19 July 1992, p. 22.
15. G.D.N. Worswick, 'Is Progress in Economic Science Possible?', *Economic Journal*, **82**(1), 1972, p. 79.

6. Individualism and the public sector

This is an area of discussion that is, or should be, of direct interest to East European 'marketising' reformers: for what ought the state, so excessively dominant under communist rule, continue to be responsible?

It is tempting, for polemical purposes, to erect an 'Aunt Sally', a kind of composite neo-liberal-anarchist or ultra-conservative, who really does consider that economic theory points to a purely 'night-watchman' state. To my own surprise, I found that Aunt Sally actually existed. As a contributor to *Critical Review* once put it, such neo-liberal ideologists believe that the role of the state should be confined to national defence and road-building, 'and one is not sure about the roads'.[1] Privately-issued money has been advocated, as has the privatisation of prisons. Private police forces already exist, though no one (to my knowledge) actually advocates the abolition of a national or municipal police force – perhaps action against criminals is subsumed under national defence. It has been reported – perhaps wrongly – that Milton Friedman can be reluctantly persuaded that traffic lights or parking regulations, installed or promulgated by public authorities, are legitimate interferences with individual freedom. Yes, he and others like him are willing to admit the existence of externalities and of other kinds of what are sometimes called 'market failures' (I am not too fond of the term, for reasons which will appear). But the neo-liberals tend to hold that actions by public authorities to deal with the resultant problems generally do more harm than good, as Friedman himself argues in the book written jointly with his wife.[2]

Let us then gradually build up a list of functions which justify either taxes to maintain them, or regulation, or both. In doing so, it is important to bear in mind an important distinction, which is sometimes blurred, between *responsibility* and *implementation*. Thus, to illustrate the point, road building and garbage collection may be carried out by private contractors, but public authorities are responsible for the road network and for ensuring that garbage in cities is collected.

Before proceeding further, it is also necessary to take another look at the neoclassicals' predilection for methodological individualism. Benjamin Ward formulated it thus: there is a tendency 'to divid[e] up choices in such a way that each act of choice, even purchase, has as little discernible impact on others as possible. This very act of division encourages a fragmented organisation of information around the choice acts, which minimises the individual's exposure to the cumulative effect of even his own set of choices'.[3] As I have argued at length elsewhere, neoclassical theory tends to *fragment*, to concentrate on increments, is reluctant to focus on systems, networks of interrelationships. *Individual* preferences dominate analysis.

We have already observed, quoting Harold Demsetz, that 'perfect competition' is really 'perfect decentralization'; in the last analysis no distinction is made between the individual and the group, which is why there have been problems fitting a theory of the firm into the neoclassical paradigm. Problems arise, too, from reconciling the paradigm with the (surely self-evident) fact that people's individual choices interrelate, influence each other in a variety of ways, and that people learn from experience and from each other. But in the present context this is not our concern. Two matters are, however, of high importance in just this context. One has been recognised in the form of the 'prisoner's dilemma', and figures in some game-theory models: individuals can in some circumstances better their individual position by collaborating or conniving, rather than each separately pursuing what appears to them their best interests, in ignorance of each others' decisions. (By extension, this can be seen as relevant to the investment dilemma identified by G.B. Richardson, already discussed in Chapter 5.) But this whole question can be formulated differently, in terms of the interests of the whole *(any* whole) and of its parts. Arthur Koestler put the point particularly well in his *Janus.* There are two undesirable extremes to see the part *only* as a subset of the whole, or to see the whole as *only* the sum of its parts. His is a philosophical point remote, in his book, from economics, but is directly applicable to economic life too. Neoclassical economics tends strongly towards the second of the undesirable extremes. And repentant Soviet planners are the more likely to fall under the spell of such doctrines because, under the old Soviet system, the *first* of these extremes predominated: people, individuals and firms were subordinated far too totally to the supposed interests of the totality, as interpreted by the oligarchy of party functionaries. A switch towards much greater concern for individuals was and is entirely proper. But it could go too far, in theory and in practice.

It is simply *wrong* to regard the interests of the whole as just the sum of the interests of the parts composing it. Examples are legion. Let us begin with the firm itself. Suppose that it is a firm with 15 branches, factories, divisions. As already mentioned when we discussed the multi-level nature of margins in the real world of business, the very existence of head office is predicated upon the belief that, if each of the fifteen pursued its own interest as seen at its level, this might frequently *not* be in the interests of the firm as a whole. This is why head office exists! Otherwise it could be costlessly abolished and money saved on salaries and office space. There is also informational economies of scale.

The same is true of a country. Suppose that the imposition of a tariff on imports of widgets would benefit the economy of (say) Pennsylvania, but that retaliatory action of the government of the widget-producing country would harm the economy of (say) New Jersey. One or other of the policy alternatives – to impose or not to impose a tariff – would have to be judged to be in the interests of the totality, in this case the United States. Whatever decision is taken is bound not to be in the interests of either Pennsylvania or New Jersey.

Other examples can be listed almost indefinitely. An elegant terrace in the town of Bath, or the Champs Elysées in Paris, represent vistas which cannot be usefully seen as merely the sum of each of the buildings of which they consist. From which it follows that altering one of the buildings (for example, demolishing it and substituting a 30 storey office block), which could be in the interest of the owner, would have profound 'external' (or 'internal') effects on the totality, and so the municipality would be justified in forbidding it. It would be odd, would it not, if we trained architects to see each building they design in isolation, ignoring its environment. But that is how neoclassical economists are trained. The word 'environment' also calls to mind the importance of ecological externalities, which serve to provide many examples of the possibly harmful effects of individual action based upon maximising individual utility.

Are the Chicago symphony orchestra, or the first battalion Grenadier Guards, or the University of Cambridge, or the Argentinean soccer team, no more than the sum of the individuals composing them; each of whom is supposed to maximise his or her own utility? Is this a useful way of looking at things, important though the role of individuals are in orchestras, universities, armies and sports?

Alfred Eichner, among others, has made similar criticisms, on 'the "fallacy of composition"– the fallacy being that *wholes* can be considered as the sum of *parts*'.[4] Interestingly, Keynes in his philosophical moments was also aware of this key methodological problem. To cite Richard X. Chase:

> In Keynes's view, the atomic theory of structure wherein the whole is equal to the sum of the constituent parts is well suited to the study of the natural world . . . However, this framework, consistent with the idea of methodological individualism, is only carefully applicable to the social world because of the possibility of organic interaction – i.e., functional interdependence – in the latter.[5]

There is a fascinating discussion of the meaning and appropriateness of methodological individualism (by P. Boettke, I. Kirzner, G. Madison) in an issue of *Critical Review*,[6] in which it is argued, *inter alia*, that while the mainstream neoclassicals take too narrow a view, the 'Austrians' do or did see individual action in its social context, though the stress is on the individual, counterpoised to socialist conceptions of community.

A powerful criticism is put forward by Rajani K. Kanth; he attacks the view that 'facts pertaining to social phenomena are reducible to facts about individuals', that 'army becomes just the plural for soldier'. The ascription of rationality and maximising behaviour does not explain *why* decisions are taken. It is 'a grand tautology', since virtually any behaviour can be described as rational after the event: 'micro statements cannot simply be added up to form coherent macro situations'.[7]

Already in Chapter 2 we have been discussing 'rationality' in the context of maximisation. The stress here is on the limitations of an 'individualism' bereft of its social context. Jerry Evensky quotes A. Etzioni's *Moral Dimension: Towards a New Economics: 'The individual and the community make each other and require each other*. The society is not a "constraint", not even an opportunity, *it is us*' (emphasis in the original), and Evensky goes on correctly to say that 'The NeoClassical community, the mainstream of modern classical liberal economic thought, has elevated *homo economicus* to a central position in the discourse about human behaviour, simultaneously relegating "community" to a marginal role.' Like Schumpeter, Evensky believes that society requires commitment to group values, to maintain the degree of cohesion and order necessary for society to function. 'Adam Smith saw humans as social animals, shaped by and shaping their society', while 'textbooks depict humans as Beckerian rational utility maximisers'.[8] Some of those ideologists who call themselves followers of Adam Smith could not have read that great man's works.

Neoclassical mainstream theory fragments, even while appearing to relate everything to everything. The bits *do* interconnect, but the interconnection is through and by the market, while institutions are seen as the aggregated total of the individuals composing them.

Chakravarty makes similar points: 'a simple reductionist position which treats the "individual" as the ultimate unit can prove very misleading, since important patterns of economic behaviour arise on higher levels of organisation.'[9] Heilbroner too rejects 'the rationally maximising individual as the irreducible building block of economic analysis', because of the importance (also to the individual) of the social context.[10]

Another common assumption, logical as far as it goes, is that any contract freely entered into must be seen as benefiting both parties, from which it follows that it is wrong to interfere with free contracts. Yet one can readily conceive of exceptions to an otherwise logical and sensible rule. Let me cite a hypothetical and a real exception. Thus suppose that we transport ourselves into the eighteenth century, when (according to Beaumarchais) the lord of the manor benefited from *jus primae noctis*. Suppose there were a price at which the lord could be persuaded to forego this right. If so, the transaction could be held to benefit the lord, the husband and his bride. All well? No. Surely, it could be argued that the institutional and legal setting were unjust. (Some might think that payment of a large rent to a landlord who inherited valuable land from a great-grandfather, and does absolutely nothing other than letting others work it or work on it, is also ethically questionable, though here too the deal benefits both parties, given the institutional and legal setting.)

My other example is inspired by a recent *Wall Street Journal* editorial in praise of Hayek, who had just died. Hayek's was indeed an intellect of formidable quality, but the example chosen by the *Journal* had him deploring measures that would stand in the way of Mexicans moving to Mexico City, since they do so to better their individual lot. Did Hayek (or the editors of the *Journal*) really not know that Mexico City is strangling itself, with huge problems of air pollution, rubbish disposal, water supply, and a population exceeding 21 million? The example can serve to illustrate the difficulty which even a highly intelligent economist, and an 'Austrian' to boot, has when faced with a problem on which methodological individualism is not easily able to focus. Of course I accept, as we all should, the proposition that men and women should be free to act as they wish, spend their money as they wish, so long as they do not harm others in the process.

Actually, this is not a satisfactory formulation, since many actions which *are* widely accepted as desirable do harm others. I have never been able to understand the relevance to the real world of the concept of 'Pareto optimality'. Naturally if anyone can improve their situation while not worsening anyone else's, then this is a suboptimal situation. But in a competitive world, with technical progress, almost *any* significant action damages someone's interests: success in competition results in loss to competitors; *any* new technology renders older technologies obsolete (the computerisation of printing put thousands of skilled compositors out of work); if the lady says 'Yes' to Mr A she may severely disappoint the hopeful Mr B; and so almost ad infinitum. So when we say that men and women are free to act so long as they do not harm others, this apparently simple phrase needs to be rather carefully qualified.

Or harm themselves? Should motor-cyclists be compelled to wear helmets? Should drug-users be free to go on using drugs? Here opinions can

differ. But if head injuries and drug-related illnesses (and the abandon-
ment of children, or their infection at birth) impose costs on others, a
case can be made for intervention. These too are 'external effects'.

One other word of caution is relevant here. Should one accept that
freedom can be limited *only* by the state? Of course, the neo-liberals do
reject slavery. Men and women are seen by them, rightly, as owning themselves. Presumably they would reject, rule out by law, anyone turning
himself 'voluntarily' into a slave to pay off a debt, or selling his or her
child. But there is no need to imagine such extreme cases. Suppose a
landowner closes off footpaths in a beauty-spot and posts private guards
to keep residents of nearby cities away. Is he not thereby restricting freedom (as much as if a government department putting up a similar
notice)? Conversely, suppose the state compulsorily purchases the land
and turns it into a national park. Is this a step on the road to serfdom? Or
is the restriction on the landlord's freedom more than compensated by
the greater freedom of thousands of others? I accept, of course, that *con-
fiscation* of property sets up regrettable precedents, as happened in
Eastern Europe; eventually not even the small owner of a house or land
could enjoy them secure from arbitrary seizure. However, many countries,
in several continents, having 'inherited' a highly inequitable land distribution, proceeded to legislate a (compulsory) redistributive land reform.
Thereby much was gained in terms of social peace and political stability
as well as equity. (I am not clear about the neo-liberals' attitude to latifundia, and to land reform generally.)

If we are to condemn intervention by reference to the sacred rights of
private property, then presumably one would also have to approve of the
(rightly) infamous 'Highland clearances', when thousands of Scots families were ordered off the land and shipped overseas, or forced to migrate to
the cities, to make room for the more profitable sheep. Here, admittedly,
there was no deal which benefited both parties. There was no contract,
and indeed this was the problem: the tenants had no title to the land, and
so could be costlessly ordered off it, until at long last Parliament passed
the Crofters' Act to give them some security of tenure. But the Scottish
Highlands and islands had by then already been depopulated.

And of course men and women do voluntarily put themselves under
the authority of their employer. In considerable degree they are free to
choose whom to obey, and this is important. However, their freedom is
thereby limited whether the 'boss' is a private property-owner, a limited
company or a state official. We will return to this question when discussing labour and 'privatisation'.

After this long digression, let us now return to a list of functions, other
than national defence and road-building, with which public authorities

should, in the view of moderates of many parties, be concerned in one way or another.

Since parks have been mentioned, let us start with them: national and regional parks, botanic gardens (for example, the beautiful one in San Francisco which I happened to have just visited), public beaches, urban gardens, or even a tree-lined boulevard giving shade to the town's citizenry in a hot climate. In practice in most countries these are seen as proper activities, which cannot be left to private enterprise to provide. It is not a 'market failure', it is simply not a 'market' matter. To expect the necessary finance to be voluntarily provided by individuals runs into the problem, frequently to be encountered in this chapter, of the 'free rider'. There would be many beneficiaries who would not pay, and this would discourage the others from contributing to the cost.

Firefighters used to be privately financed by insurance companies in eighteenth-century England. However, since fire can spread from and to the uninsured ('external effects') municipal fire services have long existed in every civilised country. In medieval Europe tax collection was farmed out to private entrepreneurs, who kept a part of the proceeds. So far no one has proposed to return to the old days in this respect, though Mrs Thatcher's advisers did think of it. After all, it is one of her appointees, in his capacity as Secretary for Education, who seriously proposed that schools hire their own inspectors from the private sector, thus proving that ideology can cause the victims to take leave of their (common) senses.

But back to local services. Street lighting confers widespread benefits, and can scarcely be charged separately to individual beneficiaries. The non-collection of rubbish (trash) becomes a health hazard, as well as an eyesore ('externality' again!), and its removal is the responsibility of public authorities just about everywhere – though in some instances it pays a private firm to do the removing. I do not see these as instances of 'market failure', any more than is the existence and maintenance of Central Park in Manhattan.

A number of other amenities are frequently provided by public authorities: golf courses, other sports grounds, swimming-pools, marinas; some of these can be and indeed are also provided by private enterprise, but usually at a price that puts them out of reach of many citizens. The same is true of public libraries and museums. Quality of life and culture can be seen as public 'goods'.

Somewhat more controversial are opera, theatre companies, orchestras, the provision of concert halls, and the like. 'Libertarians' (and also some of the extreme left) cry 'elitism': subsidies go to the 'cultured' and often affluent minority, while the masses may prefer beer, pop and football.

Why not leave it all to market forces? In the former Soviet Union, and in most of the other ex-communist countries, subsidies for the arts have been drastically curtailed or simply abolished. Culture is in dire trouble and faces closedown. Andrzej Walda, distinguished Polish film director, stated that the only films which can be made to pay in Poland are pornography. Czech playwrights have complained to President Havel, himself a distinguished playwright. Nearer home, British film-makers have begged in vain for state support for their industry. 'Market' logic is inconsistent with the survival of the BBC.

Opinions must differ as to the desirability and the magnitude of subsidies in this field. Two considerations argue 'for'. One is the value of culture as such: Bach, Mozart, Shakespeare, Pushkin, are 'goods' in themselves. The arguments are similar to those applying to the existence of public libraries, or indeed to education in the humanities. The other concerns choice. If the existence of opera, or of a concert hall or a theatre large enough to perform in, requires a financial contribution from public authority (that is, the taxpayer), then in the absence of such a contribution the citizens will be deprived of the possibility of choosing. They may vote by a large majority in favour. Does this mean coercing the minority? Some libertarians would so argue. And it must be admitted that we can all think of circumstances when a majority vote could result in intolerable oppression of a minority (for example, to confiscate the property of Chinese in Indonesia, of East Asians in East Africa, of Jews in Nazi Germany, and so on). If, with Nozick, we regard taxation as a form of legalised theft, then the concert hall would share the fate of street lighting, parks, rubbish collection or any other tax-financed amenities, however large the democratic majority in favour. One recalls the 'liberum veto' of eighteenth-century Poland: any member of the *szlachta* (gentry) could veto any act by the elected assembly. But let us also recall what happened to Poland as a result: partition. Could such a society survive?

It is relevant at this point to refer again to the concept of Pareto optimality. Neo-liberals, such as Herzog, have interpreted it as follows: 'The utilitarian will accept a change making some worse off if it yields larger gains for others; the [Paretian] economist won't.'[11] This would rule out virtually all communal or social projects financed by any form of taxation, since any taxpayer is made worse off by paying tax!

What of *public health*? When I was a student at LSE, I recall a satirical article in the student journal devoted to the not-too-mythical character called Fun Hike. His doctrines were allegedly based on strict laissez-faire, with, however, an exception: if plague broke out in the poorer quarters of the town, the infection could spread to the richer areas, so . . . The real Hayek, who was then teaching at LSE, protested against this article. The point can be treated seriously: when diseases are infectious or contagious, there are external effects: this of itself justifies public concern and remedial action, which only public authorities could take.

However, this is only a small segment of the problem. The issue could best be highlighted by two quotations. One is from a letter in the *Economist* (7–11 March 1992), from an American reader. 'Medical care is a service like any other – much as we may not like to think of it in that way. You cannot visit the local power company and claim you are entitled to electricity even though you cannot pay. Medical care is subject to the same market forces.'

In the same month, the *San Francisco Chronicle* argued editorially that 'the United States needs to establish a system of medical care that is available to every citizen. To deny anyone coverage leads inevitably to a system in which only the healthy rich can afford care – and ends up costing society more in the long run' (15 March 1992). As is known, some 37 million American citizens have no health insurance, and roughly another 37 million have insufficient coverage, while medical costs are extremely high by international standards, as are the costs of administration, public and private.

Why should health care be different from other goods and services provided by profit-maximising entrepreneurs? One reason, surely, is that the purchaser, the 'customer', is not and cannot be well informed about his or her condition or alternative treatments. So profit-maximising hospitals and/or doctors have ample opportunities to cash in on ignorance, which, in turn, is why one hopes and expects that they are not profit maximisers, but take the Hippocratic oath seriously. Whereas butchers or bakers can act in the manner described by Adam Smith, pursuing their own interests and thereby serving their customers with meat and bread of the desired quality, under competitive conditions.

A second reason is that disease imposes losses on others: by infection, through absence from work, and so on. Should the state disinterest itself from the AIDS epidemic? Or cholera? Or malaria?

A third reason is that the full cost of serious illness is beyond the purse of all but the very rich. As ex-President Reagan put it, 'the choice is between death and bankruptcy'. None of us wish to be faced with this choice, most of us prefer that our fellow-citizens also are not faced with it. Private insurance is only a partial answer, as American experience shows.[12] The point is often made that demand will exceed supply if there is no payment for treatment, and this does indeed present problems, especially with the high cost of some modern medical care. However, an adequately insured individual also does not pay, his insurance company does.

Most citizens either do or should feel enough empathy for the less for-
tunate that they would be shocked if infant mortality figures rose because
expectant mothers could not afford to visit an ante-natal clinic. My (medical doctor) mother would have been horrified to read that letter I have
quoted from the *Economist*, and I hope the editor felt similarly. Can we
really envisage a society in which a sick child is treated only after examination of its parents' wallet? There are also publicly-maintained cemeteries
in most of the world, if only for 'paupers' graves'. What is the alternative?

Perhaps the libertarians might argue that voluntary charitable contributions would be more plentiful if there were no state-financed medical
benefits. Maybe they would, but it is surely far-fetched to imagine that
they could cope with the problem. (And again the 'free rider' issue arises,
and 'charity begins at home'.)

The same point could be made in respect of old age pensions, care for
chronic invalids, orphans, and children abused at home. All this in no way
conflicts with belief in the virtue and necessity of a market economy.
Ludwig Erhard's market was a *social* market, *Soziale Markwirtschaft*, and
in 1949 Germany was not yet a prosperous country – it was still in a
process of recovery from war. Even so, the somewhat conservative
Christian Democrats under Adenauer's leadership saw the political and
social need to combine market with state-sponsored welfare. Ideological
propagandists have at times attributed Britain's post-war difficulties to the
'welfare state'. They would need to explain why the much more successful
economies of West Germany, France, the Netherlands and Scandinavia,
all had welfare arrangements at least as thorough, or more so.

A common criticism of welfare-benefit entitlements is that many go to
those who do not need them. Conservatives have frequently argued for
targeted benefits, based on some sort of means test. The idea seems
attractive, but has two defects. One is the cost of administration: many
petty bureaucrats will be engaged in assessing need. The other is the dis-
incentive effect, or what is called the 'poverty trap'. Suppose that one
receives various benefits only if one's income is below (say) £100, and
loses all or part when income rises above this level. Then a large part of
any additional earnings are lost to the recipient via lost benefits. In some
documented cases it can have the same effect on one's marginal earnings
as a 90 per cent tax rate. This is neither ethical nor efficient, discouraging
employment and effort. These kinds of 'welfare' benefits do indeed have
the deleterious effects the American conservatives point to, but they draw
the wrong conclusions.

However, let me return to the list of publicly financed functions which
most societies find to be necessary or desirable. Traffic control has
already been mentioned. 'No parking', 'no left turn', 'no large trucks',

speed limits. Without further dwelling on such (in my view) rather obvious matters, what of town planning, zoning, restrictions on the use of land? 'Libertarians' can doubtless cite examples of publicly-funded ugliness, and there are many instances of the erection of then-fashionable high-rise public housing, in cities as far apart as St. Louis and Glasgow, which pleased no one and either have been or should have been demolished. Also it is the case that land with permission to build is worth much more than land without such permission, and this could lead to windfall profits for the owner, and also to corruption. Accepting that such undesirable consequences can follow, it remains true that elementary environmental protection calls for limiting the building of factories in residential areas or conurbations, while aesthetic considerations call for preservation of ancient monuments, and architectural ensembles. The tsars issued orders that there be no tall buildings to spoil the view along the Nevsky Prospekt in St. Petersburg; successive French republics did the same along the Grands Boulevards of Paris. My own house in Glasgow is part of a terrace in which no alteration of facades of houses is allowed without municipal permission, and I accept this limitation of my property rights as rational, because such alterations can have significant external effects on my neighbours.

Perhaps the 'libertarian' believes that the market could take care of such problems on an individual basis. Thus whoever desires no change in the facades of my terrace could pay to prevent the proposed change, just as those who do not wish a factory to be built in their residential neighbourhood could pay the firm to go elsewhere. But apart from the free rider problem (why should everyone affected contribute, if they know that some can desist from so doing), there is an evident opportunity for a form of legalised blackmail: I threaten to build that factory, with the real intention of doing so, so as to get paid for not building it.

In case this sounds facetious, something similar is actually happening in Great Britain now. Landlords are being paid millions for not developing their property, in the interests of preservation, that is, they make money refraining from doing anything.

Then there is the problem of megalopolises, for example, of Mexico City and Sao Paulo, mentioned above in another connection. Their sheer size attracts people and businesses, but imposes heavy social costs and threatens environmental disaster. The manner in which one can cope with this difficult problem could vary. One can see clear objections to using the *propiska*, the Soviet police-registration method of regulating place of residence by issuing or denying permits. One could ban the setting up of new businesses, or introduce a 'discouraging' tax, reflecting the extra costs to society. But, in whatever form, it calls for action by public authority.

The ecological aspect of town planning is perhaps too well known to require space here. Just one quotation to illustrate:

> Cubatao just off the Sao Paulo–Santos highway, is one of the world's most polluted cities . . . Twenty-three factories, many producing petro-chemicals, belch fumes into clouds over the town. Thousands of trees stand bare over the surrounding hills . . . Birth defects and other health problems among the population, estimated at 90,000, are high.[13]

Surely not a case for laissez-faire? And if, as Friedman argues, one should cope with this by taxation ('make the polluter pay'), this too requires purposive action by public authority. It is a matter worth discussing where and whether a prohibition is more appropriate than some sort of monetary penalty in the form of a tax. To take noise pollution as an example, suppose one's neighbour is playing pop music fortissimo at 2 a.m. Should one pay him to desist or call the police? If effluent from chemical works poisons a river or a lake, destroying fish and making it unsafe to bathe, is not action of some sort called for, which cannot be purely fiscal or 'individualist'? Beneficiaries from the clean-up of the Great Lakes are widespread, in both US and Canada. Land reclamation (Holland), drainage, eliminating mosquitoes (France, Italy), flood control, all seem to be desirable 'public' activities, of general *economic* benefit.

The pollution which disfigures a number of industrial cities in the former Soviet Union and its ex-allies shows that concentration on growth can have appalling effects under centralised planning, if the government neglects the environment. Public authorities too can pollute, so clearly it is wrong to assume that they will always be willing to take the necessary remedial action. But it is surely their responsibility. Smog in Los Angeles is a proper concern for the local authority, and not to be dealt with by leaving it purely to market forces.

From town planning to *housing* is but a short step. Again, apart from the 'high-rise' disasters, there is the undeniable fact that rent control discourages private-sector renting and contributes to the neglect of properties. There are also examples, particularly in Britain, of excessively severe zoning regulations which so define overcrowding that – to take an example – the most elegant and sought-after quarters in Paris could be regarded as grossly overpopulated. This has had the effect of unnecessarily discouraging the private building of flats in inner London. However, given the high cost of land in cities, it is surely clear that a large proportion of low-paid employees could not afford either to buy or to rent at market prices. Consequently in most of the world's cities there is some public housing, such as the so-called HLM of the Paris conurbation, the apartment blocks which have replaced the Harlem slums in New York, and so on. All one has to do is to compare and contrast the free prices of houses with the income of (say) a postman, a railway worker, a school-teacher. 'Affordable' housing is an issue in the United States too. Roger Quillot, in *Figaro* of 12 June 1992 wrote: 'No country has been spared the phenomenon of marginalisation and ghettos. *It is the simple operation of market laws that creates ghettos.* Thus no family can buy or rent in Paris if its income is less than 25 000 francs (£2000) a month' (emphasis mine).

Mrs Thatcher's government in Britain was particularly hostile to municipal housing. It not only compelled the local authorities to sell off much of their housing stock to sitting tenants at low prices (the tenants naturally welcomed this in so far as this put money into their pockets – some unkind people saw this as a bribe to vote Conservative), but, incredibly, forbade local authorities to use the proceeds of these sales to build houses! However, even her government did see that some cheaper housing for rent was required, via what were called 'housing associations', which were non-profit making. To take the opposite extreme, in the former Soviet empire private house-building was severely limited, and state housing was let at extremely low rents, which did not even cover maintenance. Furthermore, through influence, the better-quality housing stock was all too often allocated to those with good connections with the dominant *nomenklatura*. The moral seems to be to seek some combination of private and public (or subsidised) provision of housing, as has been the case in Western Europe for many years.

Old age pensions, supplemented by private insurance, are a feature of life in almost every civilised country. So are orphanages. Social workers are employed to try to deal with problem families, child abuse, wife-beating, invalids. Steps are – or should be – taken to enable invalids to get about. Again, can private charity suffice? Unemployment pay in some form is again a feature of life in most civilised countries, though there can be wide variations in the terms on which it is offered: there can be a case made for so-called 'workfare', that is, that able-bodied recipients perform some useful work – unless, that is, in doing so they put others out of a job. But whatever is done is a matter of public-sector *responsibility*. Only in textbooks do labour markets 'clear'.

In some countries one has problems with famine. This could be of two types: harvest failure (for example, due to prolonged drought) leading to food shortage, or shortage of money (that is, food is there, but people cannot afford to buy it). This point has been made on several occasions, in writings on the third world, by Keith Griffin[14] and by Amartya Sen.[15] By definition neither can be dealt with by 'market forces'. One recalls the Irish famine of the 1840s, when many died; the then orthodox doctrine of the British Treasury led them to refuse to send relief, because of the effects this would have on prices and on the market. Nowadays virtually everyone would declare a state of emergency and send food. Interestingly, two major exceptions in this century was Stalin's Russia (1933) and Mao's China (1959–60). Not, I feel, examples for neo-liberals to follow!

At the other social extreme, one needs financial and banking regulations, to avoid or minimise white-collar fraud. In the aftermath of the Los Angeles riots of 1992, it was pointed out by several commentators that the damage done by looters there was but a tiny fraction of what was looted in the Savings and Loans frauds. Capitalists and financiers do need protection. So do small savers. Eastern Europe and Russia are bound to provide some colourful examples of fraudulent manipulation of all kinds. Indeed, some have already come to light.

What of *education*? Already Adam Smith was aware of the concept of human capital, and, as an eighteenth-century Scotsman, took for granted the responsibility of public authorities as providers, though of course not necessarily the *sole* providers. There is, to my knowledge, no country at all where the state includes itself out. The 'liberal anarchist', *pur sang*, presumably considers that education services are like any other, to be purchased in the market by those who can afford it, with private charity to help out. Though surely they too are aware that children are imperfectly informed and cannot directly purchase schooling, while their parents may or may not take a responsible attitude. So some favour vouchers, that is, they recognise the state's responsibility to pay out of taxation, but seek to ensure that the market provides the 'product', with schools competing for pupils, who bring their vouchers with them, which schools exchange into money. This way, irresponsible parents would be unable to turn the education grant into whiskey or a cruise to the Bahamas. Some British ideological advisers seek to destroy local education authorities, leaving each school to sink or swim in the marketplace. This is said to maximise parental choice. All but the most extreme recognise that education, the creation of human capital, is of direct and indirect benefit to society and to the economy. Clearly, employers benefit from being able to recruit an educated labour force. Technical training too is of great economic benefit. If the neo-liberal replies that the beneficiaries (the trainee and the employer) should pay, then, once again, the problem is the free rider. Having benefited from training, the individual can go elsewhere, to work for another firm, which has not bothered to spend on training. A relevant British example is the BBC, whose excellent training programme is of considerable benefit to the commercial TV networks. The BBC, as a public institution, none the less continues to provide such training. Surely it hardly requires formal proof that if the 'product' is free to move, private provision of technical training will be sub-optimal.

There are also problems with the voucher scheme, with independent schools competing for the money. It is yet another instance of fragmentationism. Why do school districts exist? Because the local education authority has responsibilities: to ensure that new schools are built if needed, or older ones closed if there is a decline in the school population, that special needs are met (for example, for the deaf, the mentally handicapped, the specially talented, minority subjects such as Latin, and so on). Every country has local education authorities of some sort, responsible for ensuring school places for children. If schools can choose their own pupils, what happens to the disruptive minority or to those who for any reason are rejected for admission? The notion of parental choice, while good in itself, has little meaning if the most popular schools are, as they usually are, already full. (And all too often, in inner-city areas, parents do not care). The British 'solution' of encouraging schools to opt out of local education authority control and then give them favourable treatment is a sure recipe for a two-tier, two-quality system, with the 'dregs' left to the local authority, and the result used as proof by the ideologists of the poor quality of locally controlled education. This is further reinforced by the proposal that each school independently determines the salaries of teachers. Naturally, schools in better-off areas will pay more, attract the better teachers. Again, the underclass will be driven further down. The cost of such policies, along with the neglect of housing, can be seen in the Los Angeles riots of 1992, which, it so happens, were occurring as I wrote these lines.

Scientific and industrial research is another area in which externalities *and* the free rider problem combine to justify public-authority involvement. Firms intent on short-term profit maximisation reduce their research budgets (though with a number of honourable exceptions). Even the most narrow-minded of the neo-conservatives favour large-scale investment in military research, though in theory this too could be left to the military–industrial private sector. But the vital question is availability of the results of research. Unless it is *not* freely available to others, private firms would not undertake it. Needless to say, patent laws are themselves desirable, so that 'inventive' individuals and firms can derive benefit from their discoveries. Indeed, East European experience showed that if it is forbidden to make a charge for making technical information available, there is no incentive to provide it. However, it is not only that some species of expensive research cannot be undertaken without some public support, the same is true, for example, of agricultural research, for example, into new varieties of plants, fertiliser, equipment. Incredibly, the ideologists that advised the Thatcher government argued that government financing of research in this area should be limited to where the results would have *no* practical application! (For otherwise they should be privately financed . . .) Again, this ignores the free rider problem: if the research results were available to thousands of farmers, then no one of them would be interested in financing it.

There is also a strong case of intervention to limit the cutting down of forests, and to avoid such disasters as a dust-bowl, which could be (was) created by individual farmers bent on short-term profit (and, in the USSR, by pressure to fulfil current output plans).

Next on my list, *natural monopolies*, and the linked issue of *infrastructure*, including *transportation*.

Water, electricity, gas, are examples of 'natural monopolies', in the sense that most customers cannot have choice: there will not be competing water-pipes, gas-pipes and wires under or above the same street. Furthermore the product is almost totally homogeneous: the advantages furnished by competition in providing variety or quality, or developing new products, are absent. In many countries such monopolies are publicly owned, but where private there must be, and is, regulation by public authority: otherwise profits can easily be enhanced by increased prices. The privatisation of water was one of Mrs Thatcher's least popular and least understood acts. What purpose, other than ideology, did it or could it serve? Where water supply is of major concern, for example, in California, it is taken for granted, even by right-wing Republicans, that water is in the public domain. And scholars like Wittfogel have long ago noted the importance of water supply as a ('hydraulic') factor accounting for oriental despotism. If millions of peasants, and the country's food supply, depend on the maintenance of thousands of irrigation canals, this creates the sort of problems that cannot be handled by methodological individualism.

In Great Britain the privatisation of electricity generation was accompanied by the separation of transmission lines from generating plant and from final distortions. The consequences will be discussed in a subsequent chapter.

Infrastructure includes roads, sewers, docks and airports, and some would add posts and other communications. They all yield substantial external economies and provide public services from which society derives significant benefits. Thus emergency services respond to 999 (in America 911) calls, and since Victorian times letters to every address in the land, including remote villages and islands, are carried with a one-price stamp, even though this implies cross-subsidisation (and therefore one can imagine a competitor delivering letters cheaper by providing a service between large cities only). However, new technology, for example, the fax, is transforming communications. Sewers are as important as water, and as unlikely to benefit from competition, and even the most fanatical neo-liberal can surely see that their provision and maintenance are essential public-authority functions, given the consequences of non-provision or breakdown on public health.

Airports and docks in America are generally in the public sector, and in other countries too, except in Mrs Thatcher's Great Britain, where ideology ruled. They have widespread external effects; they are local monopolies (there is most often just one airport per conurbation, for example, in Pittsburgh, Los Angeles, Birmingham, Frankfurt, and so on, and when there are several, as in London and New York, congestion is a major problem). It does appear clear (except to ideological extremists) that airports and docks should aim to serve the business hinterland and the citizens of the locality, which is not necessarily the same as maximising their own profits, whether in the long or short term.

Which brings me to *public transport*. It is a public monopoly and is subsidised in every American, Canadian and European city that is known to me, again *except* in ideologically-driven Great Britain. In the area of Oakland, California, where I am writing these lines, 'AC Transit', municipally owned, covers 40 per cent of its running costs by subsidy. Since the political colouring of the countries and the municipalities differ widely, there must be some cogent reasons. In many countries – for example, France, Germany, Switzerland, Scandinavia – the rail network is seen as a public service with the kind of universal coverage provided by the post office, with standard charges by distance, and with bus links where needed. In the case of Switzerland, these are also *postal* buses. A journey of (say) 200 kilometres in these countries will normally cost the same, even though costs and revenues per kilometre differ widely throughout the system. (Any *system-wide* fare implies cross-subsidisation). This used to be the case in Great Britain too. Indeed, at the height of Victoria's reign, by an Act of Parliament adopted in 1844, all railway companies had to operate at least one train a day stopping at every station with a third-class fare not exceeding a penny a mile. I recall paying a penny a mile in 1934 for return (round-trip) fare, anywhere in Great Britain. It was only recently that the ideologists persuaded the government to instruct the (still nationalised) British railways to charge whatever the local market will bear, that is, to exploit whatever degree of monopoly advantage they can, so that (for instance) the fare from north-east England to London is higher than the longer distance from Glasgow to London. With this 'commercial' approach, paradoxically, came the order to refer to 'passengers' as 'customers', which is symbolic of the denial of the public-service aspect of public service. And there are, with few exceptions, no connecting buses, which could link the surviving railways with

towns no longer served. The ideologists have proposed not only to privatise but also to fragment (yes, again, the fragmentationist disease): on the
same tracks there would be 'competing' trains owned by different private
companies. So no one would any more be responsible for the network, for
connections. One cannot imagine such damage being done in France or
Germany. More of this in a subsequent chapter.

In these countries, railways receive a sizeable subsidy, for their contribution to reducing congestion on roads and to a cleaner environment. The
advantages to business of the French TGV (being now copied by South
Korea, among others), and of German Inter-city, have so impressed even
conservative California that, as I write, the governor is seriously considering a proposal to build a high-speed rail link between San Francisco and
Los Angeles, with joint public–private financing, to be operated by (the
public) Amtrak. Again, in Britain alone, rail investment is supposed to
yield an 8 per cent rate of commercial return, with no subsidy, so the fares
have become some of the highest in the world, and project evaluators are
instructed *not* to make any cost–benefit analysis. (Myopia rules, OK.)

A good example of compartmentalised thinking is to be found in a specific case in Scotland. A bridge was to be built over the Dornie Firth, north
of Inverness. It would save a considerable detour, which is now followed
both by the road and the railway. The bridge is to carry only the road. The
ideologists did presumably apply cost–benefit to the road, to justify the
bridge. But when the railway asked that the bridge be wide enough to carry
its tracks, then the criterion at once became rigidly financial: since an 8 per
cent rate of return was unlikely the answer was a firm 'no'.

Urban transportation is a public and subsidised monopoly (almost)
everywhere; why? Monopoly because of the advantages of an interconnected *system*, with interavailable tickets and a unified timetable. Also
because it can be planned as a system, with investments (for example, in
metros) undertaken in the knowledge that there will be feeder and connecting services and there will not be parallel competing lines. If competitive
services were to exist, and charge the same fares, there is no advantage in
competition, while if fares vary there will be problems with ticket interavailability. In most cities there are commuter tickets, *cartes oranges* (Paris),
'capitalcards' and their various equivalents, valid on all services, which save
time and accountancy. They are usually offered at low prices for the same
reason as there is a subsidy: to ease congestion by weaning those with cars
onto public transport. A subsidy is also justified by another 'external' benefit: the effect of rapid-transit on property and house values, so that owners
gain whether or not they themselves buy bus or metro tickets. This has
been vividly demonstrated in the case of London's docklands (Canary
Wharf), where failure to provide rapid-transit contributed to the

bankruptcy of the property company. Furthermore, everywhere (except in ideological Great Britain and then only by government order) the subsidy is paid to the *network*. It can then be planned with a knowledge of the financial constraints, by persons who feel responsible for a public service, and not for maximising financial returns.

All this is understood almost everywhere, from San Francisco to Zurich, from Montreal to Munich, but not by the ideologists who advise the British government. Let us look at their counter-arguments.

First, they believe that subsidy leads to a lack of financial discipline and so to inefficiency. It is true that no scientific basis exists to determine how large the subsidy should be. There have also been instances in which public-sector unions demand higher pay, in the belief that the public purse is bottomless. However, it is hard to discern 'inefficiency' in the excellent (and subsidised) network serving Paris, Amsterdam, Munich, Vienna, Köln, Zurich, Madrid, Milan, Stockholm, Toronto and many other conurbations. To offer a *reductio ad absurdum* of their argument, let us take examples of *free* transport services, for example, in the Yosemite national park ('to reduce congestion'), and inter-terminal shuttle buses at most large airports. Must they be inefficient because free? Is there not a *prima facie* case that anything worth supplying free of charge is also worth supplying at a price below cost? If, as happens around San Francisco, bridge tolls are used to subsidise buses, in order to reduce congestion on the bridges, why should this be conducive to inefficiency?

Second, they are reared in neoclassical fragmentationism, that is, we are back in what I earlier called myopic marginalism. Each bus service, each metro line, is envisaged as a separate profit-maker. There is a difficulty for such minds to see interconnected networks or systems, a reluctance to focus on externalities, or even 'internalities'.

Third, they appear to ignore or neglect *purpose*, or rather they equate purpose with earning a profit. Only this can explain the argument (made in correspondence with this author) by one of the government's transport advisers: that such things as cheap commuter-tickets, capital-cards, *cartes oranges*, are 'a recipe for disaster'. They have as their purpose to persuade citizens to use public transport and thus reduce both congestion and pollution. They do so not only because they are cheap (subsidised), but also because they reduce the marginal cost of each separate journey to zero. A car-owner finds the marginal cost of his or her journey (once he or she has the car) is frequently less than the full fare by bus or metro, so use of the car 'pays'. But if one abstracts from purpose, and if public transport is itself congested (and investments in rapid-transport do not yield a profit), then of course the way to reduce overcrowding on trains and buses *and* improve financial results is to double the fares. The external effects can be ignored.

Yet transport is everywhere a means to an end. Consider the transport department of any manufacturing enterprise, or supermarket chain. Can one evaluate its efficiency without reference to purpose, that is, the punctual and reliable delivery of goods and materials? Can its financial results, separately assessed, be sufficient as a basis for rewarding performance?

Or take an island widely used for vacations, containing, say, several dozen hotels. Tourists arrive at the airport, or by boat. The island authority may build and operate the airport or the ships, or subcontract the task to others. But we may be sure that, unless advised by myopic marginalists, their operation will be subordinated to the interests of the tourist industry, rather than to the maximisation of the profit of the airport or ships separately evaluated.

To sum up this (frankly polemical) chapter, what kinds of functions are assigned and should be assigned, to public authorities in a normal civilised country? Some – including infrastructure, scientific research, training – benefit business through their 'positive' external effects. Then there are the widespread 'negative' effects of environmental pollution, which require state action in some form, or, in some instances, the joint action of several states. Conservation 'belongs' here, for example of fish stocks, but also architectural ensembles, ancient monuments and rainforests. Health, education, some elements of social security, confer widespread benefits or save people from disasters. Do we wish to live in a society where an ambulance will only pick up an injured person if he or she can prove that they can pay? Amenities such as parks, 'national seashores', street cleaning, trash collection, street lighting, fire services, sewers, are 'elementary' public functions, which do not require justification under the rubric of 'market failures', though some items on the above list could be categorised as involving 'externalities' and/or the 'free rider'. Museums, libraries, a public hall for meetings or concerts, encouragement of the arts and of culture, are non-commercial 'goods' that cannot be wholly dependent on charity and the begging-bowl. There are instances where loss-making culture is a precondition for (larger) profits, that is, has positive *economic* external effects. Thus the Uffizi museum in Florence, or the Edinburgh festival, loss-making as such, bring thousands of visitors to their respective cities, to the advantage of shops and hotels.

The basic question to ask is: can we expect that the pursuit of profit by separate firms and individuals under competitive conditions will provide us efficiently with goods, services, amenities and quality of life? With Adam Smith, we can answer 'Yes' in respect of a wide range of human activities. But Smith did not fail to note that public authorities should be erecting and maintaining those public works, which though they may be in the highest degree advantageous to a great society, are, however, of such a nature, that the profit could never repay the expense to any individual, or small number of individuals; and which it, therefore, cannot be expected that any individual, or small number of individuals, should erect or maintain.[16]

Is it, therefore, useful to teach ex-Soviet ex-planners that the functions of public authority should be minimised in all spheres, other than national defence? They might also pay attention to the *legal* infrastructure, to the need for financial and banking regulation to enforce contracts and avoid fraud, and also to legal aid for impecunious citizens. Otherwise, as one judge remarked, justice would be 'like the Ritz hotel, open equally to the rich and to the poor'.

Against this, the neo-liberal conservatives (the term 'liberal' has a different meaning in America) argue that men and women should have the right freely to dispose of their money, that they can judge their own interests better than can the state and its officials, so taxes should be minimised. Alas, this all too often takes the form of an appeal to straightforward human selfishness: 'why should I contribute to other peoples' children's schooling, when I have none, or they go to private schools?'. One point in favour for universal benefits is that it weakens such arguments. For example, in many European countries *all* parents have the option of sending their children to state-sponsored crèches and kindergartens; if the benefit was only available to the poor, there could be political pressure to cut the benefit.

However, it may be objected that an excessive level of taxation is not only politically unpopular but acts to diminish incentives for work and enterprise. This point could well have been reached in Sweden around 1990. Evidently, the level of public provision must be influenced, in a democracy, by what the voters are prepared to accept, and the list of potential publicly-financed projects surely exceeds the possibility of financing them all. And it is right to be reminded that, along with 'market failures', there are 'government failures'.

Eastern Europe, however, faces the opposite danger. Social expenditures have been/are being ruthlessly slashed, the health service in Russia – already underfunded under communist rule – is in a state of collapse, infant mortality rises sharply, as ante-natal services cease to be financed. Yet can we not agree that life is preferable to death? And should economists be exalting selfishness as a sort of theory-based 'good', when there is enough of it already? Should we say, with Mrs Thatcher and her advisers, that 'there is no such thing as society'? In a beautiful area of California, I saw on one side of the road a notice which read: 'Regional park, public access', on the other: 'Private property, keep out'. On which side was the Road to Serfdom?

NOTES

1. Natham Glazer, 'Is Welfare a Legitimate Government Goal?', *Critical Review*, **4**(4), 1990, p. 489.
2. Milton and Rose Friedman, *Free to Choose* (Harcourt Brace, 1979).
3. B. Ward, *What's Wrong with Economics* (Macmillan, 1972), p. 202.
4. Philip Arestis, 'Alfred Eichner (1937–1988)' in P. Arestis and M. Sawyer (eds), *A Bibliographical Dictionary of Dissenting Economists* (Edward Elgar, 1992), p. 142.
5. Richard X. Chase, 'Keynes's Dichotomy: A Methodological Escape for a Theoretic Revolution', *Methodus*, **3**(2), 1991, p. 82.
6. P.J. Boettke, 'Individuals and Institutions', *Critical Review*, **4**(1–2), 1990, pp. 10–26; I.M. Kirzner, 'Self-Interest and the New Bashing of Economics', ibid., pp. 27–40; G.B. Madison, 'How Individualistic is Methodological Individualism?', ibid., pp. 41–60.
7. Rajani K. Kanth, 'Economic Theory and Realism: Outlines of a Reconstruction', *Methodus*, **3**(2), 1990, p. 40. The author relies here on the ideas of R. Bhaskar.
8. J. Evensky, 'The Role of Community Values in Modern Liberal Economic Thought', *Scottish Journal of Political Economy*, **39**(1), 1992, pp. 21–38; quotes on pp. 21, 22, 33, 34.
9. 'Chakravarty, Sukhamoy (born 1934)' in Arestis and Sawyer (eds), *A Biographical Dictionary*, p. 80.
10. 'Heilbroner, Robert L. (born 1919)' in ibid., p. 247.
11. Don Herzog, 'Gimme that Old-Time Religion', *Critical Review*, **4**(1–2), 1990, p. 77.
12. See, for example, 'Health Care Crisis: Firms are Dumping Sick People. Insurers Weed Out Those with Medical Problems by vastly Raising Premiums', *San Francisco Examiner*, 5 April 1992.
13. *New York Times*, 25 February 1984.
14. See, for example, his entry in Arestis and Sawyer (eds), *A Biographical Dictionary*, p. 224.
15. A. Sen, *Poverty and Famine* (Clarendon Press, 1981).
16. A. Smith, *Wealth of Nations*, Volume 2 (Oxford University Press, 1909), p. 350.

7. Economics of the transition period

The title of this chapter is, of course, 'borrowed' from that of Bukharin's *Ekonomika perekhodnogo perioda*, which appeared in 1920, at the height of war-communism, and referred to transition in quite a different direction. Here we will be discussing the problems of moving from an economy based on directive planning (in which many directives were ambiguous, irrational, or distorted in execution) to one based on market. There will be a mix here of theory and practice. It will not be possible to go into detail. Many countries are involved, at different levels of political culture and economic development, different also in the degree of imbalance 'achieved' in the last years of communist rule, and in the extent to which market-type reforms and legal private activities already existed.

To take a few examples: Poland's agriculture was predominately private, some private enterprise was allowed (albeit subject to limits), but at the same time there was an economic crisis with strong inflationary pressures, so that the freeing of prices in 1989–90 was accompanied by a hyperinflationary surge. By contrast, Czecho-Slovakia inherited from the communists a comparatively balanced economy, with few shortages, but one in which virtually all private or even cooperative enterprise had long been outlawed. Hungary had introduced a 'New Economic Mechanism' already in 1968, explicitly committed to marketisation, and, though under increasing strain, the Hungarian economy in 1989 was not suffering from the degree of macroeconomic imbalance which inflicted Poland. 'Shock therapy' was therefore avoidable. Russia at the time of the coup which eliminated the Communist party was in a state of acute crisis, characterised by physical shortages, the collapse of the currency, a totally distorted price system and a soaring budget deficit, while further strains were imposed by the break-up of the Union and of Comecon. Each of the former Soviet republics presents problems of its own, and some of them (Armenia, Azerbaidzhan, Moldova) are seemingly more concerned with military action than with reform. This, most tragically, also applies to the republics that once made up Yugoslavia. Even in Czecho-Slovakia there is the issue of Slovak secession, and tension between Russia and the Ukraine (for example, over the Crimea) causes foreboding, and obstructs economically rational cooperation.

Transition to what? At first the reformers were seeking some 'third way', some form of market socialism, that is, a mixed economy with some private enterprise but with public (state, municipal, cooperative) ownership of the majority of the means of production. This kind of model I developed in my *Economics of Feasible Socialism*, which, at the time it was written, that is, 1980–82, seemed to be a radical reform programme. But now the pendulum has swung very much further. Transition is now seen as to some form of capitalism. There is not and cannot be a third way, argued Kornai and also the large majority of those in charge of the reform process in virtually all these countries, The pendulum has swung so far that even Erhard's *Soziale Markwirtschaft* is regarded with suspicion because of the sinful word *Soziale*, and articles appear attacking the welfare state (in its West European form) as excessively 'socialist'. Hayek and Friedman are extolled, advisers from right-wing or neo-conservative think-tanks are welcomed.

While I am personally alarmed and unhappy about this apparent triumph of laissez-faire ideology, this is not the place to enter into dispute about the existence or non-existence of alternatives to capitalism. Let us assume that the objective of the reformers is some sort of 'capitalism with a human face'. How does one get there? What help can be sought from economic theory? Or from the practice of other countries seeking to recover from war? The latter experience is useful for two reasons. First, in most warring countries the role of the state as economic 'controller' was very large, and the steps by which the controls were dismantled may be of direct interest to our colleagues in the 'east'. The role in their recovery of foreign help is also relevant today, recalling 'Marshall aid'. And, second, Russia, Poland, Romania and most of the republics of the former Soviet Union, face a degree of disruption analogous to what is suffered in wartime; thus the break with former suppliers and customers can be seen as a sort of equivalent of wartime supply hazards, through submarines or bombing. Some argue that the parallel with the postwar experience of Western Europe does not hold, is irrelevant, because these countries had long-established market structures, to which it was relatively easy to return. However, while true, this merely underlines the difficulty faced by such countries as Russia, where the grave economic situation (as bad as that faced by many countries in 1945) is combined with the *absence* of established market structures, which still have to be created.

I have developed at length elsewhere a critique of neoclassical theory as applied to the real world.[1] I would only quote Raymond Dietz's essay on 'Reform of Soviet Socialism': 'It may be that reforms in the east have come about not because of but despite theory. The reality of reform in East Europe and in the USSR displays a dynamic that leaves mainstream economics more or less speechless . . .'[2]

Also of great importance, and varying in different countries, is what could be called *market culture*, and those institutions and legal structures without which a market cannot effectively function. Clearly these were more developed in, say, Hungary than in Russia, more in Estonia than in Azerbaidzhan. Stimuli, such as higher prices or interest rates, can have quite different or even perverse effects in different environments.

Let us begin with the task of *macroeconomic stabilisation*. In Poland, Romania and Russia the task has been of particular difficulty, owing to the consequences of past policies. The large budget deficits had been financed by money creation. There was no way they could be financed by the sale of bonds, as the United States deficit has been; there would be far too few buyers. In the last years of the Soviet Union, problems were compounded by the gradual collapse of political authority, and by the emergence of increasingly independent republics, which spent freely, further undermining the already weak rouble. By 1991 the combined budget deficits reached 20 per cent of GNP. The formerly centralised banking system was in disarray too, weakening control over the volume of credit. Wage payments, formerly regulated strictly by the 'wages fund' limits imposed on enterprises and institutions also rose sharply, since there was no hard budget constraint to replace those imposed limits. Attempts to hold down prices led to ever-higher subsidies, and so to higher budget deficits, while shops emptied, and the collapse of the material allocation system was being replaced not by the market but by a clumsy and incomplete network of barter deals.

Clearly, no move towards a market economy could succeed without the creation of real money in the place of the rapidly depreciating currency. It was therefore entirely right to give high priority to macroeconomic stabilisation, to cutting budget deficit, drastically reducing subsidies, imposing strict financial discipline, stopping printing too much money. This task could not be separated from *price reform*, both because the subsidy bill was a major cause of budget imbalance, and because prices which reflect neither relative scarcities nor use values are useless, indeed are an obstacle, in the context of marketisation. This, in turn, raised questions of destatisation, privatisation, monopoly, incomes policy, the liberalisation of foreign trade and the convertibility of currency, which will be discussed in turn later. Of great importance too are such matters as finding the correct *sequence* of measures, and the degree of shock and sacrifice which the population can or should endure. In this connection, it may be worth citing – of all people – Hayek. It is precisely in his well-known *Road to Serfdom*, written in 1944, that he stated:

> This is perhaps the place to emphasise that, however much one may wish for a speedy return to a free economy, this cannot mean the removal at one stroke of

most of the wartime restrictions. Nothing would discredit the system of free enterprise more than the acute, though probably short-lived, dislocation and instability such an attempt would produce.[3]

Interestingly, this was cited by B. Milanovic of the World Bank, and contrasted with the view of Jeffrey Sachs, in an article on Poland.[4]

One should be aware here of a dilemma. A vital cause of the failure of Gorbachev's attempts at reform was precisely a fear of the political and social consequences of a long-overdue increase in prices, the cutting of subsidies to food and housing. Too great a concern for avoiding shock and sacrifice can be a recipe for inaction. Also, where the gap between supply and demand is as great as it became in Russia and Poland, a gradual increase in prices is no solution. Thus if meat was officially priced at 2 roubles and the free-market price were 10 roubles, there is little point in fixing a new price at 4 roubles (while continuing to print money to cover a large budget deficit). And one of the weaknesses of the plan presented to Gorbachev in 1990, bearing the names of Shatalin and Yavlinsky, was that they wished to postpone price increases until after achieving macro-stabilisation. This was an impracticable sequence, given the burden of subsidies on the budget. But more about prices later.

To balance the budget it is necessary to cut other expenditure too. Defence spending, particularly high in Russia, was an obvious candidate, and as a matter of historical fact major cuts were resisted for too long by the military–industrial complex. (This should not surprise us, given the reluctance of the United States to make any serious cuts in its huge defence budget even after the disappearance of the Enemy.) However, the conversion of defence plants to civilian production calls for considerable investment expenditures. Furthermore, while in the former Soviet Union there were many instances of wasteful investments, as well as a chronic imbalance between the demand for investment goods and the supply of those goods, leading to long delays in construction, there was no obvious short-term alternative to continuing *state*-financed investments. This was and is a problem in all ex-communist countries: privately-owned capital is scarce, or in the possession of corrupted former officials or shady dealers ('the mafia'), and, given the uncertainties – affecting politics, inflationary expectations, and in Russia also the lack of a well-defined legal order – private capital was unlikely to be invested in long-term projects. In Britain in the first postwar years there was no shortage of private capital seeking investment outlets; on the contrary, it was thought necessary to impose a form of capital rationing on the private sector, to concentrate investments on what were judged to be priority sectors. There will be more to say about the requirements of capital restructuring. For the moment it may be sufficient to note that the Russian statistical report for the first quarter of 1992 noted a decline by 44 per cent in the volume of investment, which 'threatens dire consequences in the immediate future . . . In this situation, the correct choice of priorities in investment policy is vital.'[5] But, as we shall see, ideological commitment to laissez-faire stands in the way of devising, let alone implementing, an investment policy.

Other cuts in expenditures affect social services (pensions, health, education), and also sciences, the arts, public transport and other infrastructure. An obvious difficulty is the inescapable increase in unemployment, and so in unemployment pay. More of these matters too, below.

Revenues can be increased through higher taxation of firms and individuals, the introduction of value-added tax and excise duties to replace turnover tax. However, the effect of price rises on real incomes of the population, and decline in production associated with shock therapy, and also the need to provide incentives for entrepreneurship, stand in the way of balancing the budget by raising revenues. Efforts to reduce the deficit must be made, and no painless methods exist by which this can be achieved.

Credit control presents grave problems too. These have two distinct aspects. One is the effect of the creation of a large number of commercial banks and other credit-granting institutions, which, especially in a climate of deregulation and the weakening of central authority, could not in Russia be effectively controlled. The other is a consequence of hyperinflation: a large number of enterprises in both Russia and Poland found themselves in grave financial difficulties because of a sudden and very large increase in the price of labour and materials, thus in Russia wholesale prices in March 1992 exceeded those of March 1991 13 times! Farms had been paid at 1991 prices, but faced similar, or even larger, increases in the costs of material inputs in 1992. Publishers had sold subscriptions in 1991 for 1992, but in January of that year the price of paper increased nearly twenty-fold. Firms in financial difficulties delayed payments to suppliers, and they delayed payments to *their* suppliers. Inter-enterprise debt rose exponentially, as the Table 7.1 shows.

Table 7.1 Russia: Enterprise debts unpaid (billions of roubles)

1 January 1992	39.2
1 February	140.5
1 March	390
20 March	676
End-May	2000

Source: *Izvestiya*, 28 March and *Nezavisimaya gazeta*, 17 June 1992.

The same tendency, though in less drastic form, was observed in other ex-communist countries too. The ECE Survey of Europe, 1991–92, puts this tendency in context, describing it as part of 'a pattern of reaction of economic agents in the predominantly state owned and monopolised economies to standard monetary and fiscal restrictions . . . When they are affected by a financial squeeze, firms in Eastern Europe tend to reduce output and raise prices, then they suspend payments to their suppliers, negotiate various reliefs with bank and government.' The latter find themselves unable to impose strict financial discipline in these circumstances, since even efficient and well-managed firms are beset with acute cash-flow problems, and one cannot close down a large part of the economy.

Price policy, as mentioned above, must be seen as an integral part of the reform and stabilisation process. And in countries such as Russia, Poland, Romania and Bulgaria, it had to involve a very large rise in both wholesale and retail prices, because of the large monetary overhang and the consequences of past errors of policy. Since experience shows that it is impossible to control flexibly several million prices, an essential feature of reform must be the release from any control of the large majority of prices. Some would say *all* prices, but, as we shall see, this can be impracticable in the transition period, even if all accept the ultimate aim to abandon such controls. One question frequently raised is that of monopoly. In Russia and many other ex-communist states competition is absent not only or mainly because of state ownership; it is possible to envisage state-owned enterprises competing, and some have done so – for instance theatres and literary journals. The problem, apart from such 'natural monopolies' as water, gas and electricity, is that there is frequently only one producer of some specific item, for example, an agricultural machine, or typewriters, or newsprint. Even in Russia this can be the case, and it is more likely to be so in smaller countries. Or, the several producers have been grouped into one corporation. In the latter case it may be possible to create competition by forcibly breaking-up the corporation, but plainly this is not always either practicable or desirable: would we wish to order the break-up of Du Pont or General Electric? In the smaller countries, economies of scale militate against artificially creating competing firms. Competition can, of course, come from imports, but this may not be practicable in the short run given the balance of payments constraint. (We shall be returning to the problem of the role of foreign trade and convertibility later.) Total price decontrol provides an opportunity for enterprises to use monopoly power greatly to raise both profits and wages, while not increasing output. Yet total control is unworkable and undesirable. Selective control of prices on some key items – of materials, energy, some basic foods – may prove essential in the transition period, despite problems of enforcement and the emergence of black markets. One device, used for clothing in Great Britain in the war and first postwar years, is to exempt the price-controlled items from purchase tax (the 'utility' scheme).

Great Britain was among the last countries to abandon food rationing after the war. This is not necessarily a good example to follow, for two reasons. First, it does seem that by 1949 there were no objective reasons for continuing with rationing, other than the ideological notion – which the Labour party had imbibed in the war years – that 'rationing by coupons' is somehow more just than 'rationing by the purse'. The other was the exceptionally large role of imports in the British food balance in those years, which enabled the government to maintain strict control over the allocation of (for example) meat and butter, and kept the black market to a minimum. Whereas, for example, in France, with its big peasant-farming sector, rationing was far more difficult to enforce, black markets flourished and rationing was abandoned earlier than in Britain. In Russia there was for 50 years a legal free market, alongside the state stores and with prices often much higher. However, the coexistence of several very disparate prices provides opportunities for large profits through diversion, arbitrage, bribery, and, with the decline in the power of the party and the state under Gorbachev, these opportunities could be increasingly taken. The gap between prices of various categories grew to truly astronomic proportions. Two examples can be cited. The first relates to December 1991, when this author encountered the following prices for a three-course lunch: 6.50 roubles in an 'academic' hotel, 300 roubles in a 'commercial' restaurant, 1200 roubles (if $12 were converted at the free exchange rate of that date) in a *valuta* restaurant. The second relates to April 1992 and to oil, still subject to price control. The official price was 2000–2500 roubles without an export licence, 5000–6000 with a licence to sell to other ex-Soviet republics, 8000–10 000 with a licence to sell 'beyond the further Soviet borders'. The opportunities for enrichment via corruption were all too obvious. This represents a powerful argument for a single, free price, which would eliminate or at least substantially reduce such opportunities. It may also be argued that prices should be aligned to world prices, especially for items entering foreign trade.

However, where the gap between domestic and world prices is very large, there is usually a similar gap between incomes (converted at the free exchange rate). To take a Russian example, the average wage in April 1992 was the equivalent, at this exchange rate, of at most $15 a *month*. If prices of oil and other sources of energy were set at world levels, the consequences would be devastating, in terms of individual purchasing power and industrial, agricultural and transport costs. But if they were not, then, since there is a right to acquire and dispose of foreign currency, it would clearly pay the producers and traders to sell oil and any other exportable item abroad. To prevent this it has been necessary to impose either export licensing or an export tax, or both.

Is it politically feasible to raise prices of necessities at a blow to levels that balance supply and demand? Gorbachev and his advisers felt that this was too risky, and postponed decision for far too long, so that, when the increase was decided, prices rose sixfold and more. Gavrill Popov, editor of *Voprosy ekonomiki* and (subsequently) mayor of Moscow, had proposed in 1989 a transition in which a short list of foodstuffs was rationed, while all other prices (including those foodstuffs off the ration) were freed, thus minimising hardships for the pensioners and low-paid. This proved unacceptable, and quite probably would by then have been impracticable, as the centre no longer had sufficient control. But the idea had much to commend it, as a way of avoiding social convulsions, and at least promised better than what actually was done in Russia in 1989–90, which was – nothing.

Let us now look at the effect of the 'shock' measures – fiscal, monetary, price – on *production* and then on investment. It has been a common experience in all these countries in 1989–92 that production, GNP, falls substantially. This has some evident negative effects: real incomes of the population decline, shortages are exacerbated, and/or the price rise required to bring supply and demand into balance is even higher than had previously been necessary, and budget revenues are affected because of a reduced tax-base. Why has there been so severe a fall in production? It has been severe indeed. According to the ECE Economic Survey of Europe, 1991–92, the picture was as shown in Table 7.2. In Russia the decline accelerated in 1991 and especially 1992, when total investments fell by nearly 50 per cent.

Table 7.2 *GNP and investment, 1990 and 1991 (in %)*

| | Industrial Output | | Gross Fixed Investment | |
	1990	1991	1990	1991
Bulgaria	−14.1	−27.3	−12.0	−49.3
Czechoslovakia	− 3.7	−23.1	+ 7.7	−36.0
Hungary	− 5.0	−19.1	− 8.7	−11.0
Poland	−23.3	−11.9	−10.1	− 8.0
Romania	−19.8	−18.7	−35.0	−16.8

The steep decline in living standards are reflected in the fall in the volume of retail sales, which (according to the same source) fell by 52.8 per cent in Bulgaria, 39.4 per cent in Czechoslovakia, 28.2 per cent in Hungary and 27.3 per cent in Romania, in the single year 1991. In every country the fall in output exceeded the most pessimistic expectations of the reformers and of their foreign advisers. As the ECE Survey put it: 'the market transformation was expected not only to eliminate the inefficient activities, but also to stimulate the expansion of the more efficient, so that a dramatic fall in overall production was not seen as a real possibility' (p. 46). It is true that these figures may somewhat overstate the decline, because some private activities, which have grown, are unrecorded. None the less, one can speak almost of a *zakonomernost'*, 'regularity', echoing Bukharin's 'negative expanded reproduction', to cite his *Economics of the Transition Period.*

Let us now look at causes, and consider whether this outcome was avoidable.

One, which also figured in Bukharin's book, was the short-term disorganising effect of the transition itself. People at all levels were accustomed to operate within the old system, a multitude of informal links supplemented or sometimes replaced the formal structures. The old links are weakened or abolished, the new ones cannot instantly replace them. This affects material supplies, managerial behaviour, the workers and the law-enforcement agencies. There is a lack of market culture, infrastructure, training and information flows. In agriculture, it must take time to replace state and collective farms, and meanwhile there is uncertainty and confusion, with immediate negative effects on production.

All this was exacerbated by political–territorial disintegration. The collapse of Comecon was accompanied by a drastic cutback in 'east–east' trade, with harm done to all through the disruption of supplies and the disappearance of established customers. Thus the output decline in Poland, Hungary and Bulgaria was in part due to the collapse of trade with the Soviet Union, and the former Soviet republics have suffered from the non-arrival of machines and components from their former Comecon partners. The same negative effect has followed from the disintegration of the Soviet Union, with each of the republics obstructing the free movement of goods and materials to other republics. This is occurring also within the Russian Federation. Thus 'Tatarstan' (formerly the Tatar Autonomous Republic) seeks its own sovereign right to export its oil and to keep the hard currency so earned. Oil output in Russia (including Tatarstan) is in any event declining, and the fall in export receipts has a negative effect on capacity to pay for imports. Provincial authorities also prevent the movement of goods, and engage in barter deals.

Then there is the effect on demand of deflationary policies, intended to achieve macroeconomic stabilisation. The freeing of prices has been accompanied by a much smaller rise in average incomes. This has cut back real purchasing power, and the impoverished have switched their purchases towards cheaper goods, leaving less to spend on (for example) sausages, clothing, consumer durables and luxuries. Thus in the first half of 1992, purchases of clothing and footwear in Russia fell by 50 per cent compared with the same period in the previous year, according to the official statistical report.[6] So in varying degrees the decline in production can be explained both by supply bottlenecks and by demand deflation. In Poland it is the latter that is largely to blame, but pressure to increase personal incomes has been resisted because of its likely effect on speeding up inflation. In Russia, supply disruption seems to have been more serious, though in 1992 demand also fell steeply, as we have seen.

A further cause of decline, and of rising unemployment, has been the attempt to weed out inefficient and subsidised enterprises, and those which may be producing (even 'efficiently') goods not in demand. This has been proceeding slowly in most countries, for fear of the social–political consequences of mass closures, but is set to accelerate. In all these countries a large proportion of industrial enterprises are in fact insolvent. In Poland, Czecho-Slovakia and Hungary, the move towards currency convertibility and import liberalisation has brought about a sharp rise in imports of consumers' goods of many kinds, which tend to displace the locally made products, with further negative effects on output. Thus in Poland the decline was particularly severe in 'light industry', that is, in manufactured consumers' goods, since Western goods are preferred.

Was a decline in GNP inevitable? Probably the answer is 'yes', but the scale of the decline, especially in Poland and Russia, has exceeded the expectations of the reformers and represents a cause for alarm.

This brings us to the vexed question of *investment*. It is evident that restructuring, industrial modernisation, conversion of the military sector, the building up of a sadly neglected infrastructure, call for the investment of large capital sums. So does repair of ecological damage, which in all these countries has been severe. All critics agree that the structure of the economy inherited from the Soviet-dominated past is irrational, that part of it is uneconomic and will have to close, and that one result must be a rise in unemployment. So it is essential to provide not only retraining but also new work places. Who is to do this? Where is the capital to come from?

It is a common feature of all ex-communist countries that, for evident reasons, legitimate capital accumulation in private hands is far too small, and most of the rich are suspected of having acquired their riches by corrupt means. This complicates the task of privatisation, of which more will be said below. It also severely limits the *private* financing of investment. The Hungarian economist Laszlo Casba speaks of the need to create

> an environment where putting private money into a (long term) investment – rather than consuming it or putting it in a foreign bank – makes economic sense, or at least is one of the options. 'Private' entrepreneurs of the irregular or mafia economy of the postsocialist countries normally do not risk their own money . . . productive investment would be the last thing they would think of.[7]

Clearly, even in Hungary, more advanced in such respects than Russia, Romania or Ukraine, a modern capitalist class has yet to be created, and it is wrong to assume that it already exists and will react 'rationally' to investment opportunities. In any case, in many countries the degree of uncertainty about politics, policies, rates of inflation, possible public disorder, exchange rates, plus high investment rates, are such as to deter entrepreneurial investment, diverting resources into short-term dealing. This has been particularly evident in Russia, where (in May 1992) the bank-rate has been raised to 80 per cent, which is admittedly below the expected rate of inflation, but sufficient to deter borrowing for the long term.

Investment statistics can be misleading, and not only in the 'east'. There has been a profusion of new financial institutions – commodity exchanges, brokerage houses, commercial banks – which are laying the foundations of a capital market. But so far they invest little; there is too much money to be made out of dealing and arbitrage.

If private sources of investment are highly limited – and, as we shall see, still further limited by diversion into privatisation buyouts – two sources remain: public authorities, and foreigners. If neither are forthcoming, or remain very small, then output will begin to fall because of net *dis*investment, that is, net investment will become negative, gross investment will fall below the level of physical depreciation; obsolete equipment and antiquated industries will remain obsolete and antiquated, plans to create competitive industrial structures will stay on the drawing-board. Foreign inward investment can make a significant contribution, but its scale in most countries will surely remain small, and especially so in Russia, and other countries in acute economic crisis.

This suggests the need for what could be called selective interventionism, an industrial *policy*, an investment *strategy*. There are plenty of examples, as already argued earlier: postwar Europe, South Korea, Japan, and quite strikingly the former East Germany, where investment expenditure has been massive.

There is an important gap in neoclassical economic theory, based upon general equilibrium. Long-term real investment occurs under conditions of actual or anticipated *dis*equilibrium, for example, where there is actual or anticipated market domination (temporary monopoly), collusion, and/or government-sponsored coordination and protection. The idea that the break-up of large firms in the name of anti-monopoly measures and that the maximisation of domestic and foreign competition (and so of uncertainty as to future profits) is conducive to investment, should surely be seen as a naive fallacy, even in long-established capitalist countries. *A fortiori* (or so one would have thought), in countries suffering from structural deformations inherited from the past, and little private capital, laissez-faire cannot be the remedy.

'Oh yes, it can', is, however, the answer given by most of those in charge of the transition process. For a clearly-presented view, one can refer to the article by Marek Dabrowski on 'interventionist pressures'.[8] Dabrowski writes from personal experience: he had been deputy-minister of finance in Poland. He was critical of 'the demand for a kind of government industrial policy', against any budgetary sums being allocated for restructuring, or 'state influence on the branch structure of the economy', involving 'priority in government policy' for specific branches or sectors. All he would accept would be what he calls 'active anti-interventionist interventionism'. He sees dangers of 'continuing the planning mentality', the emergence of bargaining with interest groups, undermining 'the possibility of enforcing a hard budget constraint on firms', threatening a balanced state budget, and so on. He is firmly against using 'interventionist tools as a substitute for the market mechanism.' Such sentiments echo those of V. Klaus in Prague, K. Kagalovsky in Moscow and some (but not all) of the reformers in Budapest. Klaus is reported as disapproving of the interventionist and evidently strategic activities of *Treuhand*, the institution set up to modernise, restructure and privatise East German industry and infrastructure, since this seems to resemble some kind of 'socialist' planning.

The very *scale* of West German commitment of resources to East Germany reminds one, first, of the magnitude of the gap between the two halves of Germany, from which some morals can be drawn about the relative efficiency of systems. Second, it is useful to contrast the sums involved – 150 billion DM in just one year 1991, a total sum that is likely to exceed $200 billion, this for a population of 16 million, with any likely injection of aid and credits into the rest of the eastern half of Europe, for example, with the $24 billion for all the ex-Soviet republics. Third, it is worth studying in detail how these very large sums are targeted. As also in South Korea, this is most emphatically not laissez-faire.

However, it is also worth citing another of Dabrowski's objections to 'interventionism': the lack of what he calls 'a good civil service'. (Its

importance in South Korea and Taiwan was stressed above.) The same
point was made by several of my Russian colleagues: an interventionist
policy needs efficient and reliable state officials, 'intervenors', as well as
power to implement policy. This is a very different reason for non-
intervention, a reason purely practical, not ideological. It seems to me
that, in the situation that Russia is in, if steps are not taken to impose priorities and direct some investment into key areas – agriculture, energy,
infrastructure, for instance – decline must continue, since private capital
cannot be expected to fill the gap left by the withdrawal of the state from
responsibility, in the absence of any investment strategy. Chaos and anar-
chy are already near.

One cannot sufficiently emphasise the investment problem. How can
the restructuring of these economies, the modernisation of their industries and of their infrastructure, the urgently necessary clean-up of the
environment, be undertaken without a major role for public authorities?
How, in the situation they are in, can one expect the private sector and
laissez-faire, guided by the profit motive, to do the necessary? Meanwhile,
to repeat, net investment is negative in several of these countries, and privatisation has mainly 'benefited' trade and distribution, not production.
Prospects are more promising where the inflow of foreign investment can
be expected to fill the gap.

This brings us to the important question of *privatisation*. This divides
into several parts. First, *what* to privatise, that is, what, if anything, ought
to be left in the public sector in the longer run. Second, *how* to privatise,
who should own. Third, the question of *speed*: how fast to proceed and in
what order. All this under conditions of shortage of savings and privately-owned capital.

A complication in some countries is claims to restitution of property
confiscated by the communists. This is a problem not only in such countries as Poland, Czecho-Slovakia and Hungary, but also in the Baltic
republics of the former Soviet Union. This delays privatisation, in that
many purchasers fear the appearance of a claimant, who may by now be
living in Florida or France. For example, the son of a former owner of a
farm in Hungary may now be a computer operator in Chicago; then there
are survivors of great landlords, expropriated in postwar land reforms. It
is important to dispose of this problem as quickly as possible, perhaps
best by giving a right to monetary compensation up to some limits.

The longer-term limits to public ownership are the subject of another
chapter, and will not be pursued further here (see Chapter 6).

The answer to the question referring to *how* and *who* is very difficult.
There have been many schemes. One confusion to note is between two

incompatible aims: the widest possible degree of stock-and-share owner-ship on the one hand, and the encouragement of the owner–entrepreneur on the other. All such schemes as the issuance of vouchers, either free or at low cost, which aim to ensure the direct interest of citizens in owner-ship, have two defects: one is that ownership becomes diffused, anonymous. The other is that if the stocks are underpriced and saleable, many will be sold, thereby providing additional income to the seller and thereby adding to inflationary pressure. Ignorance of the (still primitive) capital market could well cause owners of vouchers to entrust them to various kinds of capital funds and investment trusts, which may or may not exercise some control over management.

Then there is so-called 'spontaneous' privatisation, which merges with what is called 'nomenklatura privatisation', of which there are many vari-ations. They have in common the appropriation of capital assets of state enterprises by existing management, with or without the participation of former party and state officials turned neo-capitalists, and sometimes with some degree of employee shareholding. Firms can be acquired by purchase of undervalued assets at low prices, or by the creation of pseudo-cooperatives, or with the help of merchant banks. In several countries this process has been associated with corruption, insider deal-ing and other forms of fraud. Some denounce this as outrageous. Others look more tolerantly at 'primitive capitalism red in tooth and claw', and hope or expect that these new owners will learn to behave like capitalist entrepreneurs, since at least they have shown enterprise in acquiring prop-erty. It is hard to prove that assets are undervalued, since their future earning power is in any case unknown.

It may be that large accumulations of wealth achieved by dealers, in and outside of the new commodity exchanges, will one day be invested in productive activities, but meanwhile this is a (very) primitive form of primitive capital accumulation.

There is also the transformation of state enterprises into joint stock companies, with at least at first the majority of shares held by the state, directly or through a fund for administration of state property. Management is instructed to act 'commercially', with profit as the effi-ciency criterion. Shares can then be gradually sold off. A problem is what to do with those enterprises that show no profit. To close them all down would lead to disastrous cuts in output and a rapid rise in unemploy-ment. To sell off only the profitable ones would leave the state with the burden of supporting the loss-makers.

A useful intermediate stage is *leasing* properties to managers. The lease could be nominal for the less profitable, larger (a fixed sum, or a share in profits) for the more potentially remunerative. It postpones the vexed question of valuation of assets, which depend on information and prospects which, at the beginning of the privatisation process, are hidden. Leaseholders who fail could be replaced by others at the discretion of the property agency.

Sales of firms by *auction* have also been attempted. The usual criticism is that, if foreigners are excluded, purchasers will in the main be shady dealers, 'mafia' and/or corrupted officials of the old regime. And of course foreigners could act, using overvalued hard currency, via corrupted local intermediaries, or disguised in 'joint ventures'.

Giving shares away, whether to the population at large or to the workforce, has the evident defect that some enterprises are much more valuable than others, so the gains would be very unfairly distributed. But fairness is in any event unlikely.

Foreign investment is surely to be encouraged, insofar as it creates new productive capacity or modernises the equipment (and managerial practice and technical know-how) of existing enterprises. But there is understandable fear that, at highly unfavourable exchange rates (unfavourable for the domestic currency and citizenry) foreigners will buy up firms and property on the cheap, and so limits have been set on such acquisitions. Joint ventures have long been encouraged. In such countries as Russia, uncertainty about policy and confusion as to who is authorised to authorise, inhibits progress: there is still (June 1992) no clear legal order, and national republics and regions claim property rights over natural resources. Some successor republics have done better: thus Kazakstan has signed a major deal with the Chevron oil company. There is a fear, voiced for example by T. Cox,[9] of what some call the 'Latin-Americanisation of Eastern Europe', that is, the creation of foreign-controlled enclaves, 'and a less developed national sector starved of investments remaining under the control of the national elite'.

One reason for underinvestment, not yet mentioned, is the diversion of capital and savings into acquiring what already exists. This has also been a feature of British privatisation. This would not matter if the receipts from sales of public assets were used for investment purposes, but this (in Britain) has been barred by ideology; they have in fact been used as state budget revenue and/or to reduce public debt. Little thought seems to have been given to the sources of investment financing. In the United States under Reagan and (especially) Bush, the major part of domestic savings has been used to finance record budget deficits, and many American commentators identify this as a cause of America's relative decline as compared with Japan. So the problem is not confined to the Eastern half of Europe.

Finally, another form of privatisation, or more precisely, de-etatisation, must be mentioned: sale to the workforce, or the transformation of the firm into cooperative property of some kind. Here, somewhat surprisingly, some of the ideologists of the 'east' are *plus royaliste que le roi*. Thus even in Great Britain the Conservative government accepted the employee-purchase of a major (nationalised) road transport undertaking, and of coal mines by groups of miners. Yet, in his book, Kornai opposes these kinds of co-ownership,[10] and in Russia the minister in charge of privatisation, Anatoli Chubais, drafted a law which limited the employees to acquiring, on favourable terms, 25 per cent of the shares, *non-voting*. There is an ideologically-based negative view of workers' control or ownership. The weakness of political parties representing the workers lessens the pressure for this solution.

The ideologists cite the example of Yugoslav self-management and similar experiences. Yet Yugoslav enterprises were *not* owned by their workforce, and so the latter had no interest in the value of capital assets or in the long term, and naturally pressed for higher incomes. The models which analyse the behaviour of employee-managed enterprises do so on artificial assumptions. Thus the well known 'Illyrian' model of Benjamin Ward assumes perfect competition and abstracts therefore from real competition, and, as do all the models, from the possible effect on performance (and on the willingness to accept technical change) of a sense of co-ownership. Any factor that is ignored in any model has a weight of zero. This particular one can be decisive one way or the other. One should study the more positive experiences of Mondragon in Spain, and of the many millions in the United States who work for the employee-owned firms ('ESOP', Employee Stock Ownership Programme). It was odd to read articles in the Russian press written by American scholars extolling employee ownership and criticising the now-fashionable negative approach.[11] This is also my own position. It seems remarkably 'ideological' to *assume*, for instance, that the Avis car hire firm (employee-owned) must be less efficient than Hertz (not employee-owned), or that the former is less likely to invest in its own future than the latter. Yet Kornai obstinately defends the view that co-ownership only works if confined to religious or political enthusiasts (for example, the Israeli kibbutz). And, if it is objected that Russian or Polish employees are not steeped in market culture, the same applies to the would-be neo-capitalist owners too.

No doubt there is much scope for private, non-state, enterprise, for speedy small-scale privatisation, especially in the service sectors (trade, repairs, building and decorating, goods transport, and so on) and workshops of many kinds, despite the difficulties of valuing capital assets amid major uncertainties and inflationary pressures. It must not be forgotten that the value of any capital asset depends not on its initial cost, but on anticipated profitability. Getting it wrong for shops or workshops matters little. It is more complicated for the larger firms, which is an argument, along with the lack of domestic capital, for proceeding slowly.

It is worth referring at this point to efficiency criteria for those industries and firms that remain in the public sector. If a major reason for their remaining there is their 'externality-proneness' (for example, transport, docks, posts) or because they are natural monopolies, there are dangers if they are told to act 'commercially'; that is, to maximise their own profits regardless of external effects. I have written on this theme 20 years ago, referring to the British experience.[12] Externalities should not be ignored in externally-prone sectors. More of this in a subsequent chapter.

Agriculture presents problems of its own. Here Poland is exceptional, in that the bulk of its peasants were not collectivised. In other countries (except what was Yugoslavia) the issue of de-collectivisation/privatisation is on the agenda. Meanwhile existing state and collective farms are in a very difficult position, since their management has no notion of what the future holds, and investments have fallen steeply. Apart from the issue of returning land to former owners, already mentioned, there is the question of peasant attitudes: how many wish to become private farmers, if they were adequately remunerated for collective work with (for them) minimum risk and responsibility? Particularly when credit is scarce and interest rates high, there is a shortage of suitable equipment and building materials, and great uncertainty about prices of inputs and farm products. In some countries, notably Poland and Hungary, the potential market for farm products in Western Europe is barred by the Common Agricultural Policy, which is likely to remain for many years yet, given political realities in the West.

The most difficult path towards privatisation is surely to be encountered in Russia and the Ukraine. The Chinese experience is of little relevance, in that Chinese 'collective' cultivation had been on small fields by medieval methods, and de-collectivisation required little change in method or technique, while providing better incentives, so the result was positive, and quickly so. Large fields and mechanised harvesting on the Russian and Ukrainian prairies are a very different proposition. And many sources attest to 'de-peasantisation'. The short-term danger is that the disruption of *sovkhozy* and *kolkhozy* will not be compensated by the larger output of the new private farms, and that shortages of food could get worse before they get better.

In Poland the smallholders are very small, suffer from diseconomies of small scale, and also from a price policy that leaves them to swim in the cold water of the free market. Prices of basic farm products are regulated in some way in just about every country of the world. The neo-liberals ascribe this to the influence of the farm lobby, and this may well explain the level of subsidy or protection. But surely there is another reason. Agriculture approaches the 'ideal' of perfect competition; there are very many small producers who cannot directly influence price. This, plus the 'cobweb' effect, arising from the seasonal nature of farm production, could create an intolerable degree of price fluctuation, which argues for some kind of price stabilisation scheme. At the very time when private farming is on the agenda, it is being discouraged by adverse (and uncertain) price movements. Thus in Russia in 1991–92 prices of industrial farm inputs have risen twice as fast as prices of farm products.[13] Again – is laissez-faire the answer?

Next let us consider *social problems*: employment, health, education, housing. Some rise in unemployment is inevitable, linked with the closing of chronic loss-makers and a shake-out in overmanned enterprises. But, just as the decline in output is in danger of exceeding reasonable bounds, so is the rise in the number of jobless, especially if it coincides with cuts in the level of provision of public services. It has been the common experience of Eastern Europe that it has not (so far) been found possible to close down the majority of loss-makers, otherwise the rise in unemployment would have been much higher.

While some have found work in privatised services, or undertake typically third-world informal-sector activities such as selling in the street (as can be seen in Polish and Russian cities), unemployment becomes a major social problem. Apart from the threat to public order, it is also wasteful, surely an evil to be minimised. The notion that labour markets clear if wages are not downward-sticky is highly questionable even in normal times, for reasons to be discussed in the next chapter. However, at free exchange rates the average wage in Russia in April 1992 was at most $15 a month, and, in terms of the rouble prices ruling at this time, below modest subsistence levels. Job creation calls for investment, but, as already pointed out, investment has fallen steeply. In Russia matters are further complicated by the reduction in military personnel plus the arrival of refugees from some of the other ex-Soviet republics. There are plenty of essential public works that require attention, given the state of roads and other infrastructure, yet financial stringency leads the government to cut such expenditures. This way social explosion lies.

Meanwhile health services are also cut, while the idea of semi-private insurance is mooted as an alternative. In most of these countries state enterprises provided some of the social services – crèches, holiday homes, dispensaries – and these too are abandoned, or put on a cost-covering or profit-making basis, as part of the process of commercialisation. The press reports a sharp rise in infant mortality,[14] a net fall in population. (If laissez-faire leads to surplus deaths, should this not be a matter of concern?) Spending on education, scientific research, culture, is being severely reduced, particularly in Russia. Private provision is moving into the vacuum, for those who can pay. The average citizen has already suffered a decline in real incomes. (Its full extent may be overstated if one simply compares incomes and prices, since there is now a wider choice, more goods in the shops, but no one denies that real incomes have fallen). A new class of rich dealers and small entrepreneurs, and also those who have devised joint ventures which yield hard currency, are now visibly rich. The large increase in differentials suggests the need for an appropriate tax policy. However, even such non-extremist economists as Janos Kornai are so committed to encouraging entrepreneurship, and combatting what they regard as excessive egalitarianism of the past, that they advocate *lowering* taxes on high incomes.[15]

The question of an *incomes policy* is also highly controversial. In Poland there was, in 1990–92, rigid control over wages in the state sector (that is, for the large majority of workers and employees), keeping increases far below the rate of inflation. This attracted criticism from both Milton Friedman and from trade-unionists: it is an odd kind of ideology that advocates the freeing of all prices *except* the price of labour. It is also socially divisive: those whose incomes are identifiable and controllable, whether blue or white collar, are impoverished, while those who are not wage and salary earners earn whatever they can, and so benefit from redistribution in their favour. In some countries wages in the state sector remain rigidly controlled, while incomes of private entrepreneurs and of anyone employed in the growing private sector are left free. Another recipe for social conflict, though the gravity of such conflict depends on the degree of economic decline and impoverishment: thus Hungary and the Czech lands are under much less social strain than Russia. Where catastrophe threatened, it was usually found politically desirable at least to claim a degree of equality of sacrifice. In Britain in wartime the King had a ration-card. It would have made no difference to Britain's food supply if he had not, but symbolically it was important. One had the feeling that such economists as Jeffrey Sachs would not find that such an argument had meaning.

Perhaps the *pessimum pessimorum* is what actually has happened in Russia in 1991–92: in some key sectors, for example, the coal mines, the workers, by threatening to strike, have secured literally tenfold wage increases overnight, leaving far behind fellow workers outside of the coal industry, not to mention doctors and teachers, whose pay in May 1992 actually was one tenth of that of the miners. This is neither a coherent incomes policy nor a real labour market.

Finally, let us turn to the linked issues of foreign trade and currency convertibility. Here too the more naive forms of laissez-faire and free-trade ideology seem to have acquired a grip on the reformers' minds. Again, one must distinguish the short-term problems from longer-term desiderata. All these countries look forward to being included fully in the international division of labour, or more specifically in the European Economic Community. Naturally they wish their currencies to become convertible. These are aims that I for one do not wish to question. However, this was also the aim of Western European countries in the first post-war years, but, under conditions of chronic dollar shortage on the one hand, and the urgency of reconstruction on the other, there were restrictions on both trade and currency, and exchange rates were 'managed'. France and Italy retained some limits on currency convertibility until 1990.

Do or should similar considerations apply to Russia, Ukraine, Poland and the rest? Let us examine the reasons behind the restrictions mentioned above.

One was connected with the *priorities* of reconstruction. These varied in different countries, but in general there were limits set on the use of (scarce) dollars for the purchase of what were judged to be inessentials. For example in 1948 one saw very few American cars on Europe's roads. They were prevented either by import licensing (currency rationing) or by high import duties. The effect of premature import liberalisation would have been a steep decline in the exchange rates of the national currencies, since pent-up demand for imports (as for investment) was so great after wartime austerity and destruction. How different is the approach of the men now in charge in the 'east'. Here, for example, is the influential Russian economist Konstantin Kagalovsky: 'The rate for the rouble will be the same for all, and licenses and quotas will be liquidated. All foreign loans will be realised in the market and at the market rate . . . Any administrative ways of supporting critically essential imports are shown to have been totally pointless.'[16] Why? Because one ministry, when asked, wished to give priority for materials for brewing beer!

In Russia at least, this does seem a recipe for speedy disaster. For reasons already discussed above, investment has collapsed, and so have medical services, and there are acute problems with food and transport. In the short run the liberalisation of trade plus currency convertibility would have predictable effects: those who have accumulated millions of roubles (firms or individuals) will salt them away in banks abroad (which many have already done, despite the rules forbidding this), while others will buy consumer goods (panty-hose, cars, and so on) for instant resale. Foreign loans will be speedily used up, with minimum effect on the much-needed reconstruction or on the needs of the impoverished majority.

There is also the effect of import liberalisation on domestic production and investment. One recalls Nicholas Kaldor's case, which is a gloss on the long-familiar 'infant-industry' argument for protection. Industry is characterised by increasing returns. Referring to the effect of free trade on Great Britain in this century, he wrote: 'Our continued adherence to free trade meant that a lot of *new* industries . . . could not be properly established here. As the traditional industries became increasingly unprofitable, our savings were increasingly invested abroad.' Historically, as he pointed out, 'Germany, France, the United States, Japan [and South Korea too] began to foster their manufacturing industries behind the shelter of protective tariffs.'[17] How, then, is restructuring to be achieved in the ex-communist countries? Will not import competition be destructive in the short term, unless some choices are made as to what sectors should be protected or encouraged? (In fact some foreign investors have been requesting protection). To such men as Kagalovsky or Sachs such thoughts must seem heretical. They must hope that foreign investors could utilise the well-educated and low-paid labour force and put their money into industries which can speedily become competitive. Perhaps they imagine Hong Kong can be reproduced. But can it? (And Hong Kong benefited from publicly-financed infrastructure.)

So – to recapitulate. We must beware of generalisations; there are big differences between countries, in political and market culture, in levels of development, in the degree of inherited imbalance, and so in the response to be expected from shock therapy and laissez-faire policies, and from potential foreign investors. Russia is in a situation very different from that of the Czech Republic, especially if and when it sheds Slovakia. But in all of them the transition to a market economy is accompanied by a steep decline in output, in living standards, in the provision of social services. In all of them the decline in state-financed investments is not and cannot be replaced by private-sector investment. Yet there is a reluctance even to consider an investment strategy or industrial policy, as if a real capital market already exists. The problem of transition cannot be tackled or understood within the neoclassical paradigm. Though it is certainly true that elementary economic propositions are both valid and important – supply and demand, opportunity cost, the consequences of price control and of printing too much money – these propositions were not only familiar to the readers of Marshall a hundred years ago but can be traced much further back. The essentially incremental, non-institutional, timeless, equilibrium-oriented neoclassical mainstream, with its methodological individualism, is largely irrelevant. To re-cite Dietz, 'the reality of reform in Eastern Europe and in the (former) USSR displays a dynamic that leaves mainstream economics more or less speechless'. And Frank Hahn, himself a neoclassicist of some distinction, has written apropos some mainstream models: 'When policy conclusions are drawn from such models, it is time to reach for one's gun.'[18] Yes indeed. It is perhaps understandable that from the extreme of total state monopoly and state–party domination that the pendulum swings far in the opposite direction. Yet in several countries, Russia especially, it is hard to see how one can rely on a market mechanism which has yet to be created, while decline accelerates and a new 'Time of Troubles' looms ahead. To create the preconditions for a market economy surely requires purposeful action, 'interventionism', under conditions of dire emergency analogous to a war-economy, with the real supply side in such disarray as to render impossible macroeconomic stabilisation.

Meanwhile it is also appropriate to ask: what is the social basis of the policies followed by Vaclav Klaus, Egor Gaidar, Leszek Balcerowicz and their many associates? In a perceptive article, Deborah Duff Milenlovich, writing about the old system, remarked that 'ideology as an abstractly given set of goals provides an unconvincing explanation for the organisation and strategy choices of socialist societies'. She points to ideology evolving so as to 'constitute a rationale for the policies preferred by the governing elite, policies which focused on their maintaining monopoly control of all important economic and political organisations'. Yet, as she says, 'ideology is never independent of the interests of the ruling elite'. So, today, who *are* the 'ruling elite'? Clearly, the interests of the ordinary worker seem to be disregarded. The ECE Survey refers to 'a substantial fall in real wages', which 'proved economically counter-productive, socially unfair and politically dangerous'.[19] Peasants are unhappy too, even (or particularly) in Poland, as they are hit by the deflation of the their customers' incomes, high interest rates, and abolition of subsidies. The new would-be capitalists are not (not yet) in a position to influence basic policies. The old *nomenklatura* is in disarray. Into this vacuum has come – who? A segment of the intelligentsia, converted from the Marxism which most of them espoused at an earlier stage of their careers into a new religion – Chicago economics. Twenty years ago two Hungarians, Konrad and Szelenyi, speculated about 'the intellectuals on the road to class power', this being their view of the intellectuals' role in the old communist-dominated regime. I disagreed with them. But today such a view may be closer to the truth. The new Bukharins, young and committed as was the Bukharin of 1920, are convinced, as he was, of the correctness of their vision, their right to lead people into the promised land. But are they on the right road – even accepting their choice of destination?

NOTES

1. See, for example, my *Studies in Economics and Russia* (Macmillan, 1991).
2. R. Dietz, 'Reform of Soviet Socialism' in J.M. Kovacs and M. Tardos (eds), *Reform and Transformation in Eastern Europe* (Routledge, 1982), p. 22.
3. F.A. Hayek, *The Road to Serfdom* (George Routledge and Sons, 1944), p. 155.
4. B. Milanovic, 'Poland's Quest for Economic Stabilisation, 1988–91: Interaction of Political Economy and Economics', *Soviet Studies*, **44**(3), 1992, p. 511.
5. 'Svertyvanie gosudarstvennykh investitsii vedut ekonomiku k agonii', *Ekonomika i zhizn'*, No. 17, 1992, p. 11.
6. 'Sotsial'no-ekonomicheskoe polozhenie rossiiskoi federatsii v pervom polugodii 1992 goda', *Ekonomika i zhizn'*, No. 30, 1992, pp. 5–7.
7. L. Casba, 'First Lessons in the Transformation of the Economic Systems in Central Europe', *Acta Oeconomica*, **43**(3–4), 1991, p. 233.
8. M. Dabrowski, 'Interventionist Pressures on a Policy Maker During the Transition to Economic Freedom (Personal Experience)', *Communist Economies and Economic Transformation*, **4**(1), 1992, pp. 59–73.
9. T. Cox, 'Privatisation and New Economic Groupings in Hungary', Conference Paper, Glasgow 1992.
10. J. Kornai, *The Socialist System* (Clarendon Press, 1992).
11. See, for instance, J. Simmons and J. Lout, 'Trinadtsat mifov rossiiskoi privatizatsii', *Izvestiya*, 1 April 1992, p. 5.
12. A. Nove, *Efficiency Criteria for Nationalised Industries* (Allen & Unwin, 1973).
13. G. Yavlinsky *et al.*, 'Reformy v Rossii, Vesna-92', *Moskovskie novosti*, 24 May 1992, pp. 9–16.
14. Yeltsin deplores this rise in 'Deti stradayut bol'she vsekh', *Rossiskaya gazeta*, 2 June 1992, p. 1.
15. J. Kornai, *The Road to a Free Economy* (W. Norton, 1990).
16. See 'Kurs rublya budet edinym dlya vsekh, a kvoty i litsenzii likvidiruyutsya', *Izvestiya*, 6 May 1992, p. 2.
17. N. Kaldor, *Further Essays on Applied Economics* (Duckworth, 1978), p. 239.
18. F. Hahn, 'Reflections on the Invisible Hand', *Lloyds Bank Review*, **144**, 1992.
19. *Economic Survey of Europe in 1991–1992* (United Nations, 1992), p. 49.

8. Labour and productivity

UNEMPLOYMENT AND THE LABOUR MARKET

It is almost universally assumed, in neoclassical texts, that markets either do or should clear, unless prevented from doing so by 'imperfections'. The market for labour should be no exception. Unemployment is seen by some of the 'new classicals' as voluntary 'leisure preference', or else as 'job search', or what used to be known as fictional unemployment, the inevitable interval between losing one job and getting a new one. However, most mainstream economists do recognise the possibility of involuntary unemployment. Explanations as to causes, and remedies, vary. Thus Malinvaud noted that unemployment could be either neoclassical (wages too high) or Keynesian (aggregate demand too low). Since a reduction in wage levels reduces aggregate demand, the measures to be taken point, in the two explanations, in opposite directions. In all ex-communist countries there has been a sharp cut in real wages since 1989, and it is hard indeed to reach the conclusion that, to ensure full employment, they ought to be lower still. The exception is the former German 'Democratic' Republic, where sudden unification, political and monetary, did result in East German wages being too high, relative to East German labour productivity.

However, why *should* labour markets clear? It has already been argued in an earlier chapter that markets in general do not, indeed *should not*, clear, in real competitive market economies. Consumer choice, and the consequences of competition, require that nearly all the time (and not just in times of recession or slump) supply exceeds demand. There are at any given moment unsold newspapers, unfilled restaurant seats, unsold trousers and skirts, unused productive capital (that is, many firms are not utilising their equipment). Why should labour be an exception?

In fact the supply of labour, in the sense of the number of human beings capable of work, is peculiarly unresponsive to changes in demand. Let us take as counter-examples the case of horses, and then of bananas. Demand for horses fell, as a consequence of technological change. The cost of horses' subsistence was such that they could not compete with mechanical horsepower. Supply fell too – most horses were eliminated. At a much lower number of horses, one could argue that supply and demand are, or could be, in balance. Similarly, suppose there is over-supply of bananas; banana trees can be cut down and replaced by a more profitable crop. Human beings, however, cannot be treated as horses or banana-trees. Their supply is not totally fixed: some women can decide to leave or to enter the labour force as their preferences and family circumstances dictate, and immigrants can arrive, or emigrants leave. None the less, variation in supply is limited, save at the margin.

Labour can be substituted for capital equipment, and vice versa. It can certainly be argued that the price of labour can affect employment, that workers *can* 'price themselves out of a job' by demanding higher wages. It is also true – and this has in the past been an important factor particularly in Great Britain – that trade union rules on job demarcation and apprenticeships, insistence on overmanning and deliberate limits on individuals' productivity, did serious damage to competitiveness and hence also to employment in the long run, even though one purpose of the unions' actions is to preserve jobs. Paradoxically, these restrictive practices also discourage investment and technical progress: employers know in advance that innovation will be resisted by this type of trade unionist. For example, modern presses purchased by the *Daily Telegraph* remained unused for many years, because 'blacked' by a printing union. So it has sometimes been the case that unions damage employment and obstruct innovation. However, one should not generalise from what was for many years a peculiarly British disease. To take another example, much damage was done to British ports, to London especially, by short-sighted dockers, who refused to handle containers or use new equipment, but German and Dutch unions and their ports, benefited by not being so conservative and myopic. There will be more to say about the issue of how to secure the workforce's collaboration in the pursuit of efficiency and competitiveness.

While accepting that, by their behaviour, trade unions can contribute to unemployment, experience in other countries where unions are relatively weak, such as today's United States, clearly demonstrates that unions cannot be the main culprits.

What, then, of government intervention in the labour market? This takes several forms: the fixing of minimum wages and insistence on various conditions, such as equal pay for women, limitation on hours, compulsory social insurance contributions from employers, health and safety regulations, high severance pay and the like. The issue of an *incomes policy* will be discussed later.

British ideologists, inspired also by Hayek, put much blame on the unions and have sought to weaken them, while rejecting so-called 'corporatism', that is, institutional collaboration between government, employers and unions. They also oppose the 'social chapter' accepted by all other EEC countries, and the week in which I am writing these words (July 1992) have persuaded the British government to abolish the so-called wage councils, which had the power to impose minimum wages and conditions in some notoriously lower-paid sectors of the economy. No doubt the argument was that such restrictions on free bargaining were both unjust (because a bargain freely entered into must benefit both parties), and contributed to unemployment by raising the cost of labour to the employer.

If one went back 150 years, no doubt similar arguments were heard when it was proposed to limit the work day to ten hours, or prevent children from working in mines or cotton mills, or to provide paid vacations. Even today free-marketeers in America oppose laws giving any rights (to extra time off, or re-employment) to pregnant women workers. And of course at one time trade unions were illegal in Britain, and their organisers could be (were) transported to penal colonies in Australia.

Just as, in an earlier chapter, the sacred rights of private property look a little less sacred if used to expel the inhabitants of Scottish highlands and islands from places their families had dwelt in for centuries, so one cannot, surely, support in retrospect those who argued for the 'freedom' of working for twelve hours and more a day. There is underlying this philosophy the (surely absurd) belief that the individual worker and the firm have equal bargaining power, so that the former needs neither a union nor the state to protect his or her interests.

The effect of a minimum wage rate, imposed either by unions or by government, on the willingness of firms to invest is by no means a straightforward one. Apart from the point made earlier, there is the literature on third world countries which 'blames' minimum-wage legislation and relatively low prices of machinery for the adoption of inappropriate technology inappropriate for labour-abundant economies. For Britain, the effect of unions on investment is the subject of a recent study, and interestingly, the authors say that 'there has been very little work in this area'. Their evidence suggests that unions have had, in Britain, a negative effect on investment, a plausible conclusion given the traditional attitudes of British unions,[1] but which should not be generalised, given important institutional and cultural differences.

One supposes that a principal argument in favour of legislation and social charters is that it reduces the effects of competition from firms which save costs by worsening pay and conditions. This, no doubt, is what appeared to justify bans on child labour, and limits on hours of work, in the nineteenth century. A contemporary example is the effect of Mexico's inclusion in the American free-trade zone: many US companies have established plants just south of the border, to take advantage both of low wages and the absence (or non-enforcement) of laws concerning hours, health and pollution.

Mention should be made of Martin Weitzman's proposal for a sort of universal profit-sharing bonus scheme, with the basic wage forming only part of the workers' remuneration; by reducing the cost of additional employment to the employer, it could help to reduce unemployment, or even, in Weitzman's surely over-hopeful prognostication, to eliminate it.[2] Another scheme which could have similar effects is a sort of universal dividend, paid to anyone whether he or she works or not, so that employers would, so to speak, top it up, again reducing the marginal (*and* average) cost of employing anyone. However, the politics and the various interest groups involved make such solutions impracticable – though voluntary profit-sharing schemes have both a past and future.

In any case, the relationship of unemployment and the level of wages and salaries is by no means straightforward. Of course any one employer would benefit from a lower wages bill. But it would surely be wrong to assert that this is in the interest of all employers, since this would reduce aggregate demand, including for that employer's product, leading to 'Keynesian' unemployment in Malinvaud's terminology. As a student I listened incredulously to Hayek, at LSE in 1933–34, arguing for lower wages as a cure for the depression, without (so it seemed to me) taking into account the effect of such a cure on demand, and, through it, on employment. The *General Theory*, when it appeared the following year, was seen as heresy.

Why, when there is what Marx called 'the reserve army of unemployed', is there not a fall in real wages? In fact even during the Great Depression, when unemployment reached record levels, real wages actually rose for those who remained in employment. The 'downward stickiness' of wages has been the subject of much comment. Two questions then arise: first, *why* the downward stickiness, and, second, could unemployment have been *seriously* reduced if it were not the case?

There has been a sizeable literature trying to find answers to the first question. Employers seek to avoid conflict, prefer a labour force that is loyal and committed, which causes them to pay more than the market rate, especially as it would cost extra to train new recruits. The unions defend their members in employment, and have no direct interest in the fate of unemployed non-members; they have, as we shall see, some reason for not believing that by letting wage rises fall behind the rate of inflation they would in fact help the unemployed. Furthermore, especially in the Reagan–Thatcher years, the 'bosses' have been awarding themselves very large pay rises, even at times of falling profits.

The special circumstances of post-communism render experience in Eastern Europe of limited relevance in the present context. There unemployment has risen rapidly while real wages have fallen, but the causes are clearly connected with the disruption attendant upon the strains of transition and the severing of trade and supply links, which have already been discussed in earlier chapters. Insofar as wage levels have contributed, they have done so by the effects of lower real incomes on demand. However, this experience does highlight one vital aspect of the employment/unemployment issues: the relationship between job creation and investment.

Whether in east or west, little additional employment can be expected from existing capital stock if the cost of labour falls. Let us imagine, for example, that in Great Britain the government succeeds in reducing real wages by 10–15 per cent, or that market forces achieve just such a result. How many additional persons would be taken on? Note that at a time of recession/depression only 'a philanthropist or a fool', to cite Kenneth Boulding,[3] would actually offer anyone work, and, as already mentioned, a fall in consumer demand could make the recession worse. It may even be argued that the downward stickiness of wages, plus welfare benefits, reduces the impact of the recession. But leaving such considerations aside, if any equipment requires (say) three persons to operate it, it is hardly likely that a fourth will be added, if wages were 15 per cent lower. A lorry can only be driven by one person. Yes, *at the margin* one can envisage some extra jobs: say a supermarket would employ one more cashier, a botanic gardens one more gardener. There is some substitutability between capital and labour at the margin, but surely not much. Capital equipment is to a considerable extent specific in the amount of labour it requires to operate it. And even in the longer run labour-saving innovations will not be significantly deterred by the existence of a labour surplus. Examples are numerous from developing countries. If a bulldozer replaces (say) 30 unskilled labourers, a bulldozer would be worth using even if there were no minimum wage legislation, if wages were at bare subsistence (and they cannot be lower than that!). Machines cannot go on strike, which increases their attractiveness for employers. And, most important, the mere fact that there are many persons seeking work does not of itself provide any motive for investors to invest, even in normal non-necessary times. Yet the creation of workplaces does require investment. Its collapse in most of the ex-communist countries must be a cause for grave concern, at a time when the closure of uneconomic enterprises and a 'shake-out' of surplus labour in many industries call for alternative sources of employment.

As has been argued at length earlier, 'investment is profoundly mysterious under perfect competition' (Hahn), and the would-be investor would only risk the long-term creation of additional productive capacity (and so of jobs) in the expectation that there would exist a profit-creating disequilibrium, a need not met, and one which his or her competitors would not be meeting. The investor has to take into account the prospective state of the economy, interest rates, prices of inputs and wage levels too, but the mere fact that there are men and women seeking work will not figure high in the decision-making process of the investor. It must be added that especially in Great Britain, because of inadequacies of education and training, a high level of unemployment can (does) coexist with a shortage of labour of the requisite skills. It is important not to treat 'labour' (or, for that matter, 'capital') as homogenous. Drastic cuts in education and training programmes in ex-communist countries do not, therefore, augur well.

It can be argued legitimately that, whereas in a closed economy a fall in employees' income can have deleterious offsetting effects on employment through a fall in aggregate demand, this would not be the case in an open economy, unless, of course, there was a sort of competitive wage-cutting involving many countries. It is precisely to avoid such an outcome that the European Community voted in favour of the 'social chapter', affecting hours of labour and various benefits, with Britain alone refusing to accept it. Indeed Prime Minister Major actually taunted his continental opposite members: you have the social chapter, we will have the jobs. This is an aspect of international competition for inward investment: thus Japanese capital may prefer to invest in Britain rather than (say) France because social charges and obligations in France add significantly to the cost of labour. It is precisely the aim of Britain's partners in the EEC to limit such competition, and competitive devaluations too. The debate continues.

As Kurt Rothschild correctly pointed out, 'the weaknesses of neoclassical wage theory as it is presented in our textbooks' relate to the fact that 'it was from the very beginning not a wage theory or a theory of the labour market but a price theory somewhat modified to meet labour market aspects'. He contrasts this with the classics, from Adam Smith to Marx. 'This (neo-classical) analysis suffered from the very beginning from a neglect of the income aspects of wages and prices . . . The close link between wage rate and total income thus provides a reason for particularly strong resistances against radical wage reductions.' Rothschild also notes the inadequacies, in this context, of marginal productivity theory, especially in the short run: 'The idea of a monotonously falling marginal productivity curve is based on the assumption of continuous and comparatively smooth opportunities for factor substitutions', yes 'the labour input of a firm or industry is determined to a large extent by the existing capital equipment'.[4] And again: 'Neoclassical wage theory is very distinctively a child of the competitive

price model, with its assumptions of atomistic competition and the
individualistic *homo oeconomicus*'.[5]

Europe's unemployment is high and rising in 1993. It is an open question whether or how far it is cyclical, how far it is explicable by effective
Asian competition with Europe's relatively high-wage economies.
Regrettably too little attempt has been focused on possible long-term
structural changes, which do not 'fit' the neoclassical mode of thought. It
can be expressed as follows:

> The essential problem is that business success is being redefined as the combi-
> nation of superior information, identifying opportunities with temporary
> packages of capital, labour and appropriate technology used to exploit the
> opportunity and then disperse. This militates against large . . . firms with stable
> labour forces, research and training programmes. When you need, you buy in.
> There is a powerful chain effect in operation in which the shedding of costs is
> being simultaneously undertaken by both businesses and government agencies
> and other non-business organisations from armies to museums. It is a process
> of self-reinforcing impoverishment, for while the logic may seem clear for any
> individual unit, the damage done to the whole economy, and to the complex
> industrial sub-cultures which make it up, is enormous . . . It is . . . a process
> that actually *produces* unemployment, and changes full-time into casual work.[6]

If this is correct, it can have alarming consequences. But it is neither
macro nor micro, so theory can miss this effect.

Recessions/depressions ought to be accompanied by a fall in interest
rates, which should encourage borrowing for investment purposes.
Unfortunately, in many countries the strains on the balance of payments
(for example, in Great Britain in 1931 and in 1991) cause a rise in real
interest rates, which makes matters worse. However, where, as in the
United States in 1992, interest rates are repeatedly cut, it does not, it did
not, follow that borrowing for investment (and the provision of employment) will rise. There is too great a chance of losing one's money, and the
thousands of bankruptcies recorded monthly underline the danger. The
end of the Cold War and the arms race threatens the employment of
hundreds of thousands. In both the United States and Russia, one needs
investment to convert the arms industry to civilian production, and/or to
retrain the workforce for employment in other sectors of the economy,
which must then expand to absorb them. However, this runs into obstacles both financial and ideological. The United States, Great Britain
and Russia all have serious budget deficits, and the governments are committed to a laissez-faire ideology, which is opposed to the state investing
directly in other than military activities, or even to providing inducements
to selected sectors. As pointed out in Chapter 7, this is particularly unfor-
tunate in Russia, which has little private capital and a still primitive

capital market. But it is a problem in the west, too. Both the American and the British governments are under pressure to continue high levels of arms procurements, because of the effects on employment of not doing so, rather than for serious military reasons. To use the money to regenerate inner cities, or say rail electrification, is ideologically excluded.

Public works as a cure are unfashionable today, as they were during the Great Depression until 1933. It is worth recalling Roosevelt's New Deal: I am writing these words in Berkeley, and recently visited the elegant rose garden, which was erected in 1933 with federal finance via the National Recovery Administration. In 1992 in California, with unemployment at high levels, local expenditures are being drastically cut back and this garden is full of weeds. Is it necessary to prove that millions of unemployed represent economic waste and social dangers?

It is particularly dangerous to approach this whole set of problems with a mindset to the effect that labour markets will clear, if imperfections such as trade unions, or laws to protect workers, and downward-stickiness of wages were eliminated. To repeat, markets in general do not clear, even when supply is wholly flexible, and there is no reason why the market for labour should clear, with many reasons why it should not. Which is not to deny that governments can make matters worse, as well as better.

INCOMES POLICIES?

An issue which has become ideological is whether or not an incomes policy is desirable, and/or whether there should be national pay bargaining, or whether each employer should negotiate separately with each group, or even with each separate employee. At the heart of the difference on these topics is different views of trade unions. It is common to both views to recognise that, especially at times of low unemployment, the unions have power to demand higher wages, and if each union pursues its own claims separately, one can have the leapfrog effect observed in Britain in the 1960s and 1970s, while those with weaker bargaining power get left far behind. Indeed, even at times of recession, some strongly-placed groups can still demand large increases, contributing to stagflation. So what could be done? One view, which can be called 'Thatcherist', is to pass laws emasculating the unions, denouncing national wage bargaining, including for public sector employees, and embracing the fragmentationism familiar in so many aspects of policy. Such a policy has the best chances of success when there is a sharp rise in unemployment, as was indeed 'achieved' in the first Thatcher years. In the public sector emphasis is given to relating pay differentiation to results, to performance, the consequences of which we will discuss below.

The opposite view has several variants. One, associated with such countries as Sweden and (West) Germany, is to avoid leap-frogging by centralising wage bargaining as far as possible, hoping that trade unions can be persuaded to moderate their claims by involving their leaders in economic policy discussions. There were, of course, also other reasons which help to explain why wage claims and interest rates were in postwar decades much lower in Sweden and West Germany than in Great Britain, but the contrast is suggestive. The other kind of incomes policy is an attempt to impose wage freezes by legislative action, either directly or through taxation. In some instances it is associated with a price freeze, seen as a temporary measure to combat inflation. In Hungary in the mid-1970s (and in Poland in 1992) wage increases above a fixed percentage led to a steep increase in tax paid by the 'offending' employing state enterprise. In Poland in the 1970s they tried out a formula relating wage rises in the then dominant state sector to a rise in total productivity. More recently in Poland one had the drastic policy of releasing all prices *except* that of labour, limiting wage increases to 30 per cent or even 20 per cent of the rise in the cost of living, which earned the authors the reprobation of Milton Friedman.

There is one predictable consequence of the attempt to impose an incomes policy, whether in the west or east: it leads to an unintended redistribution of income in favour of those whose incomes are uncontrollable, or uncontrolled. In some ex-communist countries controls are deliberately confined to the state sector, as part of the policy of encouraging private enterprise and those who work in the private sector. But the self-employed, or those engaged in trade or other forms of dealing, or workers paid on piece-rates even in state-owned enterprises, cannot have their incomes controlled as effectively as those on fixed wages and salaries. In the former Soviet Union, where total wage payments were rigidly controlled, in practice there was a 'wage drift' in favour of piece-workers, whose take-home pay inevitably depended on local bargaining about piece-rate norms. The one more or less effective control over wage payments was the so-called 'wages fund', that is, a planned total wages bill for that enterprise or institution which it was not allowed to exceed, with the state bank acting as financial policeman to impose compliance. When, after 1989, these controls were loosened, supposedly being replaced by a link to productivity, wages soon soared.

Attempts to link wages to productivity infallibly produces anomalies, in west, east or south. One problem is how to measure it. The numbers employed should be divided into – what? This proves far from easy, as

Marxists found when they sought to apply the labour theory of value in practice. Another is to identify who was in fact responsible for the higher productivity, howsoever measured. Suppose it is due to the installation of a better machine, the reward should really go to the designer or producer of the machine rather than to its operator. And what of common overheads? Does one include not just those on the production line, but also other employees of the firm, such as computer operators, secretaries, catering staff? We shall return to the issues of performance evaluation later on.

Can real wages be 'too high'? In a closed economy, it is difficult to envisage the meaning of such a proposition. Of course, *money* wages can rise excessively, with inflationary consequences. But *real* wages are equal by definition to the consumers' goods and services available. Unless, that is, one is in a one-commodity world, such as Ricardo's 'corn'. Then, if one eats a part of next year's seed grain, then of course one damages both investment and next year's consumption. If one envisages, in a dynamic economy, a fall in real wages as a stimulus to investment, this too seems dubious in the real world: for if demand falls, why should additional investment yield a profit? Of course, the introduction of foreign trade changes the picture. Real wages *can* be excessive, in two ways.

First, as when after 1925 Great Britain returned to the gold standard at too high an exchange rate, Britain's wage levels made British goods less competitive in world markets. The same was true in 1991–92 when Britain entered the European exchange rate mechanism at too high a rate. Second, as in Chile in 1971, a combination of large increases in money wages and price controls, led to a *nominal* rise in real wages, while goods became scarce and imports rose, until foreign exchange gave out. In models based on a closed economy, such problems cannot arise, on the simplifying assumptions of such models.

One problem in measuring real wages is worth a brief mention, since economists in the 'east' are all too familiar with it. This relates both to intertemporal and international comparisons. Take, for example, Poland in 1986 and Poland in 1993. In the first of these years many goods were unobtainable at the controlled price; in the second, a wider variety of goods were available, without queuing, side-payments or influence, but at very much higher prices. A straightforward comparison of prices and money wages shows a precipitous decline in 'real wages' between these two years. There was indeed a decline, as well as income redistribution, but clearly the decline would be overstated if one did not take into account the much greater availability of goods. The same problem arises if one compares the purchasing-power of the dollar and the rouble in, say, 1989. In assessing purchasing power parity, one silently assumes that the goods one wishes to purchase are available. Suppose a given quality of cheese cost 2 roubles in Chelyabinsk and 2 dollars in Philadelphia. This suggests a dollar–rouble rate for cheese of 1:1. However, there were 50 cheeses to choose from in Philadelphia, while this cheese was only on sale in Chelyabinsk on the third Monday in the month, and there were no other cheeses. If generalised over a wide range of goods, this ought plainly to lower purchasing-power parity in Russia compared with America, because of lack of power to purchase in the former, as well as a much more restricted choice, of cheeses and of most other things. As and when Russia achieves a closer approximation to balance between demand and supply, albeit at very much higher prices, there would be a more meaningful basis for comparisons with market economies, but the same problem as with Poland will arise in comparing Russia's living standards and real wages with the 'deficit' economy of 1989. The CIA has been widely blamed for overstating the relative output and consumption of the former USSR. In my view this was primarily due to their applying standard methodology for international comparisons, though this methodology was inappropriate. Criticism must, however, be tempered with the realisation that there was no known alternative.

The same problem would arise if one compared the level of real wages in Great Britain in 1944, when there was rationing and shortages, with that of 1954.[7]

Clearly, real incomes are closely correlated with the general level of productivity (plus or minus the trade balance in consumers' goods. Thus Saudi Arabia may import nearly all of the latter.). Do wages show a tendency to equal the marginal product of labour? In an earlier chapter I had queried the use or misuse of the term 'margin', in a sequential and interconnected economy, with non-homogenous labour. This may be the place to add a thought derived from Arthur Lewis's lecture given in Glasgow on the 200th anniversary of *The Wealth of Nations*: if a truck driver in India receives (say) 15 per cent of the wage of an American truck driver, this has absolutely no connection with their relative productivity as truck drivers, which may be equal if they drive a similar truck. What pulls down the general level of everyone's income in India is the existence of hundreds of millions of peasants whose productivity (whether average or marginal) is extremely low, and their influence is expressed via opportunity-cost of labour. The same was and is true in China. Skilled workers in a Shanghai factory which I visited earned (by Western standards) a pittance, but my Chinese colleagues were worried by the big gap separating their income from that of China's peasants.

EXPLOITATION AND MARGINS

If one assumes diminishing marginal productivity, and labour were paid its marginal product, it occurred to me even as a student beginner that one can demonstrate and measure exploitation in its Marxist sense, but not in Marx's way (see Figure 8.1). If all the labourers are paid the equivalent of the marginal product of the nth labourer, then the employer pockets the quantity represented by the triangle ABC. But it also seemed to me odd (it still does) that the employer would find it profitable to employ anyone whose marginal product just equalled his or her wages. No one buys any unit of any factor of production unless it is expected to yield a profit, directly or indirectly. Why should labour be an exception?

However, it is with other misapplications of the marginal principle that I am concerned. To illustrate it, let me cite an article (by D. Israelsen) which sought to show that incentives on a collective farm would be more effective than in a capitalist enterprise, because the former would pay its workforce on the basis of average productivity, the latter on the basis of marginal productivity, which would be lower.[8] There are several reasons why such a conclusion would be questionable, reasons connected with the real nature of Soviet collective farms, which we will not pursue here. Instead let me stress two factors of general application. One is that no labourer is in fact aware of what anyone's marginal or average productivity is, and what is not seen or felt cannot act as an incentive. The second relates particularly, but not solely, to agriculture. Not only do a number of different tasks have to be undertaken in sequence, but there are rush

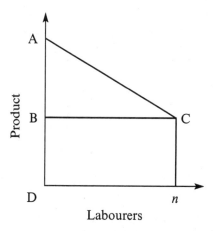

Figure 8.1

periods (notably the harvesting) which require long hours of overtime. (The Russian word for the harvest period, *strada*, has the same linguistic root as *stradanie*, 'suffering'). So motivation matters greatly. Wage-earners who work overtime usually get extra pay for so doing. But extra pay for extra hours of work conflicts with the assumption of diminishing marginal productivity! There is something amiss in applying textbook principles to real people in real workplaces.

Reverting briefly to the issue of 'exploitation', one must recall that economists in ex-communist countries were brought up on Marx's concept. Can it still be defended? As argued in an earlier chapter, if a landowner who inherited thousands of valuable acres from his forefathers can make millions by allowing others to use his land, this may cause even some of the neo-liberal worshippers of the sacredness of private property to pause before totally approving. There is no reason inherent in any economic theory which calls for us to approve of latifundia. The capitalist entrepreneur, who runs his or her own business, is another matter, since here we have work, risk-taking and responsibility. It is a matter of value-judgement whether to accept or to query income arising solely from ownership of property, or to regard or not to regard labour as just another factor of production, along with inanimate objects. This would in no way deny or belittle the importance of entrepreneurship or the entrepreneur, since that very word implies action, not sleeping. Here Marx was either wrong or confused.

There are interesting ideas on exploitation developed by John Roemer.[9] He very properly extends it to cover the situation of high officialdom in a communist-ruled country, who acquire privilege and power through rank. Though here we face ambiguity: did the *nomenklatura* officialdom's 'exploitation' equal the entire surplus which they controlled, or only that part of it which they personally appropriated in the form of goods and other privileges? (Part of the surplus may, after all, be used to finance welfare.) There is another and more questionable aspect of Roemer's concept of exploitation: he applies it not just to rank but also to ability. Thus, in his version, a talented novelist or a successful athlete or singer, who earns far more than the average, also exploits – but whom? For the term to have any meaning it seems to me that one needs an object, identifiable individuals, who are 'exploited'.

PRODUCTIVE AND UNPRODUCTIVE LABOUR

Another distinction familiar to those brought up on Marxism is the distinction between productive and unproductive labour. This has a long history behind it, very well described in a recent book by Helen Boss.[10]

Marx was not an altogether consistent follower of Adam Smith. Both included as unproductive officials, soldiers, priests, suppliers of all and any non-material services ('opera singers and opera dancers' came last on Smith's list). Marx also viewed the 'sphere of circulation' as unproductive, and indeed excluded the self-employed, because they generated no surplus value, but included anyone who did. (Bukharin quipped that prostitutes were unproductive if working for themselves, but exploited if working in a whorehouse.) However, Soviet practice treated as productive both the private activities of individuals and state wholesale and retail trade, but excluded other personal services. The Russians have now adopted the standard UN definitions of national income and GNP: anyone gainfully employed or producing any good or service is 'productive', including officials, soldiers, servants, and so on.

They have no alternative. However, they should be aware of the inadequacy of GNP as a measure. Not only because of the inevitable inaccuracies so well pinpointed by Oscar Morgenstern,[11] but conceptually too. There are anomalies such as the familiar one that a man diminishes GNP by marrying his cook. More important ones relate to state employees, bureaucrats, and so on. Here the anti-statist neo-liberals have reverted in part to Adam Smith: Helen Boss shows them as viewing civil servants as, on the whole, unproductive, parasitic, a burden. Without sharing their anti-statist ideology, can we not regard administrators, military and police, as necessary, but as a necessary *cost*? Simon Kuznets used to so regard those expenditures which yield neither product nor welfare. (A ride on an overcrowded New York subway was another of his examples.) This is quite a different distinction from that between material and non-material product. 'Opera singers', teachers, doctors, hoteliers, travel agents, hairdressers, clothes designers, all perform tasks which yield satisfaction as such. People grow apples, others transport them, sell them, eventually eat them. Policemen may be essential if apples are not to be stolen, but should this not be considered a cost? The less honest the society, the more policemen are needed. But by considering their productivity equal to their pay, and *adding* it to the national product, are we being altogether rational? If, because of the menacing behaviour of neighbouring states, it is necessary to mobilise a million men for military service, taking them away from other work, surely this could and should be seen as a minus? Yet the standard procedures add their pay to GNP.

One wonders, too, about gambling. It certainly redistributes income, but, unless gambling in itself gives pleasure (analogous to listening to an opera singer), is it a productive activity? The same thought occurred to me looking at a dealing room at a merchant banker's office: 200 men gazing at computer screens, telephone in hand, buying and selling for the purposes of buying and selling. It is not even a transaction cost, analogous to acquiring or disposing of a product. It is said that over 90 per cent of all foreign exchange transactions have no other purpose than to seek to make a profit out of the transaction. And if, as in Russia in 1992, much human ingenuity goes not into producing anything but on dealing, should this not find its reflection in GNP statistics, rather than counting the net income of the dealers as part of GNP? If house construction goes down by 50 per cent, while the number of estate agents (realtors) doubles, how should we count the net effect?

There is in practice no alternative to using the conventions accepted worldwide. But it is as well to be made aware of their imperfections.

EVALUATION OF PERFORMANCE

Here the literature on principal and agent is worth study. A hires B to act on his or her behalf, as a stockbroker, painter, works manager, repair mechanic, farm labourer, truck driver. Questions arise: of monitoring performance, of measuring output, of the possibilities of shirking and what Williamson has called 'self-seeking with guile'. Soviet economists were extremely familiar with the success indicator problem applied to firms, that is, to sub-units of the great firm USSR Ltd., and this has been referred to earlier. British economists and administrators are, or should be, aware of the importance now being attached to performance indicators for civil servants, tax collectors, teachers, medical staffs, police, and so on. There was even a proposal to pay magistrates by results; a rather comic notion which highlights the question: what are appropriate indicators of efficiency where there is no direct relationship with the market? Many of the same problems arise within the hierarchies of large private firms.

Precisely because they have been conscious of the distortions to which plan-fulfilment indicators gave rise in the former Soviet Union (for example, targets in tons stimulated excess weight of product), ex-Soviet economists should be able to see – more clearly than some of the ideologists advising the British government – that attempts to measure performance often give rise to unintended side-effects. One thinks again of Goodhart's Law: if something becomes a plan or target, then it ceases to be a good measure. If hospitals are given a target of reducing waiting-lists of patients, they will tend to refuse to put people on waiting-lists. If police are rewarded for the percentage of crimes they solve, they have a built-in incentive for avoiding taking up cases difficult to solve. Does a fall in crime represent a fall or a rise in measured police 'productivity'? Should civil servants be rewarded for the volume of correspondence to which their activities give rise? I have heard that diplomats in the Foreign Office are to be paid extra for performance, whatever that is (should they first create a diplomatic problem and then be rewarded for resolving it? It reminds one of increasing GNP by breeding mosquitoes and then making more mosquito nets and chemical repellents.) Efficient university teachers should be rewarded, and under the old system that usually took the form of recommendations for promotion. But this is regarded as inadequate by the ideologists, who believe in competition and measurable efficiency. This leads to familiar distortions: 'publish or perish', and avoiding those academic activities that do not score in the 'productivity' table. Time must be spent accumulating what a colleague calls 'Brownie points'.

I recall being asked, along with thousands of others, to fill up a form indicating how many hours per week I spent on teaching and how many on research. The reply, if sent, was inherently meaningless. Suppose I discuss an aspect of my subject over a cup of coffee or a beer with two colleagues, or lie in the bath and think of the text of my next lecture or article, or read a Russian short story about peasants, is it preparation for teaching, or research, or is it 'work' at all within the meaning of the act? If British academics were compelled to be in their offices or lecture-rooms 9 to 5 daily, would this increase their output? As was demonstrated many years ago by Tibor Scitovsky, do not people who are in control of their own time, and feel they work on their own behalf, work longer than do employees under orders?

No detailed contractual specification, no formalised and measurable efficiency criteria, can exist which do not distort the desired behaviour of subordinates. This is true in east, west and south, in sectors public and private. Another academic example, well known also in Russia: if teachers or their departments are rewarded or penalised in respect of examination results, then some poor-performing students who deserve to fail will be passed, and more first classes or As will be awarded. In fact, as any teacher would confirm, it is the same lame ducks who need most attention. The talented can mostly get first class results with little help. As also in schools, good results tell us more about the quality of student intake than about the quality of the teachers.

These issues have become extremely important in the most recent years, especially in Britain. To cite a recent newspaper report: 'professionals have lost the privilege of being trusted to do their jobs properly . . . It is management, customers and government that now determine the standards they must achieve'.[12] This has been considered with a denigration of public service, which finds its theoretical basis in 'public choice theory', which, as argued in an earlier chapter, regards public servants merely as individual utility maximisers. With this goes the attempt to reduce or eliminate job security ('goodbye jobs for life' is the headline of the above-cited *Observer* article), which already has led to the elimination of tenure in universities and to recommendations for the public and many civil-service occupations, which would have the effect of drastically altering career expectations (short-term contracts becoming the rule). This in turn is linked with 'market testing', that is, putting tasks out to tender. This puts millions of jobs in jeopardy, and the winners too are victims of job insecurity, insofar as the task or franchise is to be again 'market tested' after a few years. To cite the same article, 'there are implicit and explicit contracts between people, but if you have a contract now it means exactly what it says and no more'. It is also believed that a market-tested contract can be relied upon to ensure quality.

It is a real criticism of the economic profession that these policies and measures has produced no critical analysis, and indeed economists themselves have tamely accepted them in their own professional capacity. There are some fundamental questions which are begged by this whole package.

First, it is remarkably naive to suppose that quality of performance can be assured by detailed contract. Williamson has been cited already about the possibilities of what he called 'self-seeking with guile' on the part of subcontractors and franchisees. It seems to be foolish that the phrase 'work to rule' describes a form of strike, that the deliberate observance of all the rules is a way of bringing work to a virtual halt. The unexpected often happens. Goodwill, willingness to collaborate with others for a common goal, is essential for the efficient operation of almost anything, in public and private sectors. So is trust. And if 'professionals are no longer trusted', they will not trust the managers that do not trust them. What an oddly narrow view of human motivation!

Second, what of such qualities as loyalty, commitment, pride in one's job, responsibility. Is it really the case that they matter no more than does trust? On the face of it, this is absurd. Can it be explained by the fact that these qualities cannot be measured or 'mathematicised'? Or is it an ideological assumption that all men and women are natural shirkers?

Third, is job insecurity good for performance? Williamson thought the opposite, that job security acts as an incentive. It is true that shirkers do exist and there must be a procedure to deal with them, and the inefficient must be disciplined, and, if all else fails, dismissed. But to generalise insecurity is surely bad psychology, bad labour relations, and even bad for the macroeconomy, as it discourages commitments to consumer expenditures.

Fourth, all this is linked with performance-related pay, apart from the distortions caused by performance measurement, which has been the subject of very little attention in the profession, with the exception of Peter Smith's excellent article.[13] Smith lists the distortions by categories ('tunnel vision', 'suboptimisation', 'myopia', 'convergence', 'ossification', 'gaming', 'misrepresentation') with examples from performance criteria in the health service. But apart from point-scoring and league-table distortion of behaviour, three other factors are worthy of attention: effects on transaction costs, informal cooperation and on performance itself.

The greater the reliance on individual performance indicators, the more time has to be spent on monitoring, measurement, accountancy. This is a link with a tendency frequently criticised in these pages, fragmentation, myopic marginalism. The possibility of what Smith called 'misrepresentation, including "creative" accounting and fraud', places the need to relate differences in pay to some objective measure (to avoid accusations of favouritism, and so on) provides good reasons for employing more 'measures'.

The greater the subdivision of performance measurement (individuals, small groups, and so on), the greater the reluctance to cooperate with others, unless the effect of this cooperation is to help one's own performance indicators. Since most firms, departments and faculties generate some organisational economies of scale, internalise what would amount to externalities, the effect of separately rewarding segments of the whole can be to inhibit informal cooperation.

And lastly, what motivates performance? Is it the case that surgeons, professors of economics, parks superintendents, police chiefs and most other professionals can be persuaded to do a better job by offering them an extra sum for meeting 'targets'? We all know cases where teachers, who previously devoted hours to extracurricular activities, will no longer do so if they are told, ordered, to 'work to contract'.

All this apart from the fact that work satisfaction is a 'good' in itself, and goodwill matters, whether this is goodwill won for itself by a firm which acquires a reputation for providing quality and reliability, or goodwill at the workplace.

None of this is intended to assert that there is no inefficiency or shirking. It merely underlines the futility of so many well-meaning schemes of measurement and reward. The singling out of individuals, which seems to be a particular aim of ideologists in Britain, also inhibits teamwork.

In practice much depends on human attitudes. Bad industrial relations have done much harm, not only in Britain, but also in former communist countries. A sizeable volume can be compiled about alienation of the Soviet workforce. Here, for example, is Nikolai Shmelev: 'We have one of the lowest levels of productivity of any industrial nation . . . , since through the years of stagnation the working masses reached a stage of almost total disinterestedness in freely committed and honest labour. Apathy, indifference, thieving, have become mass phenomena.'[14]

Can privatisation be a cure?

PARTICIPATION, CO-OWNERSHIP, ESOP

The dominant view in ex-communist countries appears to favour the authoritarian model, with the employer-boss in command. Earlier commitment of reformers to various species of workers' self-management have all but disappeared. As we saw in Chapter 7, the draft law on privatisation in Russia, while it did provide for an allocation of shares to the workforce, limited this to 25 per cent and made them non-voting.

This is odd. It cannot be explained by reaction to excesses of worker participation under the communist regimes: it was nowhere more than nominal, except in Yugoslavia, and workers' 'alienation' was frequently referred to. The Yugoslav version, as many (including this writer) have long ago noted, suffered from serious defects: the enterprise was owned not by its employees but by 'society', that is in effect by no one, and the employees had no interest in its capital value. They *were* interested in increasing short-term payout, that is, the net distributable income per employee. This, plus some unwarranted deductions from Benjamin Ward's 'Illyrian' model, and other models which abstracted from human attitudes or assumed a strictly individualistic 'rationality', combined to give a negative view of any sort of employee-managed enterprise.

Yet there is a basis for the concept of 'alienation'. Performance in almost any occupation depends on willingness to work well. Whatever the methods of supervision, slackness and shirking are possible, and supervision is costly. The Japanese are well aware of the importance of loyalty and commitment, and devote much effort to further it in employer–worker relations and in the organisation of various tasks and processes, encouraging low-level participation in decision-making, spreading responsibility, teamwork. It helps to create a spirit which welcomes rather than obstructs innovation, new technology. With this goes a reluctance to dismiss workers, this being part of the cost of securing and maintaining loyalty.

Japanese firms are certainly not examples of any sort of cooperative *ownership*, and it is in any case wrong to regard the practices of the large and well-known companies as applicable to all of Japanese industry. Anyhow, it is surely the case that Japan's performance, organisational arrangements and human relations can hardly be understood without also taking into account national character and traditions. Much of the content of the present chapter falls outside the neoclassical mainstream, nowhere more than in the above sentence, which has no meaning in a world of mathematical formalism. A colleague in Glasgow once said: 'Unless one assumes that everyone responds identically to the same stimuli, one cannot have a truly scientific economics.' But everyone does *not* respond identically to the same stimuli! Thus if a shipbuilding company would suffer a severe penalty for late delivery, this is consistent with two types of response from the workforce: work harder to complete the job on time (let us call this Japanese) or go on strike to demand extra pay (British, when we still had shipyards). Away from their models, few economists would deny that to explain Japan's remarkable success we must take into account that which is peculiarly Japanese. But because it is hard to define and harder to measure, it could be ruled out as a factor outside of economics. Which, I submit, unnecessarily narrows our subject-matter.

To take two other examples: there have been for centuries (until Stalin deported them) German peasants farming in the Volga region, and for 50 years or so there have been Japanese market-gardeners in Brazil. There were and are local Russian and Brazilian farmers in the area concerned, and they remain far less productive and efficient than the incomers. The learning process, if any, has been remarkably slow.

This is relevant to international comparisons of labour productivity, as one explanatory factor among many. Thus American soil and climate plays an important part in accounting for superior productivity as compared with Russia, but, quite apart from the handicap imposed upon them first by serfdom and then by the *kolkhoz* system, one knows intuitively that most Russian peasants would not behave like most American farmers. Comparisons are of particular interest and relevance if one is dealing not only with similar natural conditions, but also the same people. Hence the value of comparing East and West Germany, North and South Korea.

But to return to the question of the role of labour in management and the possibilities of co-ownership. Interestingly, while East Germany nominally had a 'proletarian' ideology, its management structure was more authoritarian than that of capitalist West Germany, which had and has *Mitbestimmung*, employee representation. (This is regarded with suspicion by British neo-liberal ideologists, who seem wedded to the authoritarian model). There are many causes for the fact that Germany has been relatively strike-free (1992 was in this respect exceptional), but the corporatism so disliked by Thatcherites, plus *Mitbestimmung*, as well as the traditional German virtues of discipline and order, must surely have contributed. As did, in Britain, the fragmented and obsolete organisational forms of British trade unions. How can such matters be seen as lying outside the subject-matter of economics! The motto of my *alma mater* was, and still is, *rerum cognoscere causas*.

In America, there has been some significant development of co-ownership, known by the acronym ESOP (Employee Stock Ownership Program), which is said by now to cover 11 million employees. It is claimed that the defects of the Yugoslav model (that is, of 'self-management' without ownership) disappear, in a competitive environment. There is self-discipline, belief in strong management, concern for investment and market share. One imagines that, in this area as in many others, 'small is beautiful', that is, that employee ownership and other forms of cooperatives have more chance of success if the enterprise is not of the size of General Electric or DuPont. The attitude of neo-liberal ideologists is here ambiguous, or mixed, since some are committed to the spread of stock and share ownership ('people's capitalism'), and, rather comically, the effort of miners to buy their pit from the (still) nationalised British Coal was actually described as 'privatisation'.

If a sense of 'belonging', if joint responsibility, if being residuary claimants, improves labour's performance, reduces pilfering and the need for supervision, facilitates innovation, encourages teamwork and loyalty, then these are matters which should be taken into account. They are systematically omitted from models which, by abstracting from such possible effects on behaviour, give this factor a weight of zero. It may be objected that the ESOP enthusiasts tend to exaggerate the positive features, and this may be so. One cannot pronounce a verdict without carefully scrutinising the evidence. However, Kornai surely did not do so before dogmatically rejecting any such solution other than for religious or ideological enthusiasts.

After all, in a country such as Russia or Ukraine, the reformers have inherited the overwhelming predominance of state ownership of the means of production, that is, in effect ownership by no one (that is, everybody), with control in the hands of high party functionaries. Out go the functionaries. Then – what? In a sense one starts with *tabula rasa*. One has choices.

As already discussed in Chapter 7, there are complex issues involved in privatisation, when there are no capitalists and landlords. No one solution can be wholly satisfactory, and there is likely to be a mixture, within which there could be a major place for some version of ESOP. Even neo-liberals can be persuaded that human freedom can encompass also some degree of control over one's workplace. One thinks again of Tibor Scitovsky's 'Joyless Economy'. And those, like Kornai, and Friedman, who recommend organisational forms which subordinate employees to employers, who insist that efficiency requires that the latter be residuary claimants, themselves enjoy a wide area of freedom in their work, and would doubtless claim, with good reason, that their work benefits therefrom.

When, in 1930, independent Russian peasants were forcibly herded into pseudo-collectives, this was presented as a victory for 'socialism', though socialism used to be seen as involving control by the producers over their work and over their product. In agriculture, the 'eastern' reformers do appreciate the virtues of peasant ownership and independence. Strangely, they do not extend this vision to non-agricultural employment.

The Chinese experience in the past decade is relevant in the present context. There has been a boom in market-related production of goods and services carried out by a variety of ownership types: private, collective, corporate, municipal, and China's positive record in recent years contrasts with the decline in Eastern Europe. Martin Weitzman and Chenggang Xu have drawn attention to this contrast, and with it to the doubtful validity of orthodox theoretical assumptions about labour incentives.[15] These assume that if (say) 20 people jointly share the gains from their jointly-owned activity, then any extra effort by any one of them would yield only a twentieth of the result to the one who makes the effort, so he or she would shirk. Yet this is a highly dubious simplification: would such theorists therefore assert that a 'cooperative' of 20 doctors or lawyers must necessarily be less efficient than if one employed the other 19? It seems to me unnecessary to invoke the Chinese (or Russian) national character, as Weitzman and Xu do in the above paper. But it is true that in Russia there was a traditional kind of work-gang (*artel*'), and it was well known that such informal *arteli* were able to build faster and better than state construction enterprises, despite being all but illegal (they were known, in the 1970s, by the pejorative label *shabashniki*).

Surely, while private entrepreneurs are highly desirable, it is wrong to rule out ESOP and other forms of collective or cooperative ownership.

It is sometimes silently assumed that the western 'market' model is based on private entrepreneurs. So it is worth reminding the reader (again!) of the important, often dominant, role played by the corporation, the joint stock company, with ownership diffused and separated from management control. This tendency was already visible over 200 years ago, and was sufficiently significant to have been noted (and deplored) by Adam Smith. ('Negligence and profusion therefore must prevail, more or less . . .') Recent experience suggests managerial 'profusion' in awarding themselves large rewards, often unrelated to performance or pay. One recalls Kurt Rothschild's book of readings, titled *Power in Economics*, another issue neglected by the neoclassical mainstream, which presumably would treat pay differentials between chief executives and the rank-and-file of 200:1 as in some way not related to bargaining power but to productivity. Dennis C. Mueller pointed to the limitations, in this context, of the principal–agent model,

> because the fundamental premise of the principal–agent model in case of shareholder and manager is false. Shareholders do not write the contracts that

define managerial compensation, do not hire and fire managers. To a considerable degree managers select themselves and design their own contracts. The
point Berle and Means sought to make [in 1932!! – A.N.] is that *control* of the
'contract' linking shareholders to managers lies with the managers.[16]

I do not derive from this a reason for condoning the joint stock company, which has its justification. The two points I wish to make in this
context are, first, that (as already argued in an earlier chapter) we are far,
far away from textbook profit maximisation, and, second, that in recommending the joint stock company to 'eastern' reforms we should bear in
mind the differences between this and the textbook entrepreneur, especially in the context of discussing the positive and negative aspects of
employee ownership as an alternative.

Ideologists in Britain are, at the time of writing, engaged in another
exercise, called 'market testing'. Civil service, local government, and other
public-sector employments are threatened by a decision to put work out
to tender. This could be anything from cleaning to filing, from transport-
ing the sick to hospital to issuing driving licenses. The justification is: by
separately defining and contracting out specific tasks, these can be done
cheaper. The disadvantages, apart from being yet another example of
fragmentation of what used to be seen as closely complementary tasks,
tend to be neglected by the ideologists, and are worth stressing. One is the
effect of spreading job insecurity through the public sector, which is
having a visible effect on behaviour (restraining many people's willingness
to spend or borrow), as well as being a source of human unhappiness.
The second is that it disregards the value of loyalty and committed service, more likely to be rendered (as the Japanese never forgot) if one has
confidence in retaining one's job. Third, in the competition to acquire
franchises or to win the tender the temptation to cut costs (and wages)
and worsen quality is probable, and the consequences are costly to moni-
tor and remedy. Private firms, as was pointed out by Benjamin Ross, 'give
much more weight [than government procurement agencies] to past experience, and put a high value on maintaining existing relationships'.[17] But
ideologists do not usually know how real firms behave in real markets.

INCOME DIFFERENTIALS

Is there such a thing as 'excessive' income differentials? Or does the
market, left to itself, resolve the question? Hayek was always contemptu-
ous of any attempt to devise 'fair' income scales, since he (very
reasonably) argued that general agreement can never be expected about

what is fair and just. In the former USSR it was claimed that income was graded 'in accordance with work', but no objective criteria existed. If bus drivers received double the pay of medical doctors, this was not a consequence of any theory about differentials.

In Western countries progressive rates of income tax, and also inheritance tax, represent the view that the state does have a redistributive role. There is something to be learned from the counterproductive nature of excessively high marginal rates of tax on the wealthy (for example, 90 per cent), which provide a powerful incentive for concealment and evasion, though without accepting the so-called Laffer curve, popular in the early Reagan years, which purported to show that lower taxes would actually increase revenue, both directly and as a result of the greater incentives for the rich to become richer. This illusory notion made its contribution to the record budget deficits. The ex-communist countries have much to learn about taxation; income tax was low, and in some countries, such as Hungary, all but non-existent. There was no experience with value-added tax. Little was written about incidence of taxation, and for many years (for example, in the USSR) rates of turnover tax were a state secret. Tax evasion is a problem everywhere, and in arguing against any progressive rate of income tax, Kornai gives as one of his reasons the ability of Hungarians to avoid payment. But his principal argument is that potential entrepreneurs should have every encouragement for personal enrichment, reversing what he regards as excessive commitment to egalitarianism. Similar voices are being heard in Russia. It may well be that, after a long period in which 'business' was a dirty word, and entrepreneurship a tender plant in need of nurturing and encouragement, that low taxes, or even tax holidays, are justifiable. However, in all these countries, in the most recent years income differentials have soared, at a time when ordinary citizens live in real poverty, while at the same time various welfare benefits (for example, cheap crèches, subsidised holiday houses and the like, and most medical services) are being drastically cut back. Hard though it is to define or to measure, there does seem to be an almost militant denial of social justice, perhaps only possible because in none of these countries was the demise of communism followed by the creation of any sort of Labour or social-democratic party with roots in the working class.

An interesting example of a tax destroyed by hostile public reaction is the so-called poll tax in Britain. It was a head tax, which replaced the rates (that is, a property tax) as the basis of local government finance. Though the very poor were partially exempt, the effect was that, for example, a lord in his castle, or I in a smart and large house, paid the same as someone living in a bed-sitting-room in a run-down housing estate. I believe that Mrs Thatcher's objective was not to redistribute income from the poor to the rich, but rather to control expenditures by local authorities, since any of their expenditures would fall disproportionately on those least able to pay, who might (she thought) even vote Conservative in local elections. But so regressive a tax proved impossible to defend, and it was abandoned. This shows that a residual sense of social justice does exist, and tax laws (and tax theory) ignore it at their peril.

The ex-Soviet economists will be observing that the gap between rich and poor has notably widened in many Western countries, above all in the United States. Evidence has already been cited about the most incredible scale of increases in the incomes of chief executives out of all proportion to efficiency, profitability, or the income levels of their own employees. They should wish to inquire into the reasons, which are by no means clear, and certainly have nothing to do with marginal productivity. The lower pay of much more successful Japanese chief executives was much commented upon in the United States on the occasion of President Bush's ill-fated visit to Tokyo. And the level of personal savings in Japan is very much higher. ('Greed' has had a bad press after Reagan's departure, but what is the difference between greed and individual profit maximisation?)

In Britain too, the effect of policies has been to create a socially dangerous gap, with a frustrated underclass ready to launch into a British equivalent of the Los Angeles riots. All this is not an argument for state regulation of incomes, but suggests two thoughts: one is that it is not the task of economists (*pace* Kornai) to press for and justify greater income inequalities, and the other that redistributive progressive taxation (though not at counterproductively high marginal rates) can be rationally justified.

CONCLUSION

In a comment on contemporary mainstream economics, R. Kuttner wrote: 'orthodox theory has ignored the crucial variables of worker motivation and labour–management interaction'. Work on the subject, wrote Kuttner, is dismissed with such words as: 'That's very interesting – but it isn't economics'.[18] One is inclined (with Kuttner) to reply: 'Oh yes it is'. All the matters touched on in the present chapter are concerned with men and women about 'the ordinary business of life', which affect economic performance, efficiency, its measurement and its stimulation. It may be objected to, but health also affects performance and efficiency, but medicine is not economics. We can argue about disciplinary boundaries, but if there is a subject called 'economics of labour', one cannot exclude the sort of problems discussed here, even if they do not fit easily within the neoclassical paradigms. They most certainly matter greatly to economic policy-makers, in east and west alike.

NOTES

1. K. Denny and S. Nickell, 'Unions and Investment in British Industry', *Economic Journal*, **102**(4), 1992, pp. 874–87.
2. See, M. Weitzman, *The Slave Economy* (Harvard University Press, 1984) and the critical comments by K.W. Rothschild, 'Is there a Weitzman miracle?', in *Employment, Wages and Income Distribution. Critical Essays in Economics* (Routledge, 1993), pp. 173–84.
3. 'Boulding, Kenneth E. (born 1910)' in P. Arestis and M. Sawyer (eds), *A Biographical Dictionary of Dissenting Economists* (Edward Elgar, 1992), p. 51.
4. K. Rothschild, 'Alternative dimensions in the theory of wages', in *Employment, Wages and Income Distribution*, pp. 78–84.
5. Ibid., p. 89.
6. Martin Woollacott, 'Our world at risk as free trade goes into free fall', *The Guardian*, 16 June 1993, p. 16.
7. J.L. Nicholson, 'Rationing and Index Numbers', *Review of Economic Studies*, **10**, 1942–3, pp. 68–72, discusses some of these issues.
8. L. Dwight Israelsen, 'Collectives, Communes, and Incentives', *Journal of Comparative Economics*, **4**(2), 1980, pp. 99–124.
9. See, for example, John E. Roemer, *A General Theory of Exploitation and Class* (Harvard University Press, 1982).
10. H. Boss, *Theories of Surplus and Transfer* (Unwin Hyman, 1990).
11. O. Morgenstern, *On the Accuracy of Economic Observations* (Princeton University Press, 1963).
12. Margaret Coles, 'Goodbye jobs for life, hello networkers', *Observer* (Business), 30 January 1994, p. 8.
13. P. Smith, 'Outcome-related Performance Indicators and Organizational Control in the Public Sector', *British Journal of Management*, **4**, 1993, pp. 135–51, and not in an *economics* publication.
14. N. Shmelev, 'Avansy i dolgi', *Novyi mir*, No. 6, 1987, p. 144.
15. M. Weitzman and C. Xu, 'Vaguely defined Cooperatives and Cooperative Culture: A Reconciliation of a Paradoxical Phenomenon in Transitional Economies', in A. Nove and I.D. Thatcher (eds), *Markets and Socialism* (Edward Elgar, 1994), pp. 538–51.
16. Dennis C. Mueller, 'The corporation and the economist', *Economics Alert*, No. 3, May 1993, p. 3.
17. Benjamin Ross, 'What is Competition For?', *Challenge*, March–April 1988, p. 47.
18. Robert Kuttner, 'The Poverty of Economics', *The Atlantic Monthly*, February 1985, p. 80.

9. Competition, privatisation and public-sector efficiency criteria

'What is competition for?' This was the title of an article by a practical businessman. It is not a question usually approached in this way in the textbooks. But it is directly relevant both to what ought to be the concern of the public sector, already discussed at length in an earlier chapter, and to the criteria by which performance in that sector should be judged.

Let me begin by challenging a view long common among Marxists, who contrasted the competitive struggle with cooperation in an imaginary socialist commonwealth. I sought, in my *Economics of Feasible Socialism*, to show that this view is misleading. The converse of competition is not cooperation, the converse of competition is monopoly. Both consumer choice and producer choice very frequently require or imply competition. Suppose there is only one provider of a good or service, be this sausages, skirts, TV sets, dry-cleaning, travel agents, car repairs or tractors. If there is to be user choice, there should be several providers. Actual or potential producers of these or other goods and services should be free to provide them if the need for them exists, and this can normally be measured *ex post* by the profitability criterion. Naturally, decisions take time to be implemented, and errors arise because, *ex ante*, the would-be entrepreneur can have guessed wrong about demand, future prices of inputs and the behaviour of competitors. Hence bankruptcies do and must occur. While bankruptcies, like divorce, can be regarded as 'bads', they must be accepted as a consequence of free choice of business activity or of partners. The alternative, compulsory attachment to one supplier or partner, is worse. As I had argued in that book, socialists must recognise that a ban on all competitive private enterprise requires the eternal vigilance of 'socialist' police. And, in the Soviet Union, it was so for decades: the man or woman who sought to supplement the inefficient trade network by buying apples where they were cheap and plentiful and selling them where they were scarce was 'rewarded' with several years in a labour camp.

On an individual level too, there is competition to get into prestigious educational institutions, or to receive a research grant, or to be elected to parliament, or to be promoted within any profession or occupation.

Authors can repeat, with Hilaire Belloc, the desire that 'When I die, I hope it may be said/My sins were scarlet, but my books were read.'

However, let us delimit forms of competition, even in areas where it is evidently rational and necessary. One relates to 'dirty tricks', or 'cut-throat' methods. Examples: British Airways endeavoured to destabilise or bankrupt two airlines by ways which may land the firm in expensive legal proceedings. Football (soccer) is a competitive sport of its nature, but breaking the legs of the cleverest opposing player is improper. Similarly, a case was reported of a student deliberately damaging a fellow-student's experiment during competitive examinations for entry into medical school. The Mafia eliminates competition by eliminating the competitor ('cut-throat' taken literally). Adam Smith would agree that a moral code is necessary.

Contrasting with such extreme cases are instances of competitors engaging in limited forms of collaboration. The logic of these can be and has been illustrated formally in contrasting cooperative and non-cooperative games. There are a wide variety of such instances met with in real life, which are worth examining with care. To take a few individual instances of combinations of competition and cooperation, two violin players in an orchestra may both be seeking promotion to the top desk, but continue to play in harmony (or unison!). Two schools in the same area, or two departments in the same university, are or can be collabora-tive rivals. There are also instances where firms in the same industry find it pays to collaborate. This could, of course, take the form of conspiracy against the public, through cartel-like agreements to limit output and keep prices high, justifying a reference to a Monopolies Commission. One thinks also of OPEC. It is appropriate to regard such arrangements as likely to distort the market and to constitute prima facie evidence of inefficiency. However, there are counterexamples. Thus the 'Airbus' plane is the joint product (both in the R&D and in the production phases) of several European aircraft firms. This is explained both by economies of scale and the need to spread the cost and risks of R&D. There are other 'high tech' instances. William Baumol has shown that there are circum-stances in which this departure from the standard competitive model would be rational.[1] Discussing 'incentives to develop new products', Suzanne Sotchmer spoke of competition which could 'undermine origi-nal innovators' profits . . . and hence undermine incentives to innovation', while Michael Culinat spoke of 'clusters of firms to master new technolo-gies and share know-how'; 'a ban on state aid would have catastrophic consequences for Europe's high tech. industries'.[2] Here it would seem that departures from 'mainstream' assumptions are essential. Even today believers in competition *à l'outrance* argue in Brussels against various joint European arrangements, and it took until May 1993 for the British government to appreciate the need for a science policy, which was ideologically excluded in the Thatcher years when laissez-faire advice had a monopoly of access to ministerial ears.

Economies of scale can take a number of forms. Thus Viktor Keegan has alleged that 'Britain is being denied the revolutionary power of fibre-optic communication by political dogma'. Government ideology stresses the virtues of competition and so British Telecom is being prevented from achieving the degree of market dominance which alone would justify the large investments required.

> In Japan and the US industrial strategy is *object* driven. They decide what they want (a national optical fibre grid) and then decide the best way to achieve it. If competition is the best way to achieve it, then, fine. But if it isn't, they don't shirk from alternatives. The important thing for the British government is that whatever happens is decided by market forces and done by the private sector. But the method is the madness if it leads inevitably to a patchwork approach using the wrong technology.[3]

Far be it from me to claim that Keegan's views are unchallenged. My point – as so often in this book – is that neoclassical mainstream either cannot focus on this kind of problem, or predisposes to the fragmented market solution, or both. It is not good at economies of scale, or, as we have seen, in analysing the preconditions for rational investment decisions.

Similar problems arise with public transport. Already in an earlier chapter I sought to show why in most countries it is regarded as a public-sector activity, and why it should be subsidised. British residents who seldom use public transport may be unaware of the truly striking contrast between Great Britain and other countries, as regards both quality and cost. To cite two examples from my recent experience, the first class fare from Glasgow to Swindon, a distance of about 460 miles, cost far more than a first-class ticket from Paris to Florence, a distance of over 700 miles. In New York, San Francisco, Boston, Montreal, and *every* European conurbation, passengers pay two or three times less per journey than in London for similar distances. Freight is being priced off British Rail and onto even narrower Scottish Highland roads, because of a policy which disregards externalities; indeed the 'policy' is one of not having a transport policy at all. More will be said about the whole issue of externalities later. In the present context, the question to be discussed is the pros and cons of competition. British ideologists have already disrupted urban transportation networks, and are about to do the same to the rail network, and their advisers claim orthodox economic theory as justification. Competitiveness in the market-place must deliver efficiency.

So it is appropriate to ask: why is there no competition (other than with private cars, of course) in virtually every US, Canadian and European city, regardless of the political colouring of the national or municipal government? The reasons are so compelling, once one removes ideological blinkers, that one is at a loss to find a rational explanation for British policy. Does neoclassical economics predispose to just this sort of myopia? In every other country, a local transport authority plans the network, and considers whether to build a metro or electrify suburban rail lines, how many buses to run, up to what hours, ensures connections or feeder services, subject to financial constraints. There is a subsidy, for reasons already explored, and the subsidy is paid to the *network*, which establishes long-term links with suppliers of transport equipment. There is system-wide timetabling, and tickets are interavailable. Because a major objective is to reduce congestion, most systems issue cheap commuter tickets (cartes orange, and so on), which, as already pointed out, have two advantages. One is that the marginal cost of each journey becomes zero, which helps to wean users from their cars. The other is that there is economy in ticket issuing and one can dispense with conductors and not hold up the driver. Economy in accountancy is also significant. Specific segments of the system (for example, bus No. 63, or the green metro line, or whatever) are evaluated in the context of the system as a whole, no one buys tickets separately for that bus or line, tickets cover the system, or zones within it. All this is readily understood everywhere, from Montreal to Munich, from Barcelona to Boston. One can add that in most of the world there is a constitution, which does not exist in Britain. This helps to explain that an ideological British government can order the cities of Glasgow and Manchester to privatise and fragment their services in the name of competition, whereas Washington or Bonn could not issue such orders to Boston or Hamburg. (Not that they would be so foolish. And anyhow, Washington itself has a *public* transport monopoly, DC Transit.)

What are the advantages claimed for competition? In some instances one object is to weaken the trade unions, which could have succeeded in demanding overmanning and high wages. The British government has repeatedly expressed its hostility to unions and its belief in low wages as a stimulus to inward investment and to higher employment. But above all its policies reflect the naive textbook: if there is demand for a service it can be profitably provided, competitors will stimulate efficiency, there is no need for a local transport authority. Bus No. 63 can be seen as a separate profit-orientated firm. This is how things are run in some Latin-American countries, for instance in Santiago, Chile. In La Paz, Bolivia, I once saw bus No. 13 labelled 'for sale'.

Why does theory predispose to copy La Paz and not Europe and North America? To some extent I have dealt with this question in an earlier chapter. However, it may be worth showing how the thought-processes of orthodox economists, long before the advent of Mrs Thatcher and her ideologists, prepared the ground. I pointed this out over 20 years ago, and so, with apologies to the readers for so doing, would like to quote myself.

First, I found highly questionable the doctrines expounded by the then influential economist, the late Denis Munby. Speaking to the Select Committee on Nationalised Industries, he *blamed* (!!) the London Transport Authority for 'following a policy which is explicitly stated in their Annual Reports of what they call a "social contract" with Londoners, which I think makes no economic or social sense at all'. In other words, efficiency must be detached from *purpose*. If there is to be a transport authority, then surely its management should be motivated to provide the best possible service to the citizenry, and be worried (see themselves as 'inefficient') if buses or trains are uncomfortably packed or passengers have a long wait in the rain. A 'social contract' is precisely what *does* make 'social and economic sense'. This is surely how the senior managers of the San Francisco 'muni' or of Paris Regional Transport see their role, and rightly so.

A general point needs to be stressed: if anything is in the public sector for reasons other than left-wing ideology, then this must be because normal commercial criteria do not or should not apply, either because it is a natural monopoly or because of prevalence of externalities, or because of some overriding social purpose. If none of these are present, there would be no reason for the activity to be in the public sector. It could be privatised without any ill-effects. If the BBC's efficiency criteria were the same as those of the commercial TV stations, why have a BBC? Therefore Christopher Foster was wrong in arguing that nationalised industries 'should be fully commercial operations' with objectives 'no different from the main objective of private industry'.[4] Munby's view of how London's transport undertaking should operate requires it 'to say which services pay for themselves, which are the services which do not pay for themselves, where are the losses', and 'if the Greater London Council do not like the consequences . . . then the question comes: how do you subsidise this particular thing?' (the Greater London Council was subsequently abolished by Mrs Thatcher). He specifically wished to *remove* social obligation from the criteria of management, though it is surely the case that it is management that has the clearest view of alternatives, of the costs and benefits for the system. He was plainly opposed to subsidising the *system*, as distinct from specific loss-making routes.

Munby took the same view with regard to the railways: he wished as far as possible to compute separately the revenue–cost relationship of every segment of line, junction, station,[5] that is, to externalise internalities! I commented at the time:

> What is the point of having a municipal (or any other) bus monopoly other than for the provision of a system of transport? The logic of the dominant 'school' (say Alan Day or Denis Munby) is to disassemble the system, to operate only the profitable parts, and to suspend any route or service unless specifically subsidised . . . What, then, is left of the system? Why not make every bus a separate limited company, run for its own profit?[6]

Deregulated and privatised Manchester is said to have 70 bus companies operating. London is about to be deregulated too, so that there will be no coherent system at all, with no overall responsibility for London's transport. A recipe for chaos, surely, in the name of competition.

It is worth taking the opposite example, Switzerland. The Swiss railways run regular hourly services between all the principal cities, with no competing buses, and probably the large majority of Swiss would agree that this is the best way of keeping costs per passenger-mile low. There is, of course, a system-wide subsidy – though some believe that it is too high. Buses connect with trains and carry mail, and school children, to places not served by trains. Lake boats are run wherever local plus tourist needs justify it, and it makes no sense to the hard-headed Swiss to have competing boats between any two points. As I remarked in a paper presented at Lausanne University, where Walras had taught, it would surely not have occurred to him to condemn these arrangements. But those trained in Walrasian economics differ in this respect from their master. The problem is that Walrasian methodology predisposes to fragmentation.

It would also seem clear, from experience as well as common sense, that responsibility for complementary services makes their provision more likely. Thus in France and Germany, as well as Switzerland, connecting buses connect, since the railway either operates the services or hires a subcontractor. The connection is timed to do so, the bus leaves from the station, and the timetable provides the needed information, whereas in Britain this would be exceptional. More usual is the situation in (for example) Oxford and in Perth, where the bus station is distant from the railway, and the railway inquiry office does not have the bus timetables. Again, received theory does not handle well the issue of complementarities. The market, so it is thought, would automatically provide. British experience abundantly proves the contrary in respect of public transport.

The disruption of a network is taken to its logical conclusion in Great Britain by the Railways Act of 1993. In terms of ownership, responsibility and management, track is separated from trains, passengers from freight, trains and track from stations, trains from each other. A 'franchising' authority would entitle specific private entrepreneurs to run trains in competition with each other, on tracks still publicly owned. Incredibly, the minister expressed the belief that there would be a saving on 'bureau-cracy'. In other words, there are no administrative economies of scale, it is assumed without argument that 50 firms operating trains must have fewer 'bureaucrats' sitting at desks and lower transaction costs than does one such authority. Criticism in the press has concentrated on side issues such as reduced fares for pensioners; little has been said about the effect of destroying the system itself, the effect on connections to smaller towns (who would seek profit from serving places like Grimsby, Huddersfield, Halifax, Blackburn, not to mention rural areas), the effect on the subsidy bill of eliminating cross-subsidies which, despite the efforts of the ideologists, still survived, as they must within *any* network of interrelated activities. The predictable effect will be a combination of much higher fares, line closures *and* higher subsidy bills. Profitable modern trains will run from London to Birmingham, to Edinburgh, to Bristol. Much of the rest of the network will wither, with no incentive to invest or to modernise.

There are other principles involved here. One is managerial motiva-tion in non-profit organisations, whether or not these are in the public sector. There is danger here of uncritically following Tullock and Buchanan and assuming that public officials are just individual utility-maximisers with no commitment to quality of performance. French transport operators are proud of the TGVs, of their speed and punctual-ity, and in seeking to modernise the remaining lines they show a commitment to their job. If a subsidy is held to lead to inefficiency, then what of services that are provided free, such as shuttle-buses at airports? Not enough attention is paid to the motivation of more junior person-nel, on whose commitment much depends in any organisation, public, private, military. They seldom can observe, at their level, the profitability of any act or omission. Quality of performance is affected by the atti-tude of the performers. Supervision there must be, but who supervises the supervisors? This affects not only transport.

Water presents another set of problems. This is an evident natural monopoly. Its privatisation in Britain was due almost exclusively to ideol-ogy. The immediate effect was the doubling of salaries of top management, higher charges and a steep rise in disconnections for non-payment of these charges, creating a health hazard. It is true that part of the increase in charges was due to the need to cope with arrears of capital expenditure, to bring quality up to EEC-imposed standards. These arrears had built up in part because of government restriction on public spending, that is, to keep down the Public Sector Borrowing Requirement (PSBR). This in turn raises two related questions, which I will not pursue further here. One is the questionable practice of conflating public current and capital expenditure. The other is the odd belief that a given item of capital expenditure (for example, on water, or docks, or airports, or prisons, or roads) becomes somehow kosher once it can be shifted into the private sector. Yet, *ceteris paribus*, the effects on the real economy are surely identical, whoever actually owns the water, the docks, the airport or the prison. (Privatised prison construction is now a reality in ideology-driven Britain, while public-sector jails built in Victoria's reign are starved of funds.)

However, back to water. It may be recalled that the origins of public water provision, dating back to the Victorian era, were intimately connected with public health, the avoidance of epidemics. Every town-dweller, so it was believed, is entitled to the supply of clean water, and payment (in Britain at least) was through a charge which was related to the value of the property, and thus was a form of progressive (local) taxation, the so-called water-rates. Charges were unrelated to the quantity of water used. If there was a prolonged drought, administrative measures (for example, a ban on hosepipes for gardens) and not market-and-price forces were resorted to.

One recalls an incident in Brazil. A poor neighbourhood drew its water from polluted wells. So the local authority spent a sum to provide pure running water. However, it may have employed the sort of economic advisers who separated efficiency from purpose, and believed that everything should 'pay' and that subsidies were evidence of misallocation. The poor found that they could not afford the charges, and continued to use the polluted wells.

In Britain more and more water companies are proposing metering, that is, charges by quantity of water used. This is bound to have several significant effects. One is to turn progressive into regressive charges. A poor woman with two small children will use more water than (for example) I do, in my much larger house. The switch from water-rates to metering will redistribute from poor to rich in much the same way (though not to the same extent) as did the poll tax. Second, it will achieve economy in the use of water by the poor, who will soon realise that each time they have a bath or even flush the toilet their bill goes up. In most instances we should encourage economy, but is this an appropriate instance?

Where water supply is an important practical problem, such as in California, even right-wing republican governors see it as a major public-sector responsibility.

And finally, if one compares a situation where local taxes just cover the cost with one in which a private firm aims at profit, *ceteris paribus* the charge to the customer will be higher by the size of the profit margin. True believers will assert that privatisation will result in larger efficiency gain and in lower costs. Such a possibility cannot be excluded, but neither can it be assumed.

Different issues arise with electricity. In my own earlier work I treated it as a monopoly *par excellence*. It is also an example of a totally homogenous commodity. Kilowatt-hours do not vary in colour, size or model. Electricity is used by every firm and by every household. It is supplied via a national grid. Technically it is possible to envisage its generation being controlled from one centrally-located control room. The centre can be aware of the total available generating capacity, it then has the duty of ensuring that reserve capacity is available to deal with abnormal temperatures, or in case of accidents. It has the duty of estimating future demand, and taking investment decisions to ensure that capacity is sufficient to meet it. Electricity generation is thus plannable; and the centralised Soviet system was able to cope with planning it. There were, there as elsewhere, problems of choice between alternative investment projects: thermal (using gas or coal), hydro, nuclear, large or small generating plant. But the additional capacity required was estimated through a sort of future-orientated input–output table. For other reasons energy tended to be wastefully used in the Soviet Union, but generation and distribution were handled adequately by a system which in many respects resembled a Western public monopoly, such as Electricité de France.

Electricity was privatised in Great Britain, and the regulator appointed by the government was an ideologist who believed in competition. There emerged two large generator companies, separated organisationally from the grid and from distributors. The latter had monopoly over distribution to households, but industrial users could negotiate for supplies via the grid from any generator. They, and the distributors, could set up their own generating plant, or buy from a 'pool'.

It is too soon to judge the total effects of privatisation. However, the following check-list seems relevant.

1. No one is now responsible for estimating total future demand and relating it to installed generating capacity. This, as already noted, could have led to underinvestment. In fact it led to overinvestment, to excess capacity. The reasons were well set out by David Newbry, who spoke of 'considerable unnecessary investment in new capacity'.[7]
2. There is not any energy policy at all. Its absence will not be noted by neoclassical orthodoxy, since the subject falls into the gap separating

micro from macro, which leaves a gap for laissez-faire extremism to enter, and to convince Mrs Thatcher and her ministers that the state need not interfere with market forces in energy as in anything else.

3. There was the so-called 'rush for gas', when the regional electricity distributors, anxious to reduce their dependence on the two large generating companies, built their own power stations. The effect on the demand for coal, the long-term effect on the balance of payments, the possible exhaustion of North Sea gas supplies and its consequences, was not their concern. If gas prices rise, they would still recoup their profits since they have a local monopoly in supplying residents in their area.

4. The former Central Electricity Generating Board had set up a research department, which contributed to technological advances. This has been abolished and scientists made redundant, since no one company in the fragmented industry finds it would pay them to maintain such an establishment.

5. There was a sizeable increase in transaction costs, which no one has even tried to measure. Just how complex the 'transaction' structure is has been well set out by A. Powell.[8]

6. Damage has been done to major industrial users of electricity, notably the chemical industry. It is in the interests of none of the existing generators to renew the special arrangements which had been made with ICI, with the result that energy-intensive chemical production is being phased out. This may or may not be an economically rational outcome. It would be important to know the amount charged for electricity to competitors in other countries. But such considerations would not fall within the remit of the (ideologically committed) regulator or in the balance sheet of the generating companies.

It is relevant to the issue of the advantages and limitations of competition to compare electricity with gas, the latter still a (regulated) monopoly. Pressure has been exerted to break it up, but it has (so far) been resisted, for what appear to be cogent reasons. Gas, like electricity, is 'transported' by an interlinked network. Most if its users face what for them is a monopoly supplier. But to lay competing gas-pipes in the same street is plainly wasteful, and economies of scale (plus simplicity in transactions) argue against change. This highlights the importance of distinguishing between privatisation and disintegration/fragmentation. One does not need imply the other.

Also it does not follow that the public sector itself cannot be subject to competition. Thus before privatisation nationalised gas competed with nationalised electricity and (privately-owned) oil in the domestic heating market. Even in Soviet Russia, publicly-owned theatres and literary journals competed with one another. It would have been possible to encourage competition between state shops and restaurants, with penalties for failure to attract customers, if only there had not been chronic shortage. Clearly, if prices are set at a level at which demand exceeds supply, all the characteristics of a sellers' market must appear: a take-it-or-leave-it attitude to customers and lack of concern for customer preferences.

There is a sizeable literature on the question of economic criteria of performance of publicly-owned or regulated enterprises. There are basic contradictions which cannot be satisfactorily resolved in the nature of things. It is precisely because the untrammelled pursuit of profit is known to lead to 'inefficient' outcomes that public ownership, or regulation of private owners, exists in the first place. What, then, is the appropriate criterion of operational efficiency? Thus managers of British formerly nationalised industries used to complain that control over their prices, and/or imposition of specific objectives by ministers, had an adverse effect on their finances and could (sometimes did) result in losses which were in no way due to inefficiency. Since privatisation there has been criticism of the regulators for permitting a very large increase in profits, due (it is alleged) to abuse of monopoly power, and at the time of writing the Labour party is proposing a 'tax on windfall profits' of the privatised utilities. There could be conflict between profitability and purpose: thus a public transport undertaking could find it financially advantageous to pack the passengers in like sardines, and the Post Office to close rural offices and have fewer collections and deliveries in remote areas. Duties, and performance indicators, could be imposed, seeking to tie up efficiency with purpose. Thus both the public and the private sector could (do) have franchises, specifying conditions. Thus an airport could hire a catering firm to provide meals, and the terms could include hours of opening and some limitation on prices charged.

Franchises are, so to speak, second cousins to the subcontractor. It is odd how seldom the subcontractor is mentioned in microeconomic textbooks. Even Oliver Williamson, who focuses on the relative role of markets and hierarchies, seems to me to blur the distinction between a firm purchasing a good or service and subcontracting a segment of a *process* of production. In the latter case, the activity is under control, it decides what is to be done and how. A building firm, for instance, could buy paints or bricks, or hire another firm to do the painting or lay the bricks, to precise specifications it determines. Of course the subcontractor can negotiate terms and can turn down the offer. And the principal may prefer, for reasons well analysed by Williamson, to have its own employees do the work ('hierarchy').

NOTES

1. See W.J. Baumol, 'Horizontal Collusion and Innovation', *Economic Journal*, **102**(1), 1992, pp. 129–37.
2. *Bulletin of the Centre for Economic Policy Research*, April–June 1992, pp. 3, 4.
3. Viktor Keegan, 'Through a glass fibre darkly', *Guardian*, 22 May 1993, p. 26.
4. C. Foster, *Public Enterprise* (Fabian Society [sic], 1972).
5. *Cahiere de l'ISEA*, No. 130, 1962, p. 52.
6. A. Nove, *Efficiency Criteria for Nationalised Industries* (George Allen & Unwin, 1973), p. 31.
7. *CFSR Bulletin*, April–June 1992, p. 3.
8. A. Powell, 'Trading Forward in an Imperfect Market: The Case of Electricity in Britain', *Economic Journal*, **103**(2), 1993, pp. 444–53.

PART II

Markets and Socialism: Against Dogmatism

10. Political and polemical letters

To Lord Ralph Harris of High Cross, 1 December 1986, Glasgow

Dear Ralph,

Many thanks for your note and enclosures. I really do wish that a good debate could be organised. I feel that you and your Institute have really lost their way, that what was (and in the rest of the world *is*) regarded as common sense has been obscured by ideology.

First, the obvious, though admittedly not conclusive, point. In New York, Boston, Pittsburgh, Washington, Chicago, Philadelphia, San Francisco, even in Santa Monica (where I was last week), in every Canadian city, in every West German and French city, urban public transport is run as a system by a public authority. The governments, central and local, in these countries are not left wing, indeed by any reasonable standard must be regarded as conservative. I know of no serious proposal in any of these countries (or in Italy, Belgium, Scandinavia, Spain, etc. etc.) to eliminate the conurbations' transport authorities and have a free-for-all. We must not confuse two issues: the network or system aspect, and privatisation. While it is no accident that DC Transit happens to be public, it is not absurd to conceive of the District of Columbia subcontracting (enfranchising, subsidising as necessary) a private firm, DC Transit Inc., to run the system. What Mr Ridley and his fanatical ideologists (you too? surely not!!) would propose for Washington is the *destruction of DC Transit as a system*.

Do you really not see the difference between one rural route and an urban network? Apparently it is necessary to spell it out. Suppose the question arises of running a bus or minibus from (say) Howards Heath to a Sussex village, say West Hoathly. It can be separately costed, separately run, separately subsidised if necessary. Exactly this was done (often in conjunction with the Post Office and the education authority) for some rural services in Strathclyde. This (Labour!) local authority hired literally dozens of small private contractors to run the needed services, varying in size from a bus to a Land-Rover. But, say, Glasgow (like Washington, Toronto, Lyon, Munich, etc. etc. etc.) raise quite other questions, e.g.:

165

1. Congestion. Glasgow streets are jammed by competing buses. Also a major task of public transport is everywhere seen as providing an alternative to private cars. Hence subsidy. Another reason for subsidy is the effect of rapid-transit on property values, including the property of those who do not use public transport. This is taken for granted in Washington, Munich, Paris, etc. etc. etc. Does it really need to be spelt out? Does the fact that orthodox textbooks tend to neglect externalities entitle us to assume that they do not exist? Would you scrap the Washington metro and the NY subway because they do not pay as such?

2. Ticket interavailability. In all the conurbations known to me, they issue Cartes Orange, Capitalcards, tokens, etc. etc., valid on all modes of transport and at an attractive price. This is partly to attract people away from going to work by car (see congestion), partly to simplify life for passengers, drivers (no conductors needed), accounts. It also means that you can take whatever bus first comes and not (if you missed it) have to wait until one comes of the same colour of your ticket. Of course tickets cannot be interavailable if fares are different. And if they are not different then where is the competition?

3. 'Cross-subsidisation', or payments of subsidies to the network. Simple question. Can you, can anyone, meaningfully identify the separate profitability of a segment of an interconnected whole, other than by reference to the whole? One has connections, feeder services, a multitude of complementarities and indivisibilities. If one has any standard fare by zone or by distance, some services and times are bound to 'cross-subsidise' others, since revenues per passenger mile will differ widely. If it costs roughly the same to operate a train from Colindale to Edgware as from Charing Cross to Euston, and if there are four times as many passengers in the latter than in the former segment, then the latter cross-subsidises the former, unless the charge per mile is several times higher for the last stations on the line. Of course that would be nonsense. But equally nonsensical is to treat every bus, or service No. 134, or the line from Tooting to Morden, as the subject of a separate calculation and a separate subsidy. In every conurbation in the world, the subsidy, if any, is paid to the system, and this provides the financial constraint within which the system is planned.

4. I think I can pinpoint the theoretical error. Brian Loasby defined it as follows: 'Highly complex sub-systems, containing within themselves many layers of great complexity, are regularly treated as simple elements, while components of a complex system are treated as isolated units.' This really has nothing to do with public versus private. It is what I call 'myopic marginalism'. Any firm is a hierarchy. Marginal decisions are also very frequently hierarchical, in the sense of being

within other more general decisions, contexts, strategies. For example, the transport departments of Guinness or McEwans do not pursue independently their own separate profitability; their activities, their criteria of efficiency, are subordinated to the task of the profit-pursuit of their company. Were the micro-profitability of every beer-carrying lorry necessarily consistent with the profitability of their hierarchical superiors, the firm would not have a transport department! Do you really not see this? (Yes, as an alternative they could hire the services of another firm, but then the sub-contractor would be acting on the direction of the principal.)

5. John Hibbs, for whom everything is so simple (the practices of every city in the western world are just simply wrong! What self-confidence!!) quite misses the point on investment, and certainly has not read the work of G.B. Richardson. Yes, of course, buses call for much smaller investments than do railways (notably underground railways in cities). But just take the Washington metro. It makes sense to invest in it if it is seen as part of Washington transport strategy, to reduce congestion, to link the new metro stations with feeder services. To have competing buses run parallel to the line and into the city centre (thereby both increasing congestion and decreasing revenue) negates the whole purpose of the scheme. The same goes for R.E.R. lines to the Paris suburbs. Think of the effect of the proposed 'light-railway' extension to London's dockland on property values! Need I go on . . . ('Playing trains' indeed!!).

6. In Glasgow, thanks to the free-for-all, we now have no timetables – as to publish one would be to invite the opposition to run a bus from this or that suburb a minute before the announced time. Suburban railways have gained some revenue because at least some people know when trains run . . . The number of buses trying to negotiate the main business streets at rush hours has brought traffic to a halt. *Now no one is responsible* for the transport system as a whole, for information, planning (dirty word?) . . . Come on, Mr Hibbs, propose the destruction of London Transport too. Even Mr Ridley, possibly because he lives in London, would move next business . . . And is even John Hibbs happy with the congestion around Victoria coach station?

And so forth. This is not my proposed contribution to a discussion, this is just me sitting at a typewriter (and committing typing errors!). What about a place for an argument? Also when? (I am teaching in California for four months as from 5 January).

Best Regards. Sincerely.

To Lord Roy Jenkins of Hillhead, 4 January 1987, Glasgow

Dear Roy,

In common with many others, I am dismayed at the prospect of more Thatcher, which might happen, alas, if Kinnock is seen as the only alternative. How vital it is for the Alliance to make a better showing! How puzzling that things look so much worse for it than a year ago. Though I am sure I am preaching to the converted, may I just set out a few points which it should be possible for the Alliance to get across to a larger portion of the electorate?

1. The sometimes incredible unsoundness of the government's economic policy. Did you read Maurice Peston in today's *Observer*? *What* is going on is a totally cynical process of buying votes with a consumer boom, expended credit, promised tax cuts, the misuse of the proceeds of privatisation (bribing the electorate with their own money). Meanwhile nothing is done to stimulate productive investment (our interest rates are probably the highest in the world in real terms), so that the boom sucks in imports on a massive scale, preparing us for a balance of payments crisis.

2. Furthermore, the use of the proceeds of the sales of public assets as a basis for tax cuts, instead of financing much needed investments, means that within a very short period any Chancellor will face the painful choice of raising taxes or drastically cutting public spending.

3. This may be part of the strategy. People like Ridley and his advisers, all the right-wing think-tanks such as the 'Adam Smith' society (poor Adam Smith. *He* understood about infrastructure, education, etc.!), are devoted to the task of dismantling public services, the NHS, privatising by fiat the bulk of what is now done by local government. The public can be made to realise that very serious damage will be done to public services, *without* any corresponding help to the productive sectors of our economy which the government shamefully neglects in the name of laissez faire.

4. Ideology and political spite dominates attitudes to local government and local services. Hence the absurd abolition of elected authorities for greater London, Manchester, etc., opposed by many sensible Tories. Hence the nonsense over public transport: the wrecking of urban transport systems, the phasing out of subsidies. Cannot the public be made to realise that no other civilised country does some of these things? Thus public transport networks are publicly operated in New York, Washington, Pittsburgh, Chicago, Toronto, Montreal, *every* West European city without exception. Every major airport in North America is in the public sector.

5. While manufacturing declined rapidly, the city is flourishing, with scandalous fortunes made. Capital that could be used to invest in industry and infrastructure is being diverted into the purchase of existing state assets, takeover bids, investment abroad.
6. Laissez faire ideology prevents not only any action to stimulate or save industry, or to provide employment (as distinct from training people for jobs which did not materialise), it also stands in the way of devising a regional policy, to cope with the scandalous north–south divide.

I am just off for four months to teach in California. But if, after my return, you feel it worth having a wee discussion, I would be glad of it.

Wishing you all the best for 1987.

To Quentin Davies, MP (Con), 6 July 1987, Glasgow

Dear Quentin,

In offering my congratulations on your political success, may I express my dismay about current policies, dismay *not* based on socialist ideology of any description, but one widely shared by university colleagues of every political persuasion or none. Shall I call it a combination of militant cultural philistinism and economic myopia, plus a hatred of local government bordering on the pathological (by the time Nicholas Ridley has finished destroying all their finances, who on earth, of any party, would wish to serve on any council?).

Why the deliberate campaign against universities? The latest scheme financing them puts effective end to university autonomy by fragmenting the financing process (via separate bids and contracts), apparently designed to break up the possibility of coherent university-wide policies, greatly strengthening the role of central government in determining where subjects will be taught, making nonsense of the concept of the university as a living interconnected whole. Not even the late legislature of Alabama behaves thus towards its state university! I think I see a philosophical–theoretical error here, which also manifests itself in so different a question as urban transportation. The whole is seen as only the sum of its parts and nothing else. Therefore fragmentation is seen as rational, with each 'bit' supposed to be separately evaluated on a profit-and-loss basis.

Conservative administrations in *every* country in North America and Western Europe, every city (Toronto, New York, Washington, Munich, Paris, Zurich, you name it) takes for granted the necessity of an integrated public transport system in conurbations. Only in Mrs Thatcher's Britain are orders given forbidding local authorities from operating and coordinating transport. Come to Edinburgh: visitors to the Festival will be bemused: no more system maps, no more exhibited timetables, no more notices at shops telling passengers what bus goes where, because *the system has been deliberately destroyed* on ideological grounds. Can you imagine F.-J. Strauss even contemplating disrupting the public transport of Munich?

And now there is to be a campaign against public subsidies to the arts, even while the squeeze on local authority budgets (via the truly iniquitous poll tax) will prevent them from even maintaining present modest levels of support. I know well the arguments against such subsidies put up by the IEA and the 'Adam Smith' society (poor Adam Smith! He would have taken a quite different view!). For them quality of life means nothing. If Scottish Opera cannot make ends meet, why, abolish it! Munich spends more on its opera than all of England, Jacques Chirac continues the policy of subsidising provincial music and theatre, there are non-philistine conservatives.

We need a more commercially minded competitive society? Yes, but look at some of the effects of policies. Neglect of research and the brain drain are helpful to future competitiveness? The fortunes being made in the City have nothing to do with real investment in productive capacity, though this too is intimately connected with future competitiveness. Millions are being taught how to make money without working by being offered underpriced shares in nationalised industries. Millions of pounds (I mean billions, of course) are being diverted from real investment into the purchase of already-existing assets.

Adam Smith, and also most of our competitors, realised long ago that efficient and cheap infrastructure is a precondition for the efficient and competitive operation of private business (which both uses it and makes profits building it; it is not civil servants that build new docks and roads!). Here everything is sacrificed to the obsession with cutting public expenditure. In Reagan's America many a public utility is either in the public sector (e.g., *every* airport I have ever landed in!) or, unless there is competition, requires to be regulated. Already today British Telecom have understood the simple truth that bad service pays when one is a monopolist (and the public-service principle is regarded as old hat). Long queues in post offices pay too.

And now local authorities will be ordered (not encouraged or allowed, but compelled) to put services out to contract, whether or not the existing arrangements are efficient, as they sometimes are. You have been a businessman. Would you *compel* a private firm to sub-contract what they find more convenient to do themselves (and cost is not the only consideration: there is quality, reliability, employees' goodwill). This nonsense cannot happen in America, because the Constitution prevents the federal government imposing its ideological fads on Massachusetts or Boston: they are free to decide. Here local government is being quietly murdered.

Perhaps you are a member of the House committee which has pointed to another example of myopia: the endless cuts imposed upon the British Council. I would add the huge fees charged to foreign graduate students (which is compelling universities to accept ill-qualified sons of the rich in desperate effort to stave off the effects of still more financial cuts).

Have you examined the role of Japanese public authorities, in close alliance with Japanese business, in encouraging and coordinating public investments? Here anti-planning ideology asserts that all you have to do is nothing. Industrial decline? Laissez faire, or *après moi le déluge* when oil revenues decline. Cut taxes, stimulate consumption of imported manufactures, machinery, even of virtually all supermarket equipment from counters to cash registers. Does none of this make you unhappy?

Would be glad to discuss one or two of these things with you one day. With best regards.

To Professor J. Hibbs OBE, 30 December 1988, Glasgow

Dear Professor Hibbs,
The Times reported your 'economic' remarks in the context of the Clapham train crash. This reminded me of other remarks of yours, in the context of my correspondence with Ralph Harris. I find your views so puzzling that I would be grateful for a rational explanation. *Of course* if services were not subsidised and prices charged were much higher, fewer would use the railways and there would be less overcrowding on trains. To arrive at so 'practical' a conclusion all that is needed is to abstract from the purpose of public transport, and thereby adopt an attitude unknown, to my own knowledge, in any country in the world.

Everywhere, in North America and Western Europe, with no exceptions known to me, transport in conurbations is (a) public, (b) subsidised, and (c) a coordinated network, with some sort of standard charge by zone and/or distance. This is so in Washington, San Francisco, New York, Boston, Pittsburgh, Toronto, Montreal, Paris, Amsterdam, Stockholm, Zurich, Munich, Milan, Barcelona, etc. etc. etc. The political views of the governments and local authorities in these countries differ widely. Are they *all* mistaken? When I was in Los Angeles in 1987, the state senate adopted a law to set up a (public) body to coordinate (municipal) transport in the Los Angeles conurbation by 57 votes to *zero*. *Not one* senator thought that competition, privatisation and fragmentation were the way to provide the required services. (For one thing, they remembered that, as also in New York, previously existing private provision had collapsed, which is why the services were public!)

You must know the arguments for subsidies – (though admittedly they leave unclear the desirable *level* of subsidy): the positive effect on congestion permits those who do not travel to reach their destination with less delay, *and* rapid-transit facilities have a major effect on property values; in both instances, beneficiaries include a great many who do not themselves buy tickets. Has all this no meaning to you?

If there is to be a subsidy, then surely it should be paid to the *network*, enabling management to organise the network within the financial constraints. How can one subsidise specific routes when they interconnect? 'Cross-subsidisation' is the inescapable consequence of any 'network' charge, be it a Capitalcard, Carte Orange, or whatever. Revenues and costs per mile must vary. How to apply marginal cost pricing in London? *Where is the margin?* The 13 bus? The 13 bus between Golders Green and Swiss Cottage? The 13 bus after 9 p.m.? The line between Tooting and Morden, or between Leicester Square and Euston? The *outlawing* of cross-subsidisation is simply incredible, *within* a network. It is encountered repeatedly in everyday commercial life. Thus the copy of *The Times* which printed your remarks costs the same in Thurso as in Edgbaston. So, I believe, does a pint of Younger's beer. Many supermarkets subsidise (provide free) car-parking space. Arsenal F.C. 'cross-subsidises' its reserve team. Toilet paper is free in public and private WCs. And so on. *The Times* and Younger's brewery would evaluate their transport arrangements by reference to punctuality and regularity of deliveries, and not *only* in terms of the profitability of whoever actually transports the papers or the beer! Efficiency *also* relates to purpose. If a major purpose of rail transport is to relieve road congestion, then a pricing policy which drives more people and vehicles onto the roads is not quite what the doctor ordered. Or is this elementary point so controversial that it requires proof?

Why is competition almost invariably absent in urban transportation? Because its disadvantages are judged by *everyone* (outside of the minds of Ridley and Channon) to outweigh the advantages. No one is then *responsible* for ensuring that services actually operate, there is no system timetable, buses can race each other to stops (followed by a half-hour interval). This is a question only indirectly related to the private–public distinction. When I was in Stockholm I used the 52 bus, and often the actual bus was hired from one of two private contractors; but the Stockholm transport department is responsible, there was one (exhibited) timetable, there is a system map. In Glasgow (and soon in London) there is not only additional congestion, but chaos too. I cannot tell a visitor: take a No. 3 bus, since it may be painted black and white and advertise whisky. Are you unaware of the advantages of ticket interavailability, responsibility for connections, feeder services? Have you studied the experience of other countries? Would you advise the Americans to scrap D.C. Transit, the M.T.A., or the New York suburban system? How far will you go in the name of ideology?

Could we not publish a debate along these lines?

Yours sincerely,

P.S. An almost classic example of the importance of responsibility is the fiasco with privatising the Royal Ordnance factories. British Aerospace, which now owns them, finds greater profit in closing half of them, sacking the workforce and selling the sites. The effect of this on Britain's capacity to produce ammunition is not its responsibility, nor should it be. It resides in the Ministry of Defence, which ought to decide that reserve capacity is (or is not) needed. Which is why Royal Ordnance was 'Royal' in the first place. But even in defence matters ideology clouds the mind.

Copy to Lord Harris of High Cross.

From Professor J. Hibbs OBE, 17 February 1989, Birmingham

Dear Professor Nove,

You wrote to me – a long and challenging letter, which I was delighted to receive – so long ago as 30 December last. I hope you will accept, in lieu of an apology, my assurance that I have put off replying until I could do so adequately. You will I know understand the pressures involved in bringing out three books in six months, along with a fairly heavy teaching load.

First, let me say that I hope it to be true that my arguments are not from ideology. I have ever sought to argue for policies that, in my judgement, promote the best interests of individuals; and I start from the assumption that the individual is the only satisfactory person to decide what is, or is not good value for money for him, or her. Thus, as an Austrian paradigm, I am convinced that the market, as an information exchange, will, if it is not unduly constrained, tend to maximise the opportunities for the individual to obtain satisfactions.

This leads me to build my critique of policy for transport from two assumptions. (1) It is necessary to maintain, and constantly update, a framework of safety legislation, that must nevertheless not inhibit innovation. This is because technology and the nature of production in service industries prevents the consumer from assessing the mechanical condition of the service offered, *ex ante*. It is sometimes argued that the judgement of consumers, *ex post*, will ensure that unsafe provision is squeezed out of the market, since it will not be bought; I have no time for such theorising! But, in the context of the Clapham accident, I am not satisfied that the Railway Inspectorate has sufficient power to ensure safety *ex ante*, and in the case of both Clapham and Kings Cross, I am not alone in concluding that the fault lies with the politicians, who have asked for maximum carryings at fares that are not just cheap, but are so charged (through travelcards) as to distort the whole transport market. The trouble is that, having promised to provide funds for renewals and re-investment, that the customers will no longer provide, the politicians, as is their wont, prove unable to keep their word. That, in a nutshell, is the disastrous story of the New York Metro, and I fear London is going the same way. Flat fares – and travelcards are just that – are a recipe for disaster. See David Jones: *Urban Transit Policy: An Economic and Political History*, Prentice-Hall, 1985.

(2) My second assumption is that management needs a good selfish reason for finding out what individuals want, and providing it at a price that as near as may be satisfies consumer demand for (usually) low fares with producers' requirement to cover cost, including a return on capital that runs in general a few points above the market price. And here my argument becomes unashamedly pragmatic: from experience of management and from informed observation, I conclude that the only way to achieve this end is through the working of the market, with the perceived risk of failure. To paraphrase Dr Johnson, nothing concentrates a man's mind more than the prospect of bankruptcy in the morning. I have the word of a number of managers who have stated that they, and others, abused the monopoly that the pre-1985 law gave them.

And so, with that over-long preamble, let me turn to your letter. First, as to the nature of transport in conurbations.

You are correct in your statement as to urban transport in North America and Europe being publicly owned, subsidised and 'co-ordinated'. I note in passing that in Buenos Aires, a notably 'European' city, it is largely privately owned, unsubsidised, and subject to relatively low intervention – it is also popular. But in North America, urban transport has been a disaster, with cities as big as 100,000 being dependent upon taxis, for reasons well discussed in the text I mention above. To the debilitating effect of subsidy on management I will return, but to assume, *a priori*, that subsidy is good because it is there, is surely to ignore, at the least, the opportunity cost. Was it not Frances Cairncross, some years ago, who pointed out that the subsidy payments to British Rail would have built 25 new hospitals a year?

Your statement about New York I cannot allow to pass. Private provision did not collapse because it was private, but because the franchising authority (the city) extracted the provision of a low flat fare as a *quid pro quo*, and, then, for political reasons (that is, in order to get re-elected), insisted on keeping the fares low, but reneged on the promise of an adequate subsidy. I am not alone, and I include US opinion, in suspecting that Los Angeles will go the same way.

In European cities, outwith the UK, there has been the additional factor that planners have actively discouraged the use of the private car for access to the centre; with what loss of welfare no-one has ever, so far as I know, tried to calculate. But the case for subsidised networks is extremely weak, as I shall seek to show later.

Subsidy as a means of reducing congestion seems to me to be essentially regressive. If you subsidise the outer-suburban resident to this end, then you take the monopoly profit required out of the pockets of the inner-city residents, who can least afford it, and who will not be likely to use the new rapid-transit lines. Behind this lies the work done by Pryke and Dodgson, that shows that the affluent middle class is the greatest user of rail transport, and who can justify subsidising *them*? But I have the support of a growing number of economists and practitioners, and the politicians will follow, in arguing for road-use pricing as the only equitable and efficient (in allocative terms) way of dealing with the problem. As things stand, urban road use is priced zero at the margin – and all else follows. But to the extent that rapid-transit increases property values, then 'value capture' is a legitimate way of funding investment – provided subsequent operation is at market-secured fares. Your argument from external benefits I cannot except, since it is beyond the wit of man to internalise them (and the external costs), and thus minimise the distortion of resource allocation.

I turn now to your argument for network subsidy, and it is here that experience shows how dangerous that is. In Britain in 1985 massive subsidy was being given to urban transport authorities, and after its provision was ended, to be replaced by tender, the amount was reduced drastically, while the bus mileage continued at some 96% as before. Network subsidy is thus unnecessary. But its consequences are pernicious. I have heard accountants say 'now it will be our loss-making services that will make our living'. Much subsidy 'leaked' into wages and salaries, since management resistance to wage claims could be, and was met by 'you know you'll get it back'. And behind all this, network subsidy tended to take management decision-making out of the hands of bus managers, and into those of civil servants and politicians. This, a very capable manager said recently, meant that all the effort went into looking at services that were under-used, to the detriment of popular ones. Also, there is evidence that resources were actually transferred from frequent, well-used bus services, to provide marginally necessary services in councillors' marginal constituencies.

Pragmatically, I am convinced that the ideal dispensation is the autonomous management of each bus service or rail line, so that those who provide it can see the effect of their decisions. This is attainable either by franchise; or by co-ownership schemes such as People's Provincial, the bus company at Fareham; or by restructuring on a 'team' basis, as with the Go-Ahead Northern company at Gateshead.

Perhaps I should go a stage further into the issue of cross-subsidy. I learned from Gilbert Ponsonby, in my postgrad days, that true (and distortive) cross-subsidy only arises where a given quantum of service is provided at less than escapable (short-run marginal) cost, thus necessitating the extraction of an element of monopoly profit elsewhere in the system. This, as I have suggested, is usually regressive, and, as a form of tax, is usually lacking in democratic sanction. I suggest, therefore, that what passes for cross-subsidy is far more often a reflection of the inevitable consequence of joint and common costs, further distorted by the absence of elasticity-based price discrimination. No department store manager, and no Gujerati corner shopkeeper, expects the same percentage return from every item on sale, so we should expect some parts of the system to contribute more than others to fixed costs. As Ponsonby used to say, anything that covers its escapable costs, and makes a contribution, however small, to overheads, is worth running.

'Chaos on the streets' in Britain, immediately after the 1985 Act came into force, was limited to certain conurbations, where it was a direct consequence of the refusal of local politicians to allow the transport managers to plan for the deregulated future. Now there is an example of ideology – and to the detriment of their own citizens too. In the Potteries, for example, the local bus company (though then still state-owned) had its post-deregulation network in place, moving step-by-step to minimise confusion, by the end of May, for the 26th October 1986 deadline. System maps I have some reservations about, since a low proportion of people ever use more than two services in the course of one trip – i.e., demand is highly localised. And the use of buses to advertise whisky goes back many years, being developed by monopolist public operators themselves. (It should pay a competitive concern to see that its vehicles are recognisable – I note that the Derby ex-municipal company insists that 'overall advertising' leaves the front of the vehicle largely in its corporate livery, so that it can be distinguished from buses of the competitive (ex state-owned) Trent company). That seems to be a good idea. (The situation in Glasgow, with lively competition between a municipally owned operator – Strathclyde PTE – and several state-owned companies seems to me real Alice-in-Wonderland stuff!)

So no, I would not scrap Washington's DC Transit, nor the MTA, nor the New York Metro (though I would close down Miami's 'Metrofail' quickly, to stop the drain on resources that that ill-conceived investment represents). I would introduce road-use pricing, and then borrow forward on its cash-flow to drastically improve the metro lines, after which their super service should enable them to attract traffic at market-based fares, competing with the newly efficient bus lines running on the relatively traffic-free streets. And the result, in my submission, would be a dispensation in which market forces tended (1) to maximise customer satisfaction, and (2) to optimise the allocation of scarce resources.

So that shows why I have had to leave writing this letter till I had a morning free! May I say, very warmly, how grateful I am to you, on this as on previous occasions, for challenging me to justify my arguments at what I hope is a proper degree of rigour. If Ralph could arrange a 'published debate', I would love to take part.

With kind regards, and thanks once again,
yours sincerely,

PS – I hope you will permit me to use this correspondence as a discussion paper in a final year undergraduate seminar – it is good for students to see that we can argue agreeably!

Copy to Lord Harris of High Cross

To Professor J. Hibbs OBE, 4 April 1989, Glasgow

Dear Professor Hibbs
I have just returned from foreign parts and was very glad to receive your letter of 17th February. I will try and concoct a suitable reply. I suppose that the basic point relates to what seems to me to be a blind spot in the whole of your argument: totally missing from it is recognition that a large conurbation has a transport *network*, containing a large number of inter-related and inter-connected services. I have just spent two months in the German city of Cologne, where there is naturally an integrated set of services with inter-available tickets and avoidance of wasteful parallelism (i.e., there is not a bus line along a route taken by the metro or vice versa). Is there not a profound difference between an urban network and, let us say, two competing inter-city bus routes? One can go between New

York and Washington by one of two companies, but of course there is a single network both in Washington and in New York. I do not understand how your kind of analysis can handle the existence of hierarchically organised firms, or even the concept of responsibility (e.g., of punctual deliveries of newspapers and beer, to mention the examples I used in my first letter to you). You seem to me to be a truly extreme example of fragmentism. For you the whole is only the sum of its parts, which can be disassembled and hived off at no cost. When I cited your arguments to German colleagues they were frankly incredulous. There is no European equivalent of the polluted chaos of Victoria coach station in London. Why do you put the word 'coordinated' in what appear to be ironic inverted commas? Once again, does not the management of any firm coordinate consciously the activities of its parts? It is simply not true that each of these parts would be separately profitable if separately evaluated and managed, for were this the case there would be no need for the firm to contain them.

I think a debate would be most useful. Let us find a suitable context.

With best regards.

Yours sincerely.

To Professor J. Hibbs OBE, 18 May 1989, Paris (until 30 May)

Dear Professor Hibbs,

May we continue the debate? I firmly believe that you are fundamentally mistaken, that the advice which you and those who think like you give to ministers can do lasting harm. My critique is not in the least based on any sort of socialist ideology, and I am in line with the practice of every West European country and of virtually all of the United States and Canada too. It is for this reason that *you* ought to be on the defensive. Your confidence in your own arguments is astonishing to me. As I wrote elsewhere, it would simply never occur to the gnomes of Zurich, good capitalists all, to order the disruption of the Zurich transport system. Should it not bother you, Ralph Harris, Paul Channon, that in no other country are they even contemplating the sort of actions you so confidently recommend? Your view is vulnerable to attack both in theory and in its practical implications.

First may I challenge the excesses of the methodological-individualist position. Surely you must know that there are circumstances when the separate pursuit of individual advantage can result in a situation which is worse for the individuals. Similarly, there are situations repeatedly met with in real life when the interests of a part and the interests of the whole are mutually inconsistent, which is one important reason why there is a whole! (This can be a firm, a country, a football club, an economic research institute, a supermarket, *any* coordinated network of human relations.)

Secondly, infrastructure, transport especially, almost by definition has external effects of significance. Adam Smith (unlike the 'Adam Smith Society') did not fail to note them, when he drew attention to expenditures 'of such a nature that the profit would never repay the expense to any individual or small number of individuals'. Adam Smith had never heard of airports, but his ghost would have had no difficulty in understanding why in the United States *every* airport known to me (and also docks, and of course urban transportation) is in the public sector. Surely it is because their financial results, if considered in isolation from the effects on the businesses and citizens of the relevant localities, would be misleading as efficiency criteria. Hence the New York Port Authority, the Pittsburgh (municipal) airport, the Massachusetts Transit Authority, D.C. Transit and all their innumerable Canadian and European equivalents. *All* wrong? Victims of delusion and vested interest? Or could it be that Hibbs is wrong? (And if you would not destroy D.C. Transit, why destroy its British equivalents?).

Thirdly, you incredibly assert that Travelcards (and things like the Paris carte orange and all their equivalents) are a 'recipe for disaster'. Fantastic! Again, everyone is wrong except you. Let us rehearse their elementary raison d'être:

(a) To attract people onto public transport and thereby relieve congestion, their price is made attractive. By charging much higher prices one can, of course, reduce congestion on public transport, but every transport authority in the civilised world can see that by reducing demand in this manner one would drive more people to drive to work and get in each others' way.

(b) To economise on ticket-issuing and accountancy. The separate purchase of tickets for each journey requires more ticket clerks, conductors, inspectors and causes delay (have you never seen the time wasted on issuing tickets on one-man-operated buses? Or do you not travel by bus?). Interavailability is an evident convenience!

(c) Separate charging in relation to marginal cost and marginal revenue makes no sense within an interrelated *system*. What part of the revenue of the Paris metro is attributable to line No. 8, or to bus No. 63?

You quote the neglect of the NY subway, which is a fact, but it contrasts with the non-neglect of those in Washington, Toronto, Montreal, Munich, Frankfurt, etc. . . . Only a committed ideologist would or could deduce some sort of economic law from this. You will next be telling me that the sad state of London's tubes shows that escalators must be out of action whenever underground lines are in the public sector! Whereas I would deduce that if priority in a public service is given to the profitability bottom-line, quality is bound to deteriorate. The more so if efficiency is separated from purpose.

Fourthly, this brings me to the fundamental point, your truly unbelievable belief in fragmentation, your inability to see the logic of system, of network. As I already mentioned to you, how on earth can you understand the nature of any hierarchical organisation such as an ordinary private firm? To quote the Californian economist Harold Demsetz, 'coordination is itself productive'. A firm, whether in the private or the public sector, represents a bundle of interrelated activities, which react upon one another and cannot be evaluated in isolation. That is why the firm exists! The nature of the interrelationships vary widely. They may take the form of successive processes of production through time, which can include materials handling, transportation, after-sales service. Also important is goodwill: to keep a reputation for quality and good service frequently requires actions which are not in themselves profitable. If each and every part of a firm like ICI could be separately evaluated without reference to the effect of their decisions on ICI as a whole, ICI would not exist as a whole, thus saving a lot of headquarter staff salaries. If you see this argument to be the nonsense that it undoubtedly is, why cannot you see that the break-up of a closely integrated transport network in a conurbation is an absurdity? An absurdity by reference to its purpose, which is to move *individuals* hither and yon. You really do believe in 'autonomous management of each bus service and rail line', that is in externalising internalities, in making connections more time-consuming and less probable, with, it seems, no one in charge of and responsible for the network. Surely common sense and experience tells us that joint responsibility (e.g., of Swiss postal buses connecting with trains) is more likely to provide needed interlinks (needed by *individuals*!) than separate provision (e.g., at Oxford station they do not even keep bus time-tables in the inquiry office!).

Fifthly, subsidy. The question divides into two parts. Should there be any subsidy at all, and should it be paid to the network. On common sense grounds network subsidy seems logical (which is why it is virtually universal – whatever is real is often rational, if I may adapt Hegel), logical for the same reason for which one really cannot evaluate the *separate* profitability of line No. 8 or the 63 bus in the Paris conurbation. The reason for having a subsidy is known and has been rehearsed countless times. Every strike in Paris and London demonstrates conclusively that non-users of public transport benefit from its existence! Both Union Pacific and the old London Metropolitan Railway made high profits out of the increase in the values of the land that had previously been granted or been bought. You say that subsidy has 'a debilitating effect'. Yes, it can have. But look at the efficient systems which are subsidised: the Netherlands, West Germany, Switzerland, France. Neither subsidy nor the unions prevented the Paris authority from running one-man trains and replacing ticket-punchers with machines. Look at the systems in Köln, Munich, etc., etc. You may tell me that the SNCF and DB and the Paris system are costly in subsidy. They are. But 'debilitated'? Inefficient?? Your solution: road charging. Yes, I have heard Alan Day advocate this too. But does it not occur to you that the practical and political obstacles are well-nigh insurmountable? Incidentally, you puzzle me by your critical reference to 'planners who have actively discouraged the use of the private car for access to the centre' of cities. Of course they have!! Why should the 'welfare loss' be greater than that arising from pricing them out of these very centres by road charges? Or are you advocating pulling down a third of central London for car-parking? Again, you lose sight of *purpose*.

Do transport subsidies subsidise the affluent? I would have thought they were neutral, the situation varies. In Paris the 'HLM' (cheap housing for rent) tends to be outside the outer boulevards. In London you have both Howards Heath (affluent) and say Uxbridge and Ilford (less so). But in general it *is* beginning to be true that *Inter-city* rail travellers are more often affluent in Britain. The reason is simple: rail fares will soon be the highest by far in Europe and often three or more times the bus fare. In France and in Germany they have invested heavily in fast train services while keeping bus/coach competition away, thus ensuring heavy seat utilisation and so relatively modest fares. And there is no polluted monstrosity in Paris like Victoria coach station (HAVE YOU BEEN THERE??). Ah, you will say, illegitimate interference with free enterprise. But suppose the citizens of Lyon and Marseilles were asked: would you prefer the TGV or a competing coach route, you cannot have both. Is this not a legitimate question? (You may reply they were not asked. But in your philosophy they *could* not be asked.)

This brings me to competition. Again, an elementary question: it is absent in every conurbation in USA, Canada and Europe. Why? Because, surely, the advantages of having one network seem decisive. What are these advantages? First, responsibility for planning the network and coordinating the parts, just as in every firm (e.g., the brewery with a thousand pubs to supply), there is a transport department which is *responsible* (vital word, apparently not in your vocabulary) for ensuring that the goods reach their destination punctually – and efficiency criteria are related to the *purpose* (another vital word) for which transportation exists. This purpose is not necessarily identical with the profit and loss account of the transport system in isolation. Whether the lorries are owned and operated by that firm or are hired from contractors is a secondary matter, to be settled pragmatically and not ideologically, bearing in mind quality, reliability, etc. Competition in urban transportation can have some ludicrous consequences. You mention the Go-Ahead northern company. In the area in which it operates (Teesside, Cleveland) *all bus time-tables have been taken down* because the competing bus shows up just ahead. My granddaughter who is a student at Lancaster tells me that the bus from Morecambe, as well as nigh-doubling the fare, often does not stop for one passenger at a request stop if the driver sees a larger number at the next stop to which the competing bus can get before it. In Cleveland the question arose: who will run a late bus, there being no possible justification for two of them. The two companies (one was the Go-Ahead) wished to agree this among themselves, but were reprimanded for failing to compete, so there is no late bus at all, a fine example of ideology destroying service to individuals! In Glasgow too there are no time-tables exhibited, buses to the same destination start from different stops at the city centre, feeder services to suburban rail stations have been abandoned. Even I, who have lived in Glasgow for 25 years, have little idea how to get about on the buses other than on routes personally familiar to me (and even then with no idea when the actual bus will run). Visitors are totally bemused. There is of course no system map, because there is no system. It has been deliberately destroyed by ideology.

A different argument, relating to investment. I had earlier made the point that investment in (e.g.) an extension to D.C. Transit's metro makes sense only if there is a rational expectation of feeder services and no competing parallel bus. But there is another point, relating to investment in firms making buses and rail rolling stock. In Western Europe there is long-term tie-up between the big transport operators and their suppliers: Mercedes, Renault, Volvo, DAF, Siemens, Alsthom . . . Your ideology, and that of the government, seems to me to fail to notice the negative effect on investment of the fragmentation of operators, each of which puts its requirements out to tender. This is not unconnected with the decline of Leyland and AEC and of our rolling stock manufacturers, and with the huge rise in imports of buses and also equipment for the Docks light railway etc. This has made its contribution to the record trade deficit.

Finally, on cross-subsidisation. In real life it takes very many forms, and some of these you will instantly recognise as benign, or at least necessary. One relates to complementarities. Thus Arsenal plc runs a reserve team, whose losses are cross-subsidised by the first team. This is one instance of reserve capacity, loss-making as such but necessary to meet the unexpected and to retain goodwill. Note that if responsibility for reserve capacity is no longer identifiable, it may not be provided. This could be the sad consequence of the break-up of electricity generation (fragmentation of system again!). In transport cross-subsidisation is the inescapable consequence of any regular scheduled service (e.g., every hour on the hour, or any flight that leaves half full, or metro trains every three minutes throughout the day, or whatever). In the old days of private railways, may I remind you that they had a standard charge per mile throughout the system, and thought it proper to run extra trains at holiday times, for which they kept reserve capacity. Probably they thought (unlike today's management) that passenger confidence that they *would* get to their destination 'pays', even if this meant keeping 'loss-making' reserve capacity. (Only two weeks ago I flew from Teesside to London because it would probably be very difficult to get on the train at Darlington. . . .) Incidentally, on a recent visit to Liverpool Street I found that it costs a minimum of £2 to use left-luggage facilities. This is six to eight times the charges in America and Europe. And it clearly did not occur to the 'fragmentationists' intent on profits from left luggage to take into account the loss of goodwill occasioned by such outrageous overcharging. Incidentally, the old LMS and LNER would have considered it positively immoral to charge more to go to Teesside than the much longer distance to Glasgow, or they would have been forbidden such discrimination by the Railway Rates Tribunal. Now – charge what market will bear, ignore considerations of regional policy, bugger the north-east . . . But I am wandering off the subject, though not altogether: again efficiency is separated from social and public purpose in a public utility's operations. It is the same 'logic' that allows the scandalous condition of London's escalators: in a choice between profit and public service . . . But then government ideology systematically denigrates public service as a concept, embracing the Buchanan philosophy according to which public servants seek (95 per cent of the time) to maximise their own personal utility. No nonsense about job satisfaction, commitment, pride in work well done. And therefore no need for managers, in public transport or elsewhere, to secure the confidence and the willing collaboration of the managed. But that is another story. Or is it? (Needless to say, efficiency in the private sector also depends in large part on human attitudes, loyalty, etc. The Japanese know it. Marks and Spencer know it. Economics textbooks do not.)

Enough is enough. What about a debate some place?

I will copy this to Ralph Harris.

Best wishes.

Sincerely.

To Professor J. Buchanan, 6 November 1990, Glasgow

Dear Professor Buchanan,

I am most grateful to you for sending me copies of your papers, and for your letter of 4 October. All very thought-provoking. May I try to formulate the points of disagreement?

I too reject 'the hypothesis of a common good', and devote a whole page (18) of my *Economics of Feasible Socialism* to the issue. I enclose a xerox of that page. Where I disagree is on your exclusive stress on the individual. The librarian of the University of Glasgow (and of George Mason) must surely be seen as committed to the library, rather than to personal wealth maximisation (though no doubt he, like you and I, is not averse to making a little more money). Where, in your conception, is team work, the team spirit, commitment to the job? I see that GM has borrowed some Japanese notions on this subject and applied them with some success in their new factory. A member of the Scottish rugby team plays for the team (or for Scotland) as well as for himself, and all this without being 'altruistic'. I do not think that public choice is 'immoral', I think it is inaccurate.

Of course you recognise that the individual exists within society, that his or her preferences and actions are influenced and affected by what other individuals do, that organisational structures and alternatives matter. But you rebel against the use of such terms as social or collective utility, here you are an individualist *pur sang*. And here I cannot quite follow you. May I take as a parallel an architectural ensemble. It could be the Piazza Navona in Rome, a terrace in Bath or in the street where I live in Glasgow. Yes, the totality in each instance consists of the individual houses of which it consists. Yet the ensemble is more than just the sum of its individual parts, which is why public authority RIGHTLY prevents the owner of one house from making major changes or demolitions. Similarly, a transport network in a conurbation (be it Washington, Zurich, Munich or Stockholm) is an interrelated whole, and any change in any part must be seen in the context of the whole. This MATTERS, because the extremist advisers that surround Mrs Thatcher have persuaded her to order the disintegration of transport networks in British conurbations. If the whole is only the sum of its individual parts and nothing else, such disintegration will be seen as costless. How do you handle the many kinds of collective enjoyments: a reliable transport network, public parks, a municipal concert hall (without which the individual citizens of Glasgow were unable to choose to enjoy a visit from the Los Angeles Philharmonic or the latest pop group), or even just clean streets (collecting rubbish requires public expenditure).

Also individuals may suffer pain at the sight of homeless sleeping in cardboard boxes in London. Some sort of collective action is called for, given the level of free market rents. Meanwhile in today's Britain the building industry is suffering acute recession, with rapidly rising unemployment. Keynes might well advocate a public housing programme in such circumstances. I can confidently forecast that the British government will cut public expenditure on housing and actively prevent local authorities from developing any municipal housing programme (the government here does have such powers). I think they are wrong. Do you?

Why do you appear to be hostile to 'paternalistic, merit goods arguments'? Are there not some rather obvious instances where total reliance on 'voluntary market exchanges' are inadequate? You yourself say, and rightly, that no ordered society would be possible if all were of the *homo economicus* motivation. Slum clearance, tree planting, street cleaning, the already-mentioned concert hall, a walkway along the river Kelvin in Glasgow (along which I shall walk in ten minutes' time!) may all be motivated by a commitment to and pride in one's city, and all call for some 'collective interference' because these things do not and would not happen through 'voluntary market exchange'. The municipal officials and politicians who advocate these things are not wealth-maximisers, nor is it intuitively obvious that tax-financed expenditures for such purposes are in some sense inferior to private expenditures of the same sums for other purposes.

At no point in any of the papers which you sent me do you mention initial property distribution as a relevant factor. Suppose that a duke owns a large part of London's west end is thereby a multimillionaire. Suppose further that his title and his land were awarded to a remote ancestor for services rendered in bed to King Charles II. It is true that, GIVEN the existing situation, any agreement to rent land from him, voluntarily entered into, benefits both parties. However . . .

I am also a little concerned with your almost exclusive emphasis on what you call 'trading interactions'. Far be it from me to deny their importance, but investment and production are required so that the things traded are made. Here the role of public authority can be significant, as for instance in Japan and South Korea. I was impressed by the argument of G.B. Richardson, in his book *Information and Investment* (OUP, 1960): the nearer one gets to perfect markets, the less basis there is for investment decisions, since a profitable opportunity perceived by all will cease to be profitable. (If too many people know that a horse will win the race at odds of 10 to 1, the odds will not be 10 to 1.)

Lastly, are you really justified in employing just 'one set of behavioural postulates' across all institutions? Of course I do see why you argue thus. But it seems to me, as I am sure it does to you, that a professional gambler, or croupier, or foreign exchange dealer, or fruit merchant, will behave and respond quite differently from, say, a High Court judge, the Lord Provost of Edinburgh, the head of the Securities and Exchange Commission, the head librarian at George Mason, or for that matter the guy in charge of a research laboratory in DuPont, Inc. Of course, let us remove the 'benevolent despot' from our assumptions, if only because we have too many examples of malevolent despots. However, the most malevolent – Hitler, Stalin, let us say – were most emphatically NOT individual wealth maximisers.

Counter-attack welcomed!

With my best regards. Sincerely yours.

11. Policy and the 'mainstream' – a critique

'When policy conclusions are derived from such models,
I reach for my gun' (Frank Hahn)

Should not Frank Hahn have opened fire more often?

The object of this polemical note is to try to relate actual or potential dubious policies to blind-spots which have roots in theory: I will agree in advance that in many, perhaps most, instances a properly understood or interpreted theory could not be used as a *pièce justificative*. It is not a matter of false doctrines, rather a consequence of emphasis, of what is not said, omissions due in many cases to the fact that on certain matters nothing precise or rigorous *can* be said. However, that which is omitted from consideration is given a weight of zero. I will illustrate with one 'introductory' example. According to the then manager of a major American shipyard, a vice-president of the corporation addressed the shipyard's employees as follows: 'We are not in the business of building ships, we are in the business of making profits.' Nowhere in neoclassical economics is it stated that the attitude of people to their work is a matter of no importance. However, his training gave emphasis to 'the bottom line', and probably his teachers in business school treated such considerations as the morale of technicians, designers, skilled workers, as an imprecise irrelevancy.

Let me begin with transport policy. First, should there *be* a transport policy? Those who have successfully persuaded the British government (unlike those of most other European countries) that there is no need to have any such policy are no doubt fortified by what received theory says (or, more properly, does not say) on this subject. Located in the gap between micro and macro, the very question can hardly be asked, let alone answered, in orthodox terms.

Focusing more narrowly on urban transportation, there is a clear contrast between the British government's belief in deregulation, even now for London, and the practice of virtually every other country: in almost every Canadian, American and European city there is an integrated public transport network, subsidised as a system. Subsidy can be justified by reference to externalities (for example, congestion, effect on property values, and so on). Reference to exernalities, positive and negative, are to be found in the textbooks, along with 'public goods'. However, all too often such references are treated as exceptions, worth a footnote or two, and in 'Friedmanist' presentations there is a warning that government intervention to correct for externalities would do more harm than good. Belief in such a version of the neoclassical paradigm helps to explain why the British government's advisers do not sound the alarm when fares on public transport rise to double or treble those encountered elsewhere. (Compare New York, Boston, San Francisco, Montreal, Paris, any German city, with London). Furthermore, uniquely in Britain an attempt is made to outlaw cross-subsidisation, so that subsidy, if any, is paid not to the network, as is the case elsewhere, but to specific routes deemed to be socially in need of it. The part is emphasised, not the whole. Yet it is hard even to envisage a network of routes with any standardised fare structure (for example, by zone or distance) that does not involve a degree of cross-subsidisation, while routes and passengers intermingle.

This tendency to disintegrate also shows itself in the declared intention to destroy the railway *system*. Surely this is not unconnected with the theoretical posture well summed up by Brian Loasby: 'Highly complex subsystems, such as firms or even whole sectors of the economy, containing within themselves many layers of complexity, are regularly treated as simple elements, while components of a complex system are analysed as isolated units.'[1] Or by Peter Earl: 'The neoclassical theorist sees aggregative concepts as if they are simply the sums of their component elements'.[2]

As in the case of urban transport networks, so with the railway system, the advantages of integration (interchangeable ticketing, connections, investment planning, time-tabling, and so on) are ignored or downgraded. Why this blinkered attitude should be unique to Britain is a puzzle. What should concern us in the present context is its links with theory. There is, in my view, a dual connection: with methodological individualism, and with general equilibrium.

Let me begin with the latter. On the face of it, this should argue against my contention: far from fragmenting, general equilibrium theory teaches us that everything depends on everything else. True. But this interdependence is conceptually achieved *through the market*. As Harold Demsetz has correctly observed, perfect competition equals perfect or total decentralisation. Subsystems, networks, the advantages arising from conscious coordination of related activities, do not readily fit the paradigm. Persons trained to think in such terms would be predisposed to see the No. 1 bus from Lewisham, or even the bus departing Lewisham at 1.53, or the 10.30 train from Euston to Manchester, not as part of

London's network of buses, or of the British rail system, but as a separate profit centre. London's transport, the railway, is the sum total of such units or centres. It can then be costlessly disassembled, with a gain seen in reducing administrative bureaucracy and stimulating competition. The loss escapes attention, because theory does not draw attention to it.

This view is reinforced by methodological individualism. Arthur Koestler, in his *Janus*, warned of two kinds of excess: to see the part as no more than an element of the whole, and to see the whole as no more than the sum of its parts. Mainstream economics tends strongly to the second of these extremes. There is no wood, there are only trees. Army is the plural of soldier. A university is no more than the sum of its colleagues or departments of which it consists. (And, of course, there is no such thing as society.) Others have written on 'the fallacy of composition – the fallacy that *wholes* can be considered the sum of *parts*'.[3] Therefore, with such a world-view, one can see only advantages in disintegrating transport networks, or schools districts, or London, or separating electricity generation from distribution, or letters from parcels, or rail passengers from freight, or trains from tracks, or track from stations, or to subject any segment of any formerly integrated whole to 'market testing' (of which more in a moment).

This tendency could be labelled 'myopic marginalism', or a disregard for what, in an article, I called 'internal economies'. Each act, or decision, or transaction, is envisaged as profitable in itself, for otherwise there would be irrational cross-subsidisation. It also underlies a blinkered attitude towards externalities. Examples are all too readily to hand. Thus in every European country except Britain there are pricing policies designed to get more freight off the roads and onto rail. Here, as any rail traveller can observe, goods trains have become as rare as swallows in winter, and in this as in past years freight is being priced off rail (even onto narrow Scottish Highland roads) because of a prescribed rate of return. Other examples: most countries see the indirect economic advantages of them having a film industry, or foreign graduate students. The outgoing head of the British Tourist Board complained bitterly of a negative attitude on the part of the Treasury, once again contrasting with less myopic attitudes elsewhere. It was not an economist, but a *Standard* cartoonist, who vividly illustrated the ill-effects on the reputation of British business of the contrast between a French TGV emerging from the Channel Tunnel and the half-speed the train would achieve between the coast and London. (The government's economic advisers seemed to have been concerned primarily with the profitability of the line, and/or its privatisation, plus, of course, minimising political damage on the route.) Taking a very different example, a British car firm, now deservedly defunct, took the view that it was cheaper to repair under guarantee than to test the cars thoroughly before they left the factory. Since hardly a single textbook on microeconomics even mentions goodwill, the error may not have been identified by that company's economist, even if they had employed one.

The omission from textbooks of goodwill or reputation, despite its obvious importance in the real world of real competition, may be explicable because if perfect competition is assumed, the firm can by definition sell all its (homogeneous) products at *the* price, whereas under monopoly the disgruntled customer cannot, also by definition, go elsewhere. Or possibly because it cannot be rigorously defined or measured – though it can be sold.

To pass to a totally different question: how was it possible that the British government's economic advisers in the 1980s failed to challenge (or may even have sponsored) the notion that the decline in manufacturing did not matter, that the future lay in services? Dissident voices, such as that of Wynne Godley, cried for years in the wilderness. A non-economist had and has no difficulty in appreciating that if (despite oil) Britain has a trade deficit in manufactures (importing most vehicles, other consumer durables capital equipment, ships, textiles, clothes, electronics, and so on), a balance of payments crisis or bottleneck would result, and that this would matter; one cannot borrow for ever to cover chronic deficits. The essential distinction here is not between material and non-material products, but between tradeables and non-tradeables. Britain had for several generations a current trade deficit financed by invisible earnings. However, as statistics show, invisibles now contribute much less, and can turn negative if interest on borrowed capital exceeds the revenues arising from British investments abroad. (Revenues from shipping are vanishing together with the merchant fleet.) How many economists, other than Godley and a very few other honourable exceptions, have actually sought to study and analyse the commodity composition of British foreign trade? When was an article on the subject last published in any economic journal? Who has sought to disaggregate statistics on imports of capital goods, and of capital inflow? Capital goods imports can be seen as a counterpart of increases in investment, but they may or may not have as their consequence a subsequent improvement in the balance of trade. Purchases of imported lorries, ships, buses, all count as investment, though they may be replacing domestic production of these items, whereas imports of equipment designed to expand output of these or other products can have a corrective effect on the trade deficit.

Similarly, inward capital movements could be of at least three kinds:

(a) Short-term deposits to take advantage of higher interest rates, but which could depart at any time.

(b) The purchase by a foreign company of an existing British firm, for example, of Rowntree by Nestlé.
(c) Real investment, as when Nissan erects a factory in the north-east to make cars.

The impact of each of these on the real economy is far from identical. When were these things last analysed by an academic economist? They too fall into the large gap that separates micro from macro.

At this time we are (or ought to be) concerned with the impact of devaluation on the balance of trade and payments in the next years. This must depend decisively on the existence of spare productive capacity. When a decline occurs, as in the slump of 1980–81 and in more recent years, it matters greatly whether capacity is scrapped, or merely mothballed or 'laid off', and thus capable of resurrection. Does anyone in the profession, does the Treasury model, base any conclusions on a study of how much spare capacity has survived, and of what it consists? Thus no degree of devaluation, or change in world-market conditions, could revive coal production from an abandoned pit, or cause ships to be built in a dismantled shipyard, or lorries to be made by Leyland if the works no longer exist. Far be it from me to criticise those economists whose concerns are elsewhere, but is it not a serious criticism of the profession that so few can be weaned from their models? Once again, these problems fall into the gap between micro and macro.

A related point: what was the actual context of the investment boom of the second half of the 1980s? It has sometimes been alleged that the bulk of it went into construction of offices and retailing complexes, that little was in fact invested in manufacturing. Was this so? Has the British economy suffered from underinvestment, and, if so, why, given that British capital invests heavily abroad? Is there an institutional problem, linked with the traditional remoteness of British banks and financial institutions from industry, in contrast with Germany and Japan? Financial journalists such as the *Guardian*'s Will Hutton have been raising such questions. For those economists concerned with the efficiency of investment and of financial institutions, these are surely matters of high importance. When were they last given 'academic' attention in any journal? (Papers on 'random walks' and stock exchange valuations are, in this context, only of tangential concern.)

Mention of investment highlights another series of potential blindspots, whereof mainstream theory is largely silent. This may be attributed to the difficulty of 'fitting' investments into general-equilibrium analysis: in equilibrium there can be no expectation of a return higher than the current rate of interest, and so there is no motive to invest. In real life there is 'risk, uncertainty and profit' (or, of course, loss), and profit arises out of taking a risk under conditions of uncertainty, the profit being in effect conditional upon a *dis*equilibrium. Either the investment was due to an existing or anticipated disequilibrium (which may or may not have been linked with technological innovation), or else the investment itself is expected to be disequilibrium-creating. 'Animal spirits' are not enough: the animal must have some basis for optimistic expectations. One cannot in this context assume perfect knowledge of the future, not only because it is far from real life, but also because it then removes an essential element in investment decisions. It is not only that future prices (or wages, or interest rates) are not known. If they were known, and known to all, then – as G.B. Richardson pointed out long ago, the profitable opportunity would no longer exist, and indeed agents' responses would alter future prices. If a price in five years' time would yield a 20 per cent return on capital, and this was known, then the action of other agents would ensure that it would not do so. If it is widely known that a horse would win the race at odds of 10:1, the odds would not be 10:1.

Real investments in real capacity to produce a future flow of goods and services occur, as Richardson (1960) pointed out, because of so-called market imperfections: imperfect knowledge, anticipated market dominance, long-term links with suppliers of capital, material inputs and customers, coordination by or through government, selective protection, cartel-like agreements with potential competitors, and so on. It is astonishing that Richardson should have had so little impact on mainstream textbooks, despite the efforts of Loasby and a few others.

The gap in theory prevents adequate appraisal of the role of the state in such countries as Japan, South Korea, Taiwan, or in the postwar 'recovery' decade in Western Europe (not even the most recent economic history figures in economics lectures and reading lists in most universities). The gap is part-explanation of the 'hands-off' advice given to British governments since 1979. It underlies too the advice given to Russian and East European governments since 1989. Investments there have in most instances fallen below replacement levels, capital markets are still in an early process of formation, and there is little legitimate private capital. While the need for a fundamental restructuring is (or should be) obvious to all, there too there is an ideologically-based resistance to the very notion of an investment or restructuring strategy. This resistance finds support (or, better, does not find refutation) in textbook economics.

Nor does either micro or macro theory, as taught, draw attention to the consequences for investment of fragmentation – of public transport, for instance. In France, or Germany, or Italy, large public undertakings have a long-term relationship with the providers of vehicles and equipment. This provides a 'confidence base' for investment commitments. In Britain there has been a notable shrinkage in both output and investments in these sectors, directly connected with the break-up of the urban and railway networks. One sees the effects in the trade accounts, in the form of a sharp rise in imports. It is my contention that these effects were not foreseen. It is, of course, unreasonable to ask of theory to provide ready answers to practical questions. It is, however, a valid criticism if theory pays no attention to issues that are likely to arise.

Consider the example of Rolls Royce aero engines. The firm was recently dealt a severe blow by the decision of British Airways to buy American engines instead. According to press reports, the decision was not due to the relative price or quality of the engines, but to other financial deals. No doubt the net effect was judged by Lord King to be beneficial for British Airways shareholders. But suppose, as happens frequently in Germany and Japan, and could happen anywhere, there were interlocking shareholdings: suppose Rolls Royce held a significant packet of shares in British Airways, or British Airways in Rolls Royce, or a financial institution had substantial holdings in both. It seems highly probable, does it not, that the decision would have been different, and there would have been investment, not disinvestment, in the British aero engine industry, with consequences for both the balance of payments and the future of high-technology industries. In what textbook, in what journal article, has attention been drawn to this kind of issue?

Conversely, one reason for 'the rush for gas' in electricity generation is that electricity distributors *have* invested in gas-fired power stations, which naturally affects their choice between coal and gas, with consequences we know to be by no means trivial. It is a fairly safe bet that this outcome took the government's economic advisers by surprise. Nothing in our training or our courses draws sufficient attention to the fact (a surely evident fact) that what appears to be the rational thing to do is affected by the decision-maker's area of administrative or financial responsibility; for this defines what for him or her is an externality.

Re-reading a forgotten book of my own (forgotten even by its author), I find that virtually all the points made here, on fragmentation, investment, externality and 'internality', the theoretical gaps and their consequences, were made over 20 years ago.[4] Already then I noted that if it is regarded as rational that each segment of a transport network should 'pay', as was then recommended by Munby and other advisers (and this long before Mrs Thatcher came on the scene), then why not break up the network . . . I duly emphasised also the negative effect of fragmentation (theoretical and organisational) on investment decisions both in the public and the private sectors.

This is true of investment in public transport itself. For example, DC Transit (Washington) or the Paris regional RER could invest in extensions to rapid-transit lines in the knowledge that feeder services would be provided, and there would be no competing service. Clearly whosoever has drafted the scheme to disintegrate British Rail has given no consideration to the effects of fragmentation on decisions to invest in upgrading track, when the advantages of so doing would accrue to other companies, who, in their turn, would have no incentive to invest in track if their competitors could have a free ride. A 'transport strategy for London' cannot exist if fragmentation rules, but once again what warrant is there in conventional theory for even contemplating a transport strategy? And this despite the catastrophe of Canary Wharf, with bankruptcy a visible consequence of omitting to incorporate transport in a major investment project. In that just mentioned work published long ago, I sought to draw attention to the fact that many (most?) investment decisions are part of a larger whole, and that in such cases it is wrong to assess their profitability in isolation. The question to be answered, in many instances, is not 'whether' but 'how'. Instead we teach students the difference between internal rates of return and discounted cash flow, though the practical effect of the difference between them is trivially small.

It is possible that the tendency to disintegrate, to downgrade indivisibilities and complementarities, is also connected with a reluctance to focus on increasing returns to scale, which could be (often are) informational and organisational rather than technological.

Which brings one to 'market testing'. A major change in administration in Britain has proceeded amid the silence of the profession, on the advice of those who seem able to see only its advantages. These are undeniable and measurable: if any task can be separated and opened to competitive tender, it can frequently be done cheaper. This establishes a *prima facie* case in favour, with ample theoretical as well as practical justification, reinforced if needed by elements of 'public choice' theory, references to rent-seeking, or to obstruction to productivity increases and shedding of surplus labour by public-sector unions.

It is the negative side, or cost, of such policies that tends to be overlooked, and it is true that these negative consequences do resist rigorous measurement or definition. They are none the less present and we ignore them at our peril, or at our cost.

The first of these can be tackled by using Oliver Williamson's apparatus.[5] Hierarchies can be preferred to markets, that is, in-house preferred to subcontracting, in circumstances that he analyses. Not the least of them relates to the cost of monitoring, the opportunities for what he calls 'self-seeking with guile'. The cost may more than cancel the economy. That is a matter for empirical investigation, and not theoretical–ideological prescription.

A business source, Benjamin Ross, a Washington consultant, noted that in private industry 'they give much more weight to past experience and put a high value on maintaining existing relationships . . . Most purchases are made on the basis of existing supply relationships rather than on actual comparison of bids.' He noted that 'as government procurement is reformed to increase competition', the amount of real competition declines, as government officials' discretion to reward or punish their contractors decreases; 'choosing a new contractor to replace the incumbent becomes more difficult and time-consuming . . . The profits yielded by a successful relationship must considerably exceed those which would be obtained in perfect competition.'[6] Neither private nor public enterprise ought to disrupt existing arrangements if they are satisfactory. To change them imposes costs and risks. Quality and reliability matter.

'Market testing', the substitution of an outside bid for 'in-house', has several other consequences, or rather the same consequence has several effects. The more work is put out to tender, the greater the uncertainty of employment; job insecurity is a source of human unhappiness. It may at once be conceded that total job security is also undesirable, inconsistent with labour-market flexibility and work discipline. However, in most countries people who choose public service, where rewards are generally modest, do so because of greater security of employment. This applies also to many in the academic profession. To put their jobs at risk, while at the same time holding down their pay, seems a sure recipe for reducing the quality of recruitment and stimulating the drain of the best brains into the private sector, or abroad. (The ban on security of tenure in British universities contrasts with the practice of most other civilised countries.)

Insecurity of employment also has a 'macro' effect, by discouraging long-term commitment, which helps to depress the housing market and the demand for expensive durables. And it involves neglect of morale, loyalty, commitment, pride in one's work, and the link between these and productivity and quality of performance. Would a Japanese firm dismiss employees in order to get work done cheaper by an outside contractor? Is Japanese practice feudal, paternalistic, 'irrational' economically, or, on the contrary, a significant contribution to productivity through good labour relations? Mainstream economics appears to justify, indeed call for, the minimisation of labour cost (along with other costs), and this can be measured, while 'morale' and all that goes with it seems woolly, unscientific, non-rigorous – and yet surely when we lift our eyes from textbook models we know that it affects performance, of anyone from a cleaner to a professor of economics.

Research on the consequences of 'market testing' is urgently needed, and it should also focus on the additional transaction costs arising out of this, and also out of 'internal markets', imposed by ideologists increasingly on public bodies, from hospitals and the BBC to universities. Are the savings more than offset by extra accountancy? It is surely important, and not only for economists, to know whether, and in what circumstances, it is so.

One recalls the work of Scitovsky. He was particularly concerned about the treatment of the labour process in orthodox theory. He pointed out, citing statistical examples, that men and women who feel they are working for themselves, and/or control their own work time, tend to work much longer hours than do ordinary employees. There is an effect on job satisfaction, and through it on productivity and performance. Yet the still-dominant theory regards the employee as a work-minimising shirker. This underlies the views of the property rights school, and of those who urge the imposition of performance indicators and tighter work schedules, also in universities.

This school of thought is having considerable influence in Russia and Eastern Europe, where the reformers have tended to prefer outright privatisation to cooperative ownership or employee buy-outs. For example, in Russia employees do have access to shares on a privileged basis, but only up to 25 per cent, and even they are non-voting. Yugoslav experience is cited in justification, yet there was no employee *ownership* in the Yugoslav model.

Intuitively, it would seem that size matters. If one imagines a workforce of twenty, it seems over-simple to follow the doctrines of the property rights school and to assert that efficiency requires that one of them employs the other nineteen, whether the business is a restaurant, a fleet of taxis, a repair workshop, a medical practice or an Oxford college. Larger scale brings with it other problems, including the probable separation between ownership and management.

It would, of course, be wrong to assert without proof that the feelings associated with joint ownership, participation, co-responsibility, necessarily bring positive results. (Some do shirk, even in universities!) But is equally wrong to give such considerations axiomatically a weight of zero.

CONCLUSION

Questionable policy decisions find support in aspects of the neoclassical paradigm. These include fragmentation (for example of transport), neglect of both externalities and 'internalities', the disintegration of public services through 'market testing'. Theory handled investment adequately, and so misses out on the effects of fragmentation on investment through disrupting established links and increasing uncertainty. This affects also the balance of trade and payments, on which received theory does not adequately focus, due also to their falling into the gap between macro and micro. Problems arise not because mainstream theories are mistaken, but rather because of what is not emphasised or passed over in silence. More attention to such matters would bring more relevance to economics as a discipline.

NOTES

1. B. Loasby, *Choice, Complexity and Ignorance* (Cambridge University Press, 1976), p. 30.
2. P. Earl, *The Economic Imagination. Towards a Behavioural Analysis of Choice* (M.E. Sharpe, 1983), p. 61.
3. P. Arestis, 'Eichner, Alfred (1937–1988)' in P. Arestis and M. Sawyer (eds), *A Biographical Dictionary of Dissenting Economists* (Edward Elgar, 1992), p. 142.
4. A. Nove, *Efficiency Criteria for Nationalised Industries* (George Allen & Unwin, 1973).
5. O.E. Williamson, *Markets and Hierarchies. Analysis and Antitrust Implications* (Free Press, 1975), and *Economic Organization: firms, markets and policy control* (Wheatsheaf, 1986).
6. Benjamin Ross, 'What is Competition For?', *Challenge*, March–April 1988, p. 47.

12. Public choice, rent seeking and Cainesianism

This note grows from a desire to comment on M. Gradstein's 'Rent-seeking and the provision of public goods',[1] and on the theory of public choice in some of its interpretations.

Gradstein's declared object was 'to introduce realistic factors', yet in the whole of his article there is not a single reference to any specific public good or service. His model relates to some undefined composite. Yet there is a wide variety of public goods, and a wide variety too of market failures and some instances where the words 'market failure', and indeed 'lobbying' and 'rent seeking' seem inappropriate. In those instances where private provision is plainly out of the question, the comparison between private and public provision cannot meaningfully be made at all. In some others, for instance education, the social impact is different, one is not comparing like with like. Still others, such as urban public transport, are complicated by the presence of externalities and possible economies of scale in monopoly provision (for example, one authority, as in Paris, versus 60, as in Manchester). There are problems too in defining efficiency criteria, and in assessing the motivation of those who supply public services of all kinds. This last point relates also to the issue of 'performance-related pay'; currently being introduced into the public sector. However, this controversial question was not the subject of Gradstein's article, and we will leave it aside.

Let us begin with the example of street lighting. For evident reasons in this instance private 'market' provision is virtually excluded – though of course the local authority can subcontract the work. There may be pressure from citizens worried about inadequate lighting at night, and, since local budgets are limited, there may be a vote on whether there might be not more urgent purposes on which to spend the money. There is no universally acceptable objective criterion to judge between alternatives. But, in this situation, who are the lobbyists, who seeks rent? The decision, when arrived at, cannot be shown to be optimal, there being no operationally valid criterion of optimality. Since money spent on purpose A cannot be spent on purpose B, any decision is by definition not

Pareto-optimal, since someone is being deprived. For Gradstein as for Buchanan, rent-seeking and lobbying are pejorative terms, producing misallocation. This implies that there could exist a different and preferable kind of decision-making process. What is it?

Quite a different situation obtains when we come to road-building programmes. Here the rent-seekers and lobbyists are all too clearly visible, seeking to exert influence on public expenditure and on transport policy, and in Britain (unlike, say, France) the railways lose out. Unfortunately the road lobby receives help from those economist–ideologists who are now in the process of destroying Britain's rail network. They tend conceptually to disintegrate networks, to treat each segment in isolation, to see nothing but harm in cross-subsidisation. But this is another sad story.

With education the scene changes. The arguments for public provision have been known for centuries, and there are indeed pressure groups of many kinds: teachers, ideologists of left and right, women's groups demanding more nursery schools. Demands for more resources (new schools, smaller classes, laboratories, higher pay for teachers, and so on) inevitably compete with other calls on public expenditures and with pressures for tax cuts. But is rent-seeking an appropriate basis upon which to understand the process of decision-making and the motivation of those directly concerned? Can meaningful comparisons be made with wholly private 'market' provision, which would be a very different kind of educational system?

In discussing motivation, it seems important to query an element in public choice theory. In so doing, I have no wish to quarrel with some of its key propositions. Yes, the public interest is usually a vague and operationally ambiguous concept. Yes, public servants at all levels are human, and have interests of their own. Yes, one cannot speak of market failures without also considering failures by public authorities. Lobbyists and rent-seekers do exist. To stress these aspects is entirely legitimate. But there also enters a (perhaps unconscious) philosophy or ideology, derived from methodological individualism.

If I understand Buchanan and Tullock correctly, each public servant is seen by them as an individual utility-maximiser. There is a sense in which this must be so, since each of us, including the author of this note, must at all times be doing what he or she prefers. But if one departs from tautology, then the concept is too narrow. Most individuals tend to identify with their task, their area of responsibility. The librarian, the parks superintendent, the police chief, the official in charge of technical schools, the head of San Francisco 'muni', are concerned not only with themselves, but seek to advance the purposes of the library, parks, policing, technical education and San Francisco passengers respectively. Just as the head of research, or marketing, or transport, in any private corporation is committed to research, marketing, or transport. They all tend to make a case for resources to be devoted to their areas of knowledge and responsibility. It is then someone else's job, in a firm, or the municipality, or the government, to adjudge the validity of the respective claims on scarce resources.

It is surely misleading to refer to claimants for resources for 'their' area of responsibility pejoratively as 'lobbyists', thereby equating them with, say, the National Rifle Association, and to treat their efforts as 'wasteful'.

The same definitional problem arises in assessing the role of professional associations, such as the British Medical Association and teachers' or police organisations. In one aspect of their being they are interest groups, a form of trade union. They are, however, also concerned, as are their members, for medicine, policing, and education. Crudely understood public choice theory may be used to justify the assault on such professional groupings on the part of recent British governments, and provides support for 'Cainesianism', that is, the attitude well represented by such men as Caines, with their unconcealed hostility to those who are seen by them as defending narrow professional self-interest of nurses, doctors, teachers, police officers.

This same philosophy underlies the policy of 'market testing', which is at present transforming a large segment of the British civil service (amid the silence of the economics profession). If public servants are seen as individual utility maximisers, and such qualities as loyalty, commitment, pride in work well done, responsibility, are regarded as imprecise and unscientific irrelevancies, then one can see only advantages in unsettling the careers and prospects of millions. Job insecurity must seem to such ideologists to be efficiency-enhancing. Labour relations in Japan, whether in the public or private sector, must for them be quite incomprehensible, as was the reaction of the police to the Sheehy report, a report which gave full expression to what I have called Cainesianism.

But to return to Gradstein. Comparisons between public and private provision require him, surely, to differentiate. To take some further examples, let us look at urban public transport, medical care and water supply. Transport is externality-prone, as are other forms of infrastructure. In most countries, urban rapid-transit fares are set at levels below full cost, there is a public tax-funded subsidy, because of the desire to reduce congestion and to take into account the effect on property values. The recent spectacular bankruptcy of the Canary Wharf project, due in large part to failure to provide rapid-transit links, should remind us of the importance of infrastructural externalities. What is the alternative to subsidised public provision, such as exists in much of the civilised world, from San Francisco to Stuttgart, from Montreal to Madrid? Is the choice between subsidy and full-cost (or marginal-cost) pricing, or between subsidised public and subsidised private provision, or between a single network, such as exists in most cities in the world, and the fragmentation now being imposed in Great Britain? And where, in considering such alternatives, do 'influence costs' and wasteful 'rent-seeking' enter the picture? Are the managers of San Francisco transport, or their municipal superiors, seeking rent? May they not be attempting, within financial constraints, to improve the public transport system? The employees may, of course, press for higher wages, but that is common to all sectors, public and private. The tendency, in Great Britain, of newly-privatised public utility executives to award very large salary increases to themselves fits poorly into the implication that rent-seeking is peculiarly to be found in the public sector, since in their previous employment (in the same job) in the public sector they were paid so much less.

Then, medical care. An article in the *New England Journal of Medicine* documents the much lower administrative and transaction costs in Canada, where there is a state system, as compared with the United States.[2] There are counterarguments, which this is not the place to pursue. My point is a simple one: how does Gradstein's methodology enable one to focus on the relevant questions? In this case, the rent-seekers may well be the powerful lobby in America, led by the insurance companies, which seek to preserve the status quo and to defend it from state intrusion.

Finally, water. One reads of a large increase in charges and disconnections, while metering leads to a reduction in bathing and even in flushing the toilet by poor families. History tells us that public provision of water supply (for example, the setting up in London of the Metropolitan Water Board) was due to the felt need to ensure the supply of pure water, since disease is catching and has evident external effects, as well as being a 'bad' in itself. Water is also a natural monopoly; there are no benefits from competition. One must not abstract from *purpose* in assessing the performance of public utilities, whoever owns them.

Public (or national, or regional) parks exist in most countries, and in hot ones trees are planted along roads to provide shade. Are they, or the existence of New York's Central Park, or Yosemite in California, to be attributed to 'market failure'? Are those who urged their creation, or now seek their preservation, to be seen as yet another variety of lobbyist?

My contention is that public choice theory has been used, or misused, in the campaign to denigrate the public-service concept and to provide a rationale for privatisation and 'market testing' of public services. It seems important to stress the diversity of publicly funded activities, both by sector and by form of provision, and also the variety of purposes served.

Privatisation may or may not lead to greater efficiency, but, *pace* Gradstein, this cannot be analysed or measured other than in relation to specifics. And even these may greatly differ as between countries. Thus 'free' medical care can turn out to be a sick joke where bribes have to be paid to doctors. There are cases when the public-sector unions can demand overmanning and excessive wages – though some of the worst British examples (for example, printing, shipbuilding) occurred also under private ownership. In Russia today many state and municipal functions are directly associated with corruption.

A more down-to-earth research programme is called for.

NOTES

1. M. Gradstein, 'Rent Seeking and the Provision of Public Goods', *Economic Journal*, **103**(5), 1993, pp. 1236–43.
2. S. Woolhandler and D.U. Himmelstein, 'The Deteriorating Administrative Efficiency of the U.S. Health Care System', *New England Journal of Medicine*, **324**(18), 1991, pp. 1253–58.

Index